The Campus History Series

LANDER UNIVERSITY

ON THE COVER: Lander students in athletic attire stream out of Willson Hall while posing with sports equipment in this photograph from the early 20th century. Sports at Lander during this time were intramural. The 1933 *Naiad* describes "a keen spirit of rivalry between class teams, and a spirit of true sportsmanship and loyal enthusiasm characterize the college athletics." The *Naiad* was the name of the Lander University yearbook, published from 1923 to 1991.

The Campus History Series

LANDER UNIVERSITY

Dr. S. David Mash and Lisa A. Wiecki

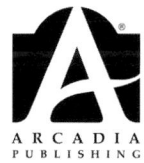

Copyright © 2022 by Dr. S. David Mash and Lisa A. Wiecki
ISBN 978-1-4671-0798-3

Published by Arcadia Publishing
Charleston, South Carolina

Printed in the United States of America

Library of Congress Control Number: 2022930632

For all general information, please contact Arcadia Publishing:
Telephone 843-853-2070
Fax 843-853-0044
E-mail sales@arcadiapublishing.com
For customer service and orders:
Toll-Free 1-888-313-2665

Visit us on the Internet at www.arcadiapublishing.com

This book is written in commemoration of Lander University's 150th year and is dedicated to the Lander community: students, staff, faculty, administration; past, present, and future.

Contents

Acknowledgments		6
Introduction		7
1.	A Wellspring of Learning at Williamston	9
2.	The Mental Stream of Learning	17
3.	The Social Stream of Learning	41
4.	The Physical Stream of Learning	61
5.	The Aesthetic Stream of Learning	91
6.	Conclusion	121

Acknowledgments

The year of this publication marks the sesquicentennial anniversary of Lander University. As part of the celebration of our 150th year, the administration of Lander University under the leadership of Dr. Richard E. Cosentino, 12th president of Lander University; Dr. Scott Jones, executive vice president for academic affairs and provost; and Mike Worley, vice president for university advancement and executive Director of the Lander Foundation, provided the freedom and financial support to pursue this project. We owe a debt to these leaders for the opportunity to enrich the lives of the Lander community by discovering and sharing forgotten splendors of the school's beginnings.

The completion of this volume would not have been possible without the skilled and cheerful assistance of the full staff in the Lander University Library. While some helped research details for photograph captions, others helped by taking on extra tasks for those doing the research. For their invaluable help, we extend our heartfelt gratitude: Caroline Jenkins, Russ Fitzgerald, Trish Clark, Grant Stone, Casey Anthony, Jean Thrift, and April Akins.

Thanks also to Dr. Jim Colbert of the Lander faculty for help solving a science mystery in one of the photos. Finally, we especially appreciate the generosity of Allie and Glen Williams of Greenwood for permission to use photos from the scrapbook of Alice Spencer, a Lander faculty member in the 1940s.

Images are provided courtesy of the Lander University Archives unless otherwise noted.

INTRODUCTION

In 1871, Rev. Samuel Lander left his post as a professor at Spartanburg Female College (SC) and accepted a Methodist pastorate in Williamston, South Carolina. The church, having no parsonage and very sparse funds, had asked for a single man. Reverend Lander was married with seven children.

No vacant houses were available in the town. A local hotel stood vacant, though, so Reverend Lander agreed to forgo a salary if the church would pay the expenses for his family to live in the abandoned hotel. To earn an income, Reverend Lander and his wife, Laura, renovated the building so that he could open a college for women. Faculty were recruited and on February 12, 1872, Williamston Female College began instruction with 36 students, with 17 boarders and 19 residents.

By the end of the first year, enrollment doubled and boarding capacity in the hotel was exceeded. To ensure stability and resources for future growth, Reverend Lander organized a stock company, bought the hotel property, received a charter from the state, and initiated the construction of a new building to expand the original campus.

The town of Williamston was established around a chalybeate spring, discovered by West Allen Williams in 1842. In 1872, the first academic catalog for Williamston Female College included a half-page description of the spring, a short 200 yards from the college campus. The "medicinal qualities" of this "Fountain of Health" are described with a detailed chemical analysis of the water and the assurance that the boarding students "have the privilege of visiting it twice every day." Each subsequent catalog—until the college moved to Greenwood, South Carolina, in 1904—included similar highlights about the fountain, adding that it "sends forth its healing stream, free, constant, and inexhaustible."

In 1884, as the number of alumnae and supporters grew, Reverend Lander began publishing a monthly journal. Issues included news and information about the college, short articles on interesting topics, humor, alumni updates, and other incidental matters of possible interest to the readers. The eminence of the spring in the life of the college is reflected in the title chosen for the journal: the *Naiad*.

As explained in the first issue, the ancient Greeks and Romans believed in a class of female divinities called nymphs. Various classes of nymphs included the naiads, given to the care of fountains. Reverend Lander linked the beneficial flowing waters of the Williamston Spring to the benefits flowing from the college: "About twelve years ago, there sprang into existence near this fount of health, the fountain of learning which since then has sent forth copious streams of mental and moral culture to gladden and adorn full many a happy heart."

The first yearbook was published in 1923, long after the college had moved from Williamston to Greenwood to become Lander College. Yet, the name given to the yearbook until its last year of publication in 1991 was the *Naiad*. In the 1923 edition, the forward is devoted to a beautifully written recollection of the Williamston Spring and the naiad of the spring. The continuity of the theme through the decades is reflected in the affirmation that "when the college was moved to Greenwood, the Naiad forsook her native haunts that she might remain the guardian spirit of Lander girls."

Again in 1949, the yearbook forward recalls and expands on the naiad theme: "In students of Lander there is a friendly and lively spirit similar to a mythical nymph called a Naiad which inhabits and enlivens streams and fountains. The difference is that students live in a stream of learning, developing mentally, socially, physically, and aesthetically." These four streams formed the structure of the 1949 yearbook.

To honor Rev. Samuel Lander and the ethos he encouraged for the college in its earliest days, this history of the early years is organized according to the various fountains of health, the streams of learning that still flow at Lander University, 150 years later.

One

A Wellspring of Learning at Williamston

Williamston Female College opened in February 1872 with thirty-six students, eight faculty, and twelve areas of instruction: Latin, Greek, natural sciences, mathematics, English, belles-lettres, French and English literature, geography, history, music, and art.

An emphasis on both scholarship and piety is illustrated by the first two student organizations described in the 1872 academic catalog. Students could join the Erosophic Society and the Young Ladies' Christian Association.

The Erosophic Society was organized for the "prosecution of important literary studies which are not included in the College Course." It had its own meeting room and library in addition to the general student library.

The Young Ladies' Christian Association offered a weekly Bible study. The college was founded as a private enterprise, independent of any religious affiliation. Nevertheless, Rev. Samuel Lander—a Methodist minister—intended the school to be infused with Christian ideals, though without compulsion for any student to accept Christianity. The 1873 academic catalog states, "We stand solemnly pledged not to exert or allow any proselytizing influences upon the youth committed to our care."

Just one year after opening, in February 1873, a contract was signed to build an addition to the original facility. The new 19,000-square-foot building was three floors high with three meeting rooms and twelve dorm rooms.

Between 1875 and 1880, the college operated a kindergarten according to the educational philosophy of Friedrich Froebel, the founder of the kindergarten movement in Germany. The movement was still young, and kindergartens were uncommon in the United States. The one in Williamston was only the second (after Charleston) to open in South Carolina. College students could elect to learn Froebel's methods as part of the curriculum.

On December 9, 1898, Reverend Lander proposed a new governance structure for the college by way of a partnership with the South Carolina Conference of the Methodist Episcopal Church. The proposal was accepted, and the board of directors was restructured to comprise five chosen by the Conference and four chosen by the stockholders. This arrangement broadened the support base for the school and continued for the duration of the Williamston years.

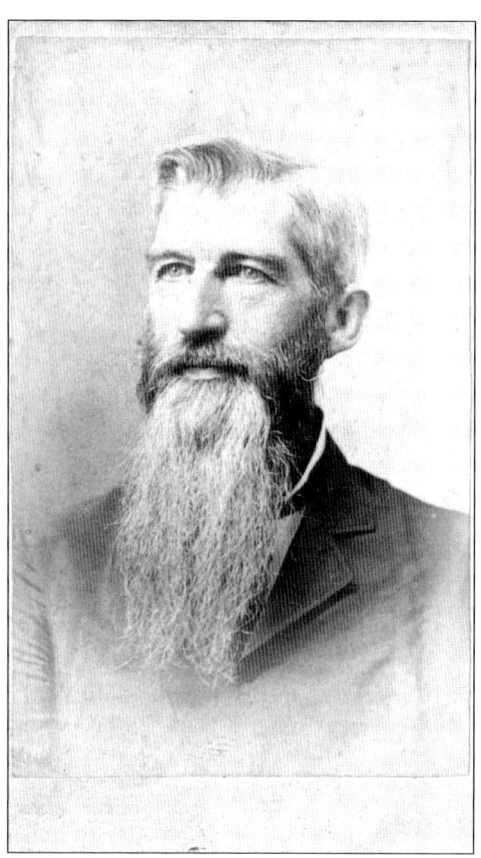

This distinctive undated portrait of Rev. Samuel Lander was taken by the photography studio of W.A. Reckling of Columbia, South Carolina. The 1932 annual describes Lander's modesty: "He sought no honors; he hated pretense. He wanted no monument but to live again in the lives of those whom he taught, and he strove to lay the foundations of his school broad, deep, strong that it might be for generations to come the living embodiment of his ideals, Christian culture and Christian character."

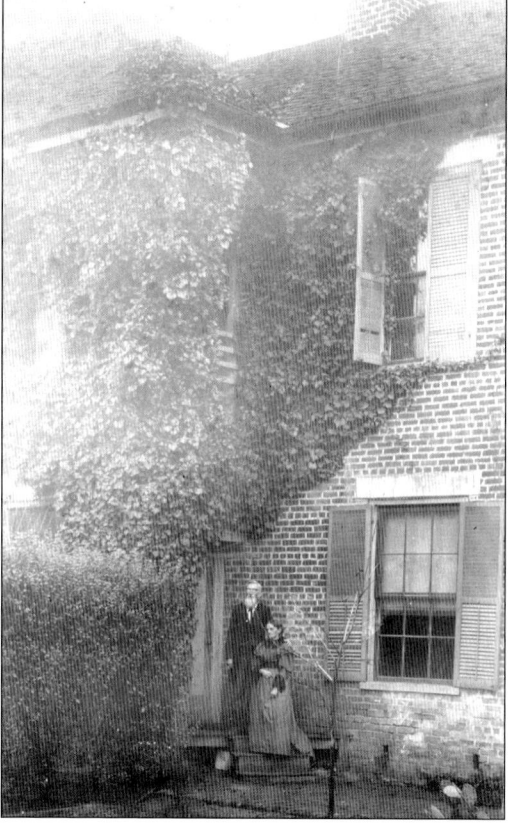

Rev. Samuel Lander and his wife, Laura McPherson Lander, pose on the east side of the Williamston campus in 1900. According to the 1923 *Naiad*, "They loved and prayed and played and worked with a single aim. Who then can say, 'Behold what he hath done. Behold what she hath done?' We would rather say, 'Behold what God hath wrought through them!'"

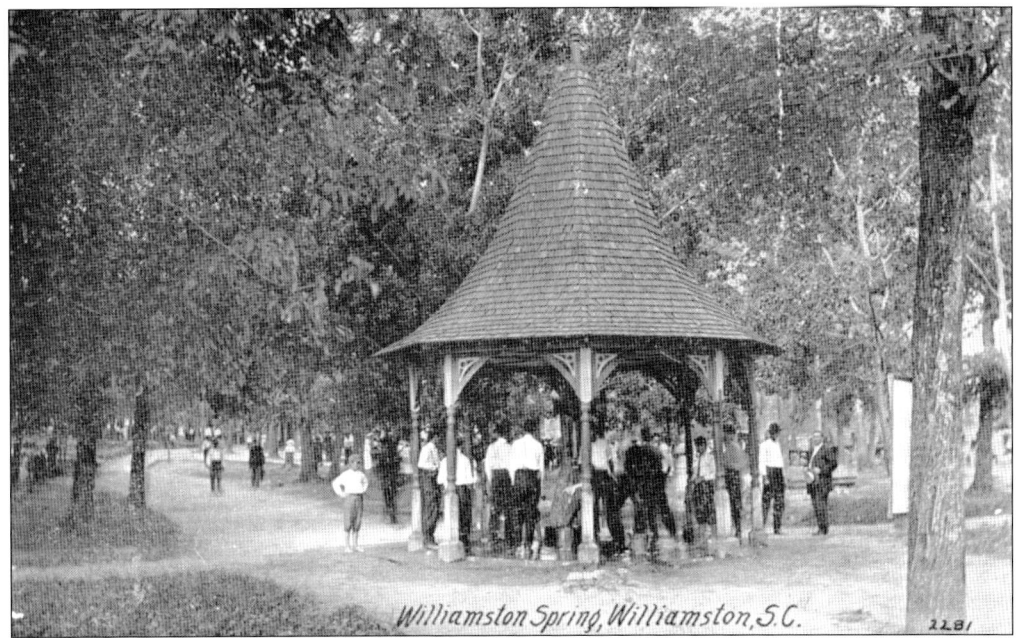

People gather under a gazebo built over the Chalybeate Spring in this early-20th-century postcard image of Williamston Spring Park in Williamston, South Carolina. The fountain can still be visited, and one can drink from the spring. A replica of the gazebo, built by master craftsmen employed by Lander's physical plant, was erected on Lander's campus near Laura Lander Hall in the early 1900s.

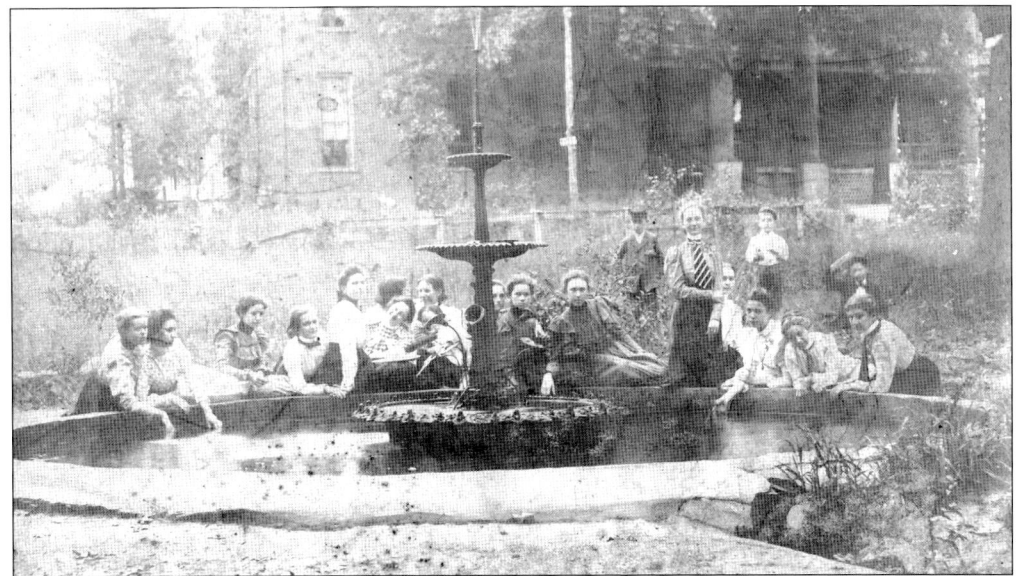

This undated photograph was taken in the early years of Williamston College. Students, young children, and perhaps a faculty member are gathered at this ornate cast-iron fountain fed from the Williamston Chalybeate Spring. Carvings of small bullfrogs encircle the basin of the fountain and the base of its finial is embellished with water lilies. The college can be seen in the background and stood 200 yards away, making daily visits to the fountain an easy excursion.

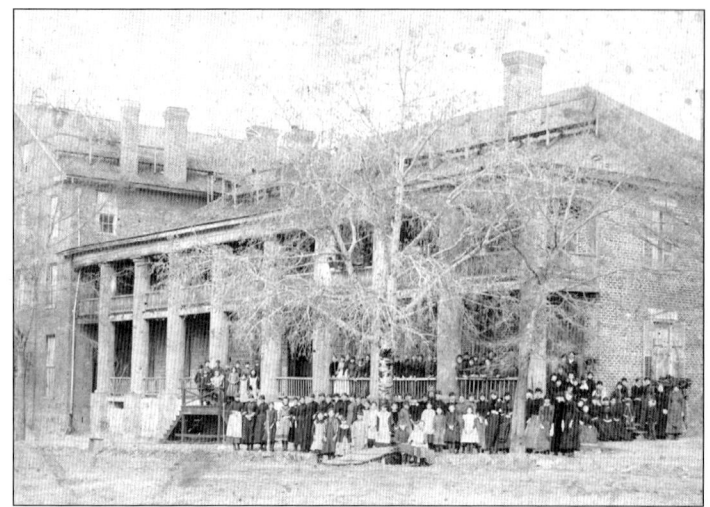

This is believed to be a gathering of students, alumnae, and alumnae children on August 27, 1885, to celebrate the 12th anniversary of the laying of the original cornerstone of Williamston Female College. Rev. Samuel Lander stands directly to the left of the second tree from the right. A pastor, possibly Rev. W.D. Kirkland, sits directly to the right of the third tree from the right.

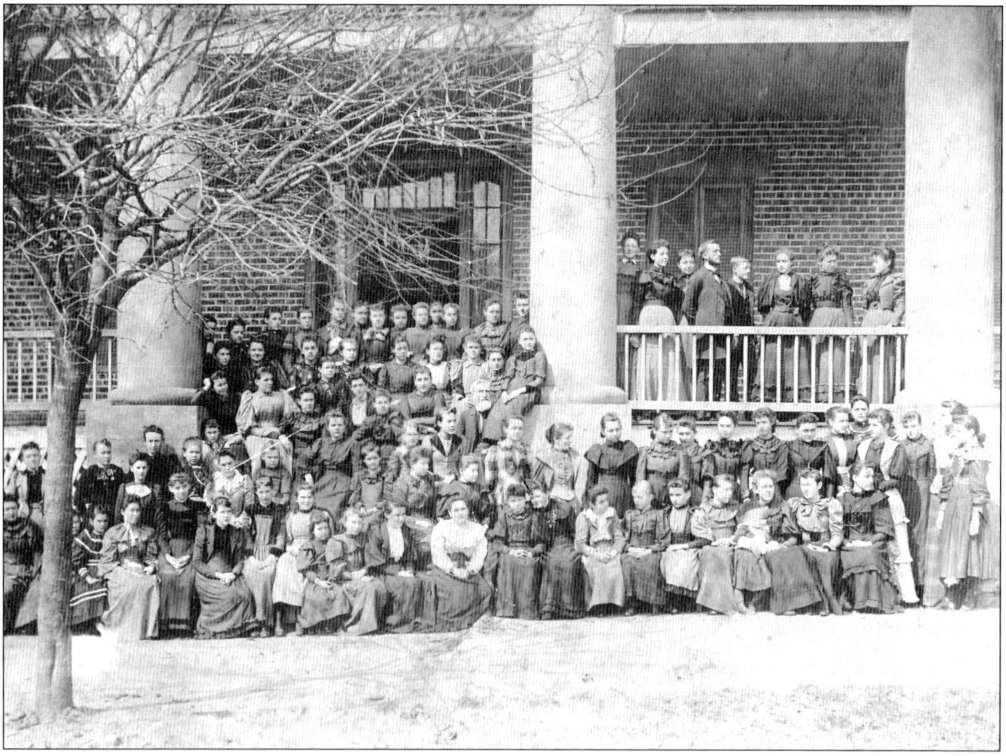

Rev. Samuel Lander stands to the left of the student seated at the base of the center column in this 1899 photograph of the student body, which may also include kindergarten students. While many of the people in this photograph look away from the camera, which was common due to the slow shutter speeds of the camera equipment at the time, some look straight at the lens and are smiling. Perhaps this is due to Reverend Lander's instruction in the art of gratitude. In undated sermon notes, he writes, "The habit of gratitude looks on the bright side, and makes allowance for the dark, finds a silver lining to any cloud and begets the habit of cheerfulness, which is the secret of happiness." Reverend Lander's sermon notes are housed in the Lander University archives.

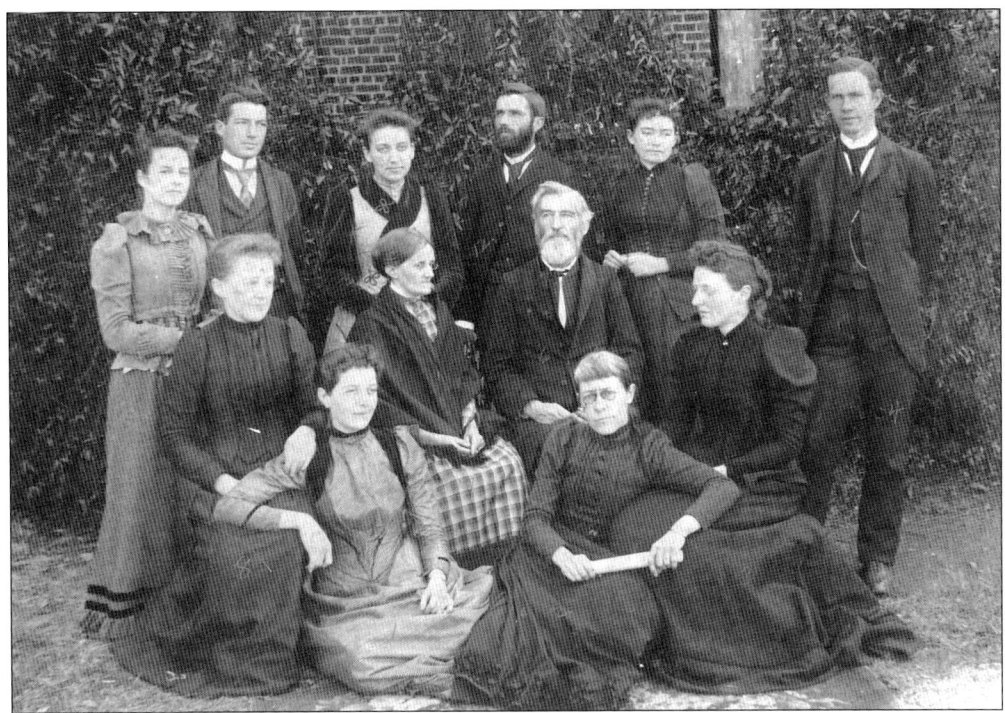

Williamston Female College faculty members are pictured in 1887. From left to right are (first row) Kathleen Lander Willson and unidentified; (second row) Laura Ellis, Laura McPherson Lander (guitar), Rev. Samuel Lander (Latin), and Hanna Keely (art); (third row) Mrs. W.T. Lander, Malcolm Lander, Frances Mattice (music), William Tertius "W.T." Lander (literature), Elizabeth Alexander (math), and Clyde Horton.

The library reading room at Williamston Female College is pictured here. According to the college catalog, the reading room "receives regularly quite a number of valuable periodicals, religious, secular, scientific, literary, weekly, monthly, from North, East, West, and South. By the payment of a small fee, any pupil may hereby learn what is going on in the world and be stimulated to exert herself to keep up in the march of improvement."

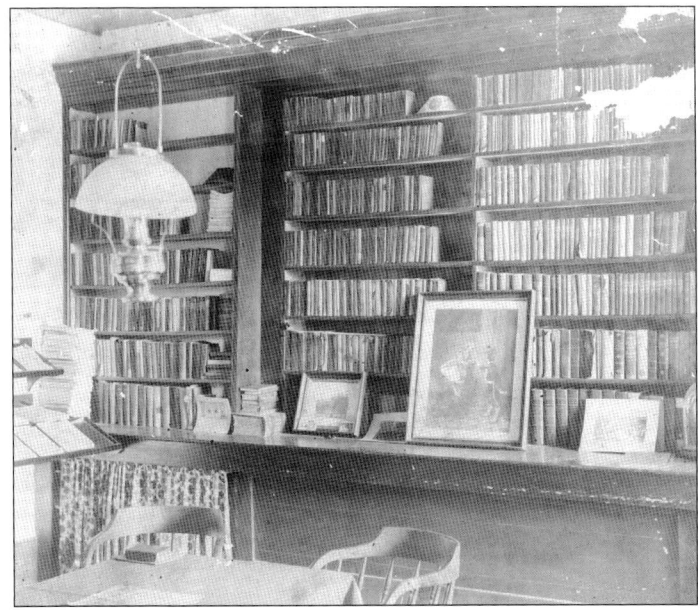

13

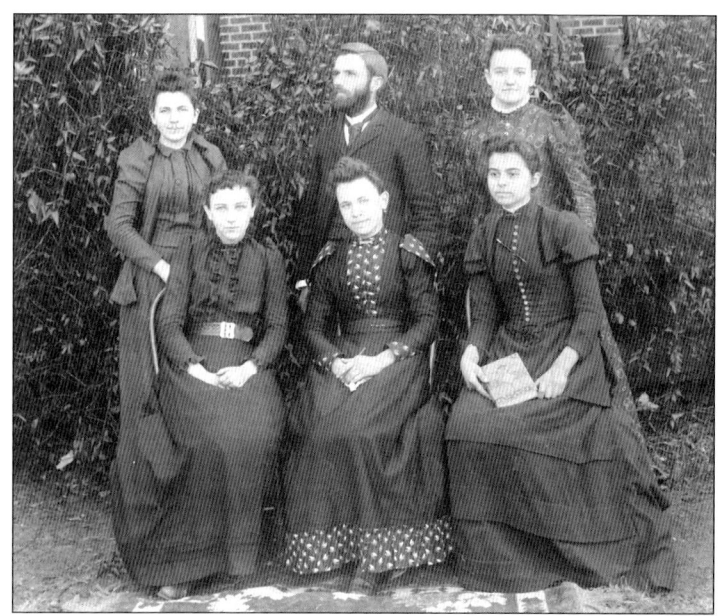

Professor of literature W.T. Lander, son of Rev. Samuel Lander, is pictured with five students during the spring session of 1892. From left to right are (first row) Bertha Anderson, from Williamston South Carolina; Daisy Crymes, from Williamston South Carolina; and Leta Tatum from Barnwell County, South Carolina; (second row) Mattie Connor, from Berkeley County, South Carolina; and Minnie Wood, from Georgia.

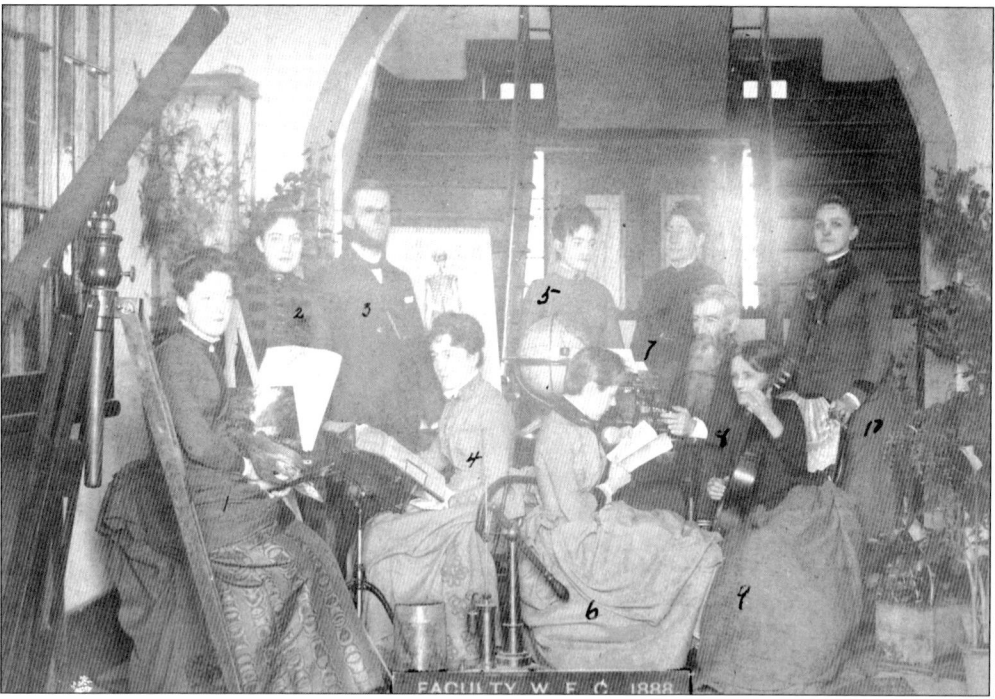

Each Williamston Female College faculty member is posing next to an object that represents their area of academic expertise in this 1888 portrait. From left to right are (first row, seated) Hanna Keely, Mrs. John M. Lander, Margaret Langdon (Rev. Samuel Lander's sister, teacher of Hebrew), Rev. Samuel Lander (with a typewriter), and Laura McPherson Lander; (second row, standing) Roberta Mooney, Rev. John M. Lander (later missionary and college president in Brazil), Elizabeth Alexander, unidentified, and Julia Wood. The objects in the photograph reflect the college's commitment to a broad education in the sciences, literature, and the arts.

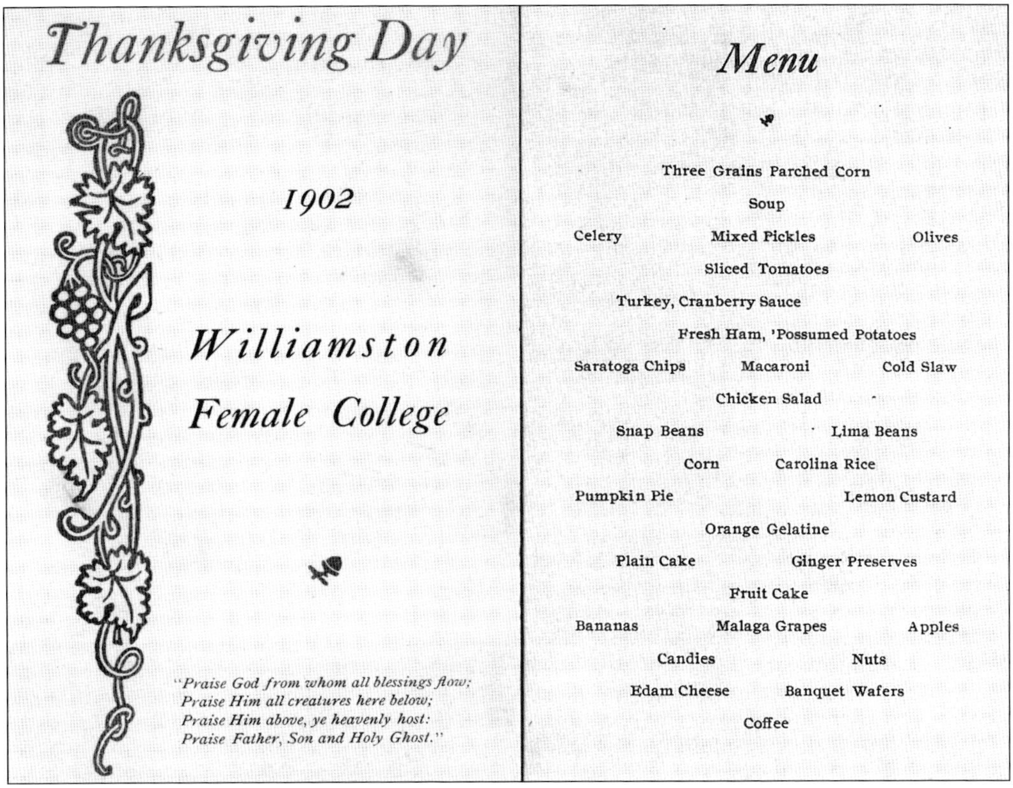

Thanksgiving Day

1902

Williamston Female College

*"Praise God from whom all blessings flow;
Praise Him all creatures here below;
Praise Him above, ye heavenly host:
Praise Father, Son and Holy Ghost."*

Menu

Three Grains Parched Corn
Soup
Celery   Mixed Pickles   Olives
Sliced Tomatoes
Turkey, Cranberry Sauce
Fresh Ham, 'Possumed Potatoes
Saratoga Chips   Macaroni   Cold Slaw
Chicken Salad
Snap Beans   Lima Beans
Corn   Carolina Rice
Pumpkin Pie   Lemon Custard
Orange Gelatine
Plain Cake   Ginger Preserves
Fruit Cake
Bananas   Malaga Grapes   Apples
Candies   Nuts
Edam Cheese   Banquet Wafers
Coffee

Seen here is a menu from a Thanksgiving meal. According to a description of the holiday in the *Naiad* newsletter, Thanksgiving Day "was duly and joyously observed in our village, and especially in our College household. From dawn to curfew, including the holiday, the service in the church, the stately dinner, — with the inevitable Boston baked beans, the traditional pumpkin pie, the turkey with cranberry sauce, and the countless other luxuries from far and near, — the free and easy interchange of homely courtesies, and the closing reunion in the Erosophic Hall, everything went merry as a marriage bell."

A portrait of Rev. Samuel Lander hangs above the working fireplace in the festively adorned college dining room. The oil lantern-style chandelier indicates the building may not have had electricity. When the campus later moved to Greenwood, South Carolina, the earliest promotional materials emphasize that the newly built facilities were equipped with electricity.

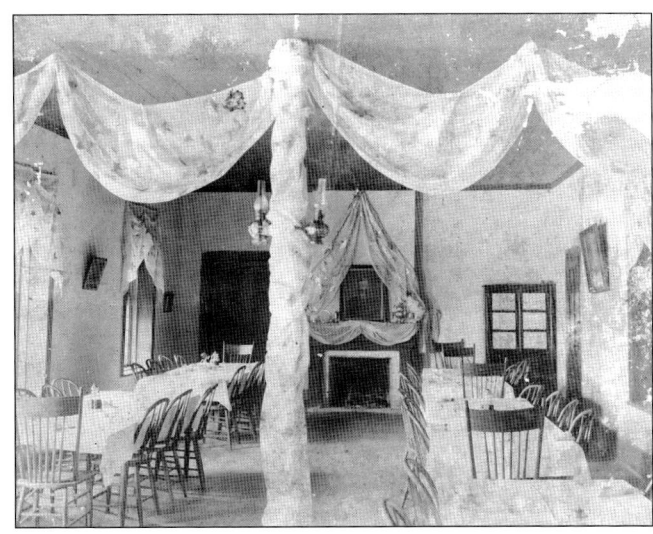

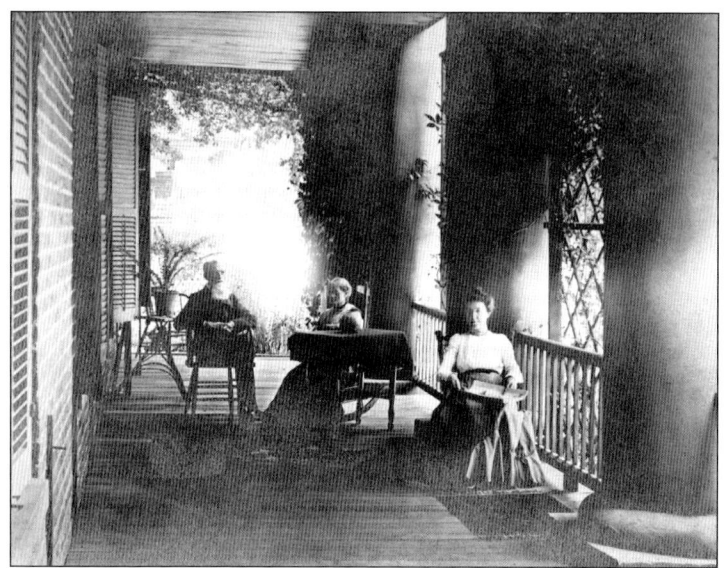

Rev. Samuel Lander, his wife Laura McPherson Lander (center), and an unidentified woman are seated on the front veranda of the Williamston Hotel in this postcard image of the school. The town of Williamston was once known as "the Saratoga of the South" before the Civil War, and the hotel had many visitors who wanted access to the healing waters of the town's wellspring. It was torn down in the 1940s.

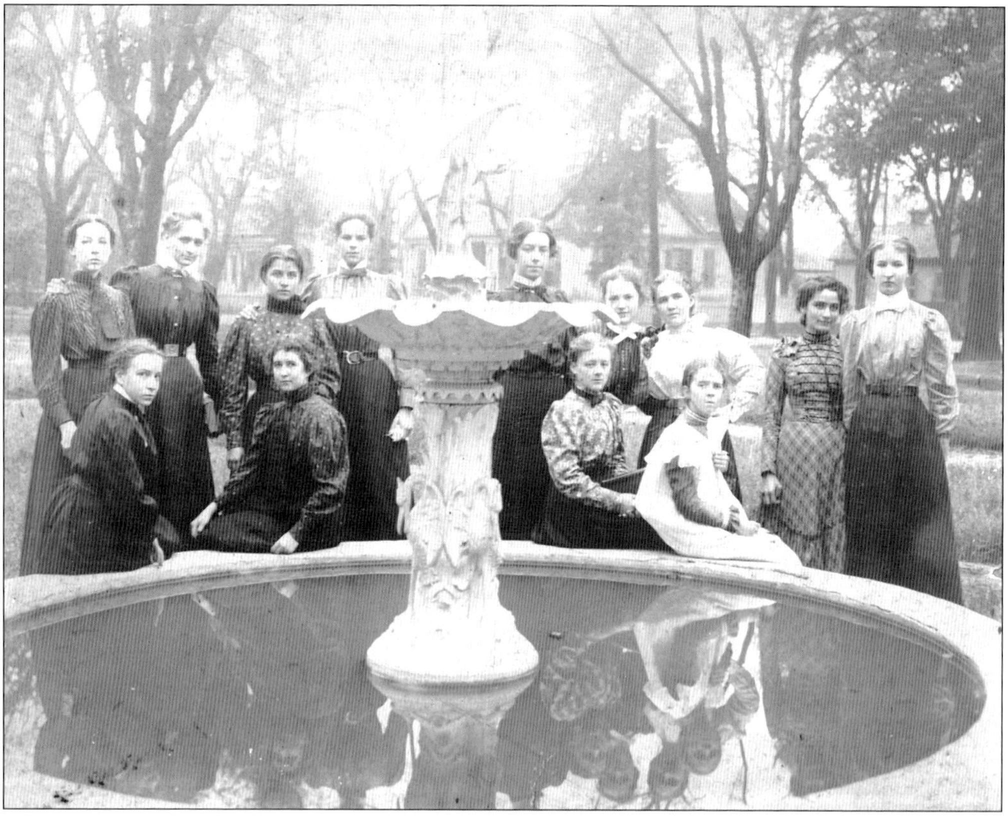

Modest dress was encouraged at Williamston Female College. The pupils in this image wear simple clothing cut from calico cloth. One well-known example of Williamston pupils' preference for modesty was when the class of 1878 wore simple calico dresses at their commencement ceremony. Every woman in attendance dressed in the same fashion, and this was known as "the calico commencement."

Two

THE MENTAL STREAM OF LEARNING

As the college continued to grow, options for physical expansion in Williamston became limited. In 1903, the administration accepted an offer to relocate to Greenwood. From the 1904–1905 academic catalog (condensed):

> As a result of the unparalleled generosity of the good people of Greenwood and vicinity, the Williamston Female College will be removed during the summer from its original location in Williamston to its elegant new home in their progressive city.
>
> Early last year, they proposed to present to the College an eligible site to erect thereon a first-class, up-to-date building containing all necessary apartments for the use of the College with dormitories; the whole property to be offered to the South Carolina Conference of the Methodist Episcopal Church, South.
>
> [The people of Greenwood purchased] 18 acres on which they are now erecting an elegant building, with accommodations for about one hundred and thirty boarders. This building is to be furnished throughout with steam heat, electric light and water works.
>
> As we are erecting this new home for the College, we embrace the opportunity of expanding our scholastic plans. We are strengthening the faculty, extending the course of study, and aiming to make the institution in every respect more worthy of patronage than ever before . . . it will be the same institution "revised, improved and enlarged."

In May 1904, Rev. Samuel Lander personally removed the cornerstone from the Williamston campus and transported it to place along with the cornerstone for the first building on the new campus in Greenwood. Reverend Lander died two months later, on July 14, in Williamston. The opening of the first academic session in Greenwood, on September 27, 1904, was led by Rev. John O. Willson, a son-in-law of Reverend Lander (married to Kathleen). Reverend Willson served as president until 1923.

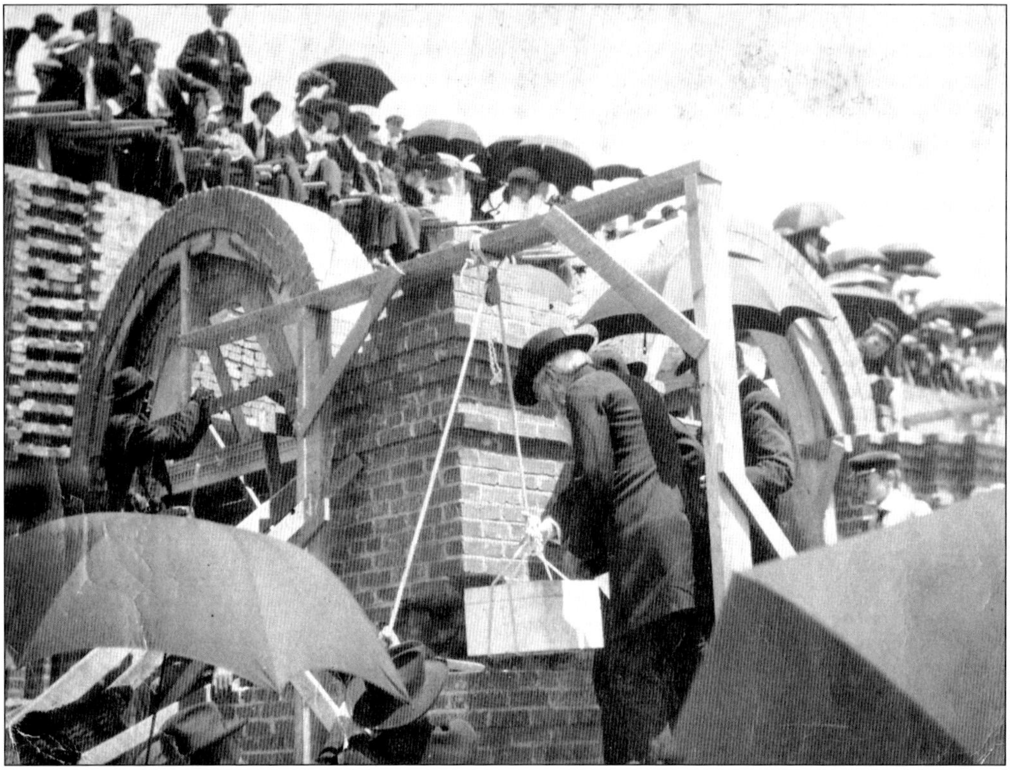

This iconic photograph shows Rev. Samuel Lander placing the Williamston cornerstone on the Greenwood building. The placement, on May 10, 1904, was beautifully described in the local newspaper *The Evening Index* on May 12, 1904: "[The mason] having placed the stone in position tried it with the level, plumb and square and found it true and well formed. The cavity in the stone was then filled with the following articles: the program of the day, a list of the subscribers of the fund to build the college, list of students and faculty of the college, list of the enterprises of Greenwood, one copy each of the papers published in Greenwood. The stone was then closed and having had poured over it wine, corn, and oil, was left to be closed forever."

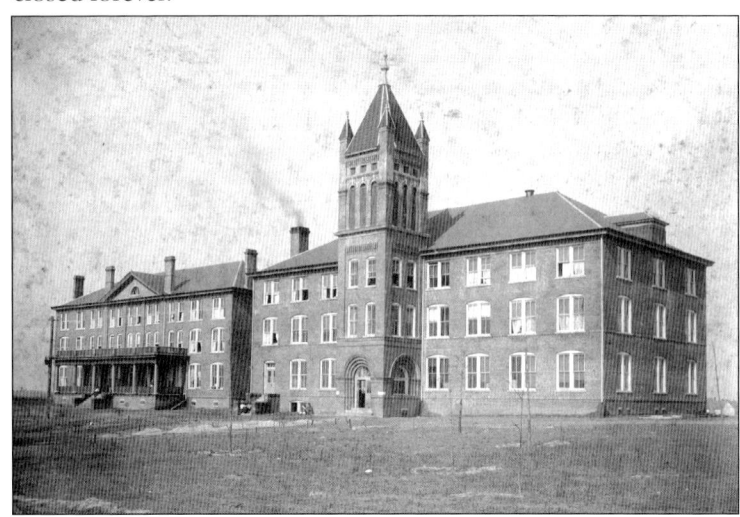

In this very early photograph of the first buildings on the Greenwood campus, tiny saplings can be seen as stick figures across the front of the lot. An electrical utility pole stands to the far left, and the Williamston and Greenwood cornerstones are visible on the left and right of the door at the base of the tower.

18

This photograph shows Rev. John O. Willson, Lander's second president, participating in the Foch Day celebration in Greenwood on December 9, 1921. Ferdinand Foch, the supreme allied commander during World War I, was greeted in the town square by 20,000 people—including many state dignitaries—and he was treated to the singing of the Marseillaise in French by Lander College students. Greenwood was the only town in South Carolina visited by Foch on his tour of the United States.

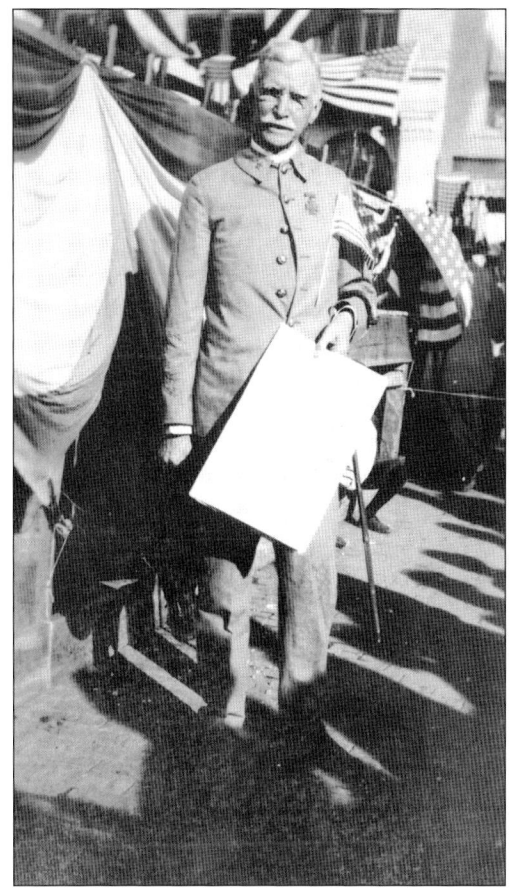

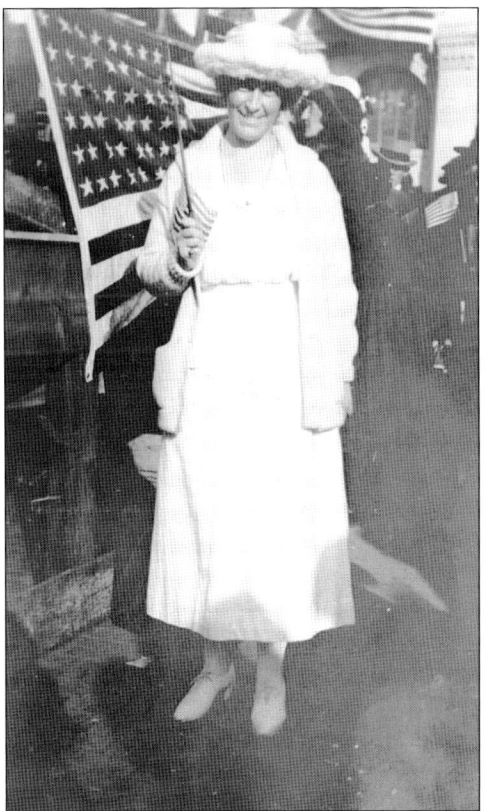

Kathleen Lander Willson is pictured at the Foch Day celebration in 1921. Willson was the youngest daughter of Rev. Samuel Lander. She was an alumna of the college and worked as the recorder for the college and as the alumnae secretary until her death in 1955. In the spirit of her mother's commitment to campus beautification, Willson wrote a descriptive survey of the plants on the Lander campus that was included in a publication on South Carolina natural history.

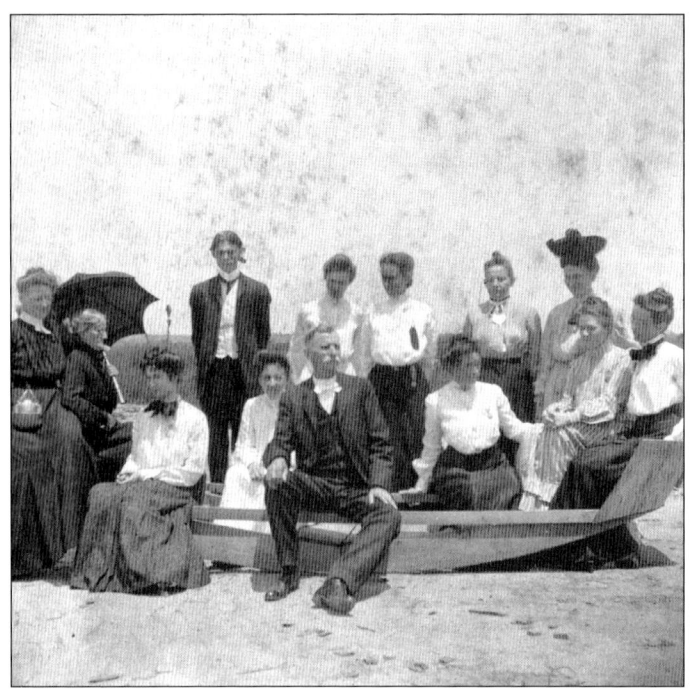

This interesting photograph was taken on the Lander campus in 1910. Rev. John O. Willson, the second president, is seated in the center. Laura Lander, the wife of Rev. Samuel Lander, is holding the umbrella to the left. The photograph also illustrates the barren landscape of the campus at that time. In contrast to the barrenness, President Willson had a pet peacock that roamed the campus and in 1922, the students gifted him with a peahen for his birthday.

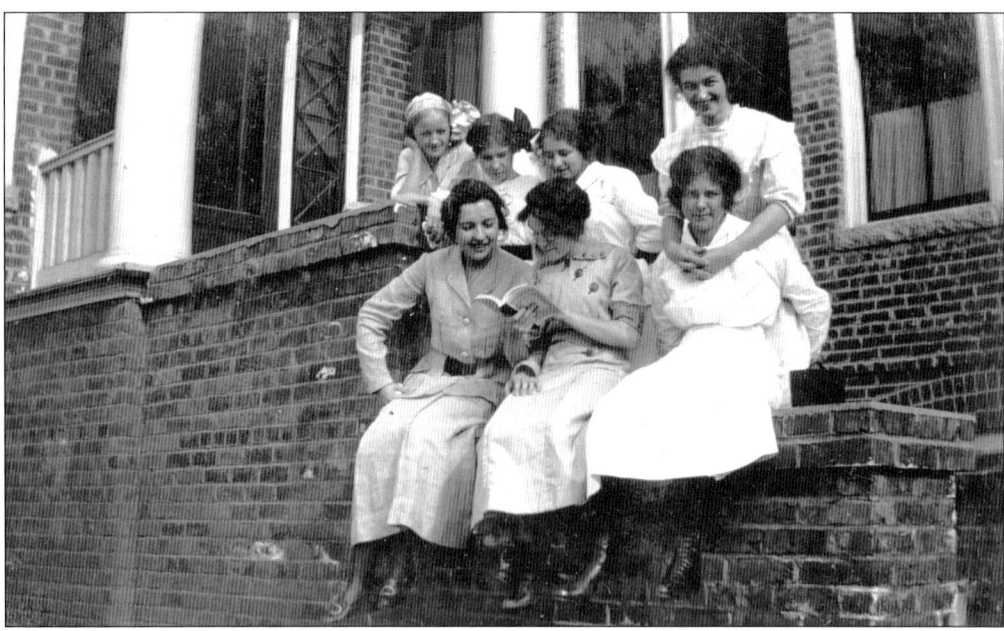

Students gather on the steps outside of Willson Hall to share some camaraderie as well as a book in 1912. The college catalog describes "the home-like atmosphere that pervades the college" that was due largely because "there is very little red tape in the management." The catalog goes on to describe "the rules are simply those of any well-ordered home, and they are made for conscientious girls who are in sympathy with the spirit of the college. Pupils are expected to make good use of their opportunities, to be neat, punctual, truthful and courteous. We believe any reasonable girl will be happy here. And unreasonable, unruly girls are not desired."

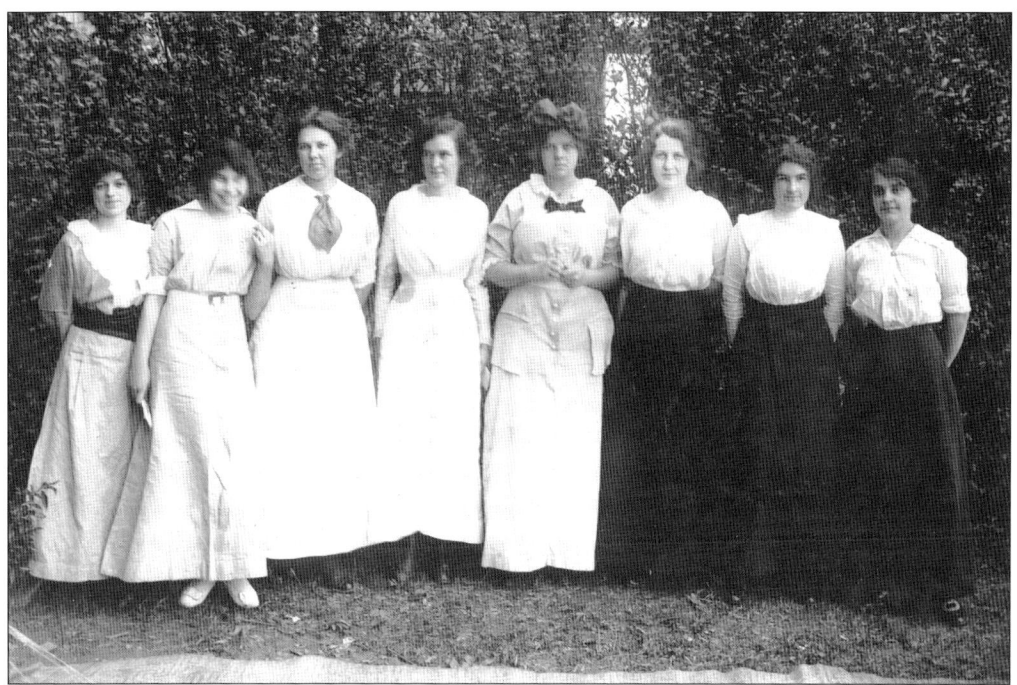

The Lander College catalog of 1912 begs of its readers "to save any possible embarrassment, patrons (parents) are requested to read the following paragraph carefully. We ask that they will please provide their daughters with high shoes and proper clothing for winter wear. Dresses with low necks, and sleeves shorter than elbow length are not allowed at any season, and we urge the wearing of medium heels on all shoes. The lady principals or any teacher will request a change in dress if it is contrary to the dictates of good taste or injurious to good health. For commencement and for all college functions the students are required to wear simple white dresses and black shoes." In this group photograph from 1912, the student second from the left, the only one with white shoes, has a broad smile and appears to be laughing.

This 1930s-era photograph shows the library with Elizabeth Alexander (head librarian 1924–1934) seated at the large service desk in the center. The 1930 academic catalog states that the library was stocked with 8,000 volumes in addition to "daily and weekly papers, and the most important American periodicals." The light fixtures were a gift of the class of 1915. The class of 1917 gave two tables and 12 chairs for the library.

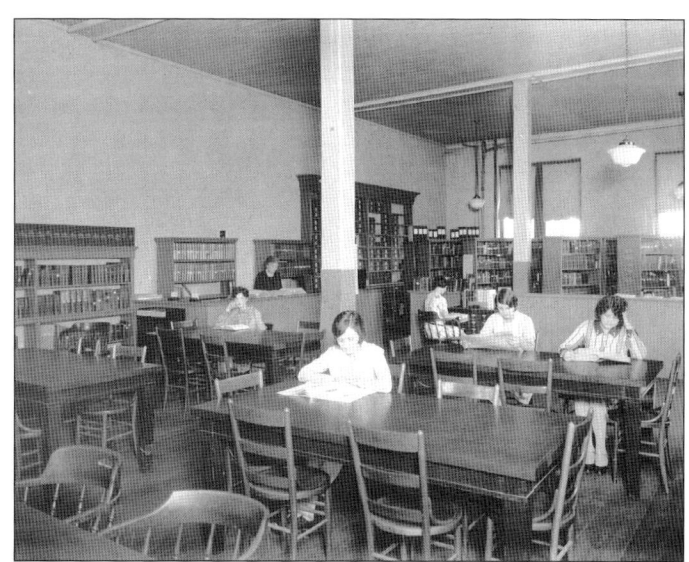

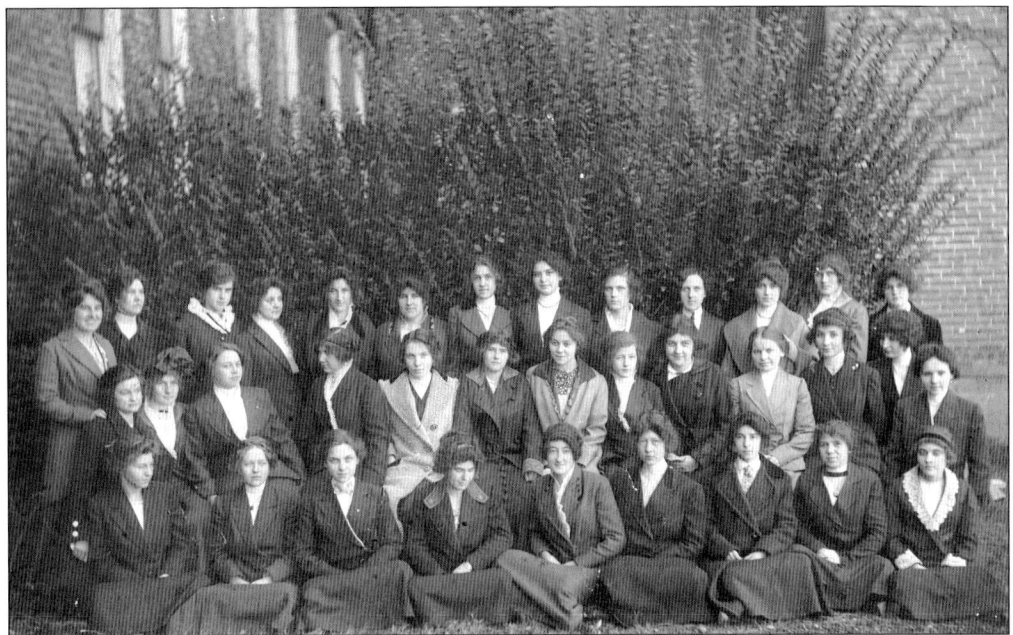

The class of 1914 is shown in this group portrait. The 1914 college catalog contains a special note to the parents of the students attending Lander: "May we not ask that you leave with us the entire management of your child while with us? Embarrassing situations occur when parents at home ask for things to be done that are entirely contrary to the good judgement of those on the ground. We earnestly ask the help and co-operation of the parents. It will help very much. But please do not try to direct the work of your child from your home."

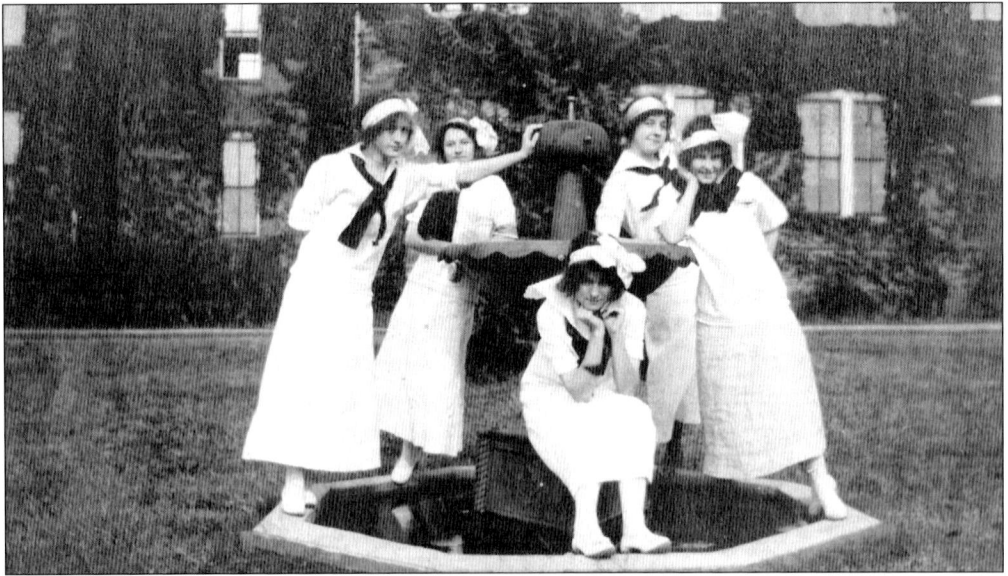

In this 1914 photograph, students are posing around the campus fountain, a gift from the class of 1912. Students enjoyed having their photographs taken in front of Lander landmarks, many of which were class gifts. This iron fountain calls to mind the habitation of the naiad in the wellspring at Williamston. It figures prominently in many subsequent photographs as part of campus ceremonies.

Students from the class of 1915 hold a pennant that says "Lander" and wear simple white dresses, which were required for commencement ceremonies. The Lander College catalog of 1915 describes the moral atmosphere of the school, "It is not popular to be loud or fast, but gentle refined courtesy is inculcated in every way. It is gratifying to believe that our girls deserve the reputation they have made for themselves by their quiet, lady-like behavior on railway trains and everywhere."

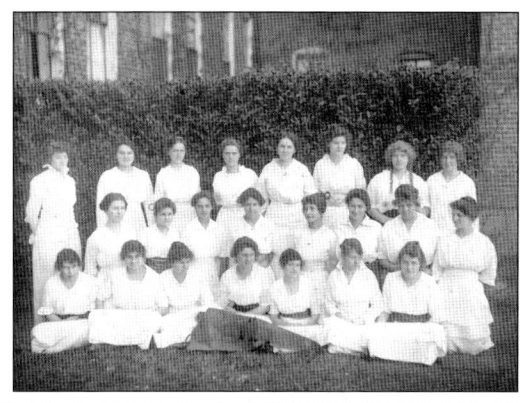

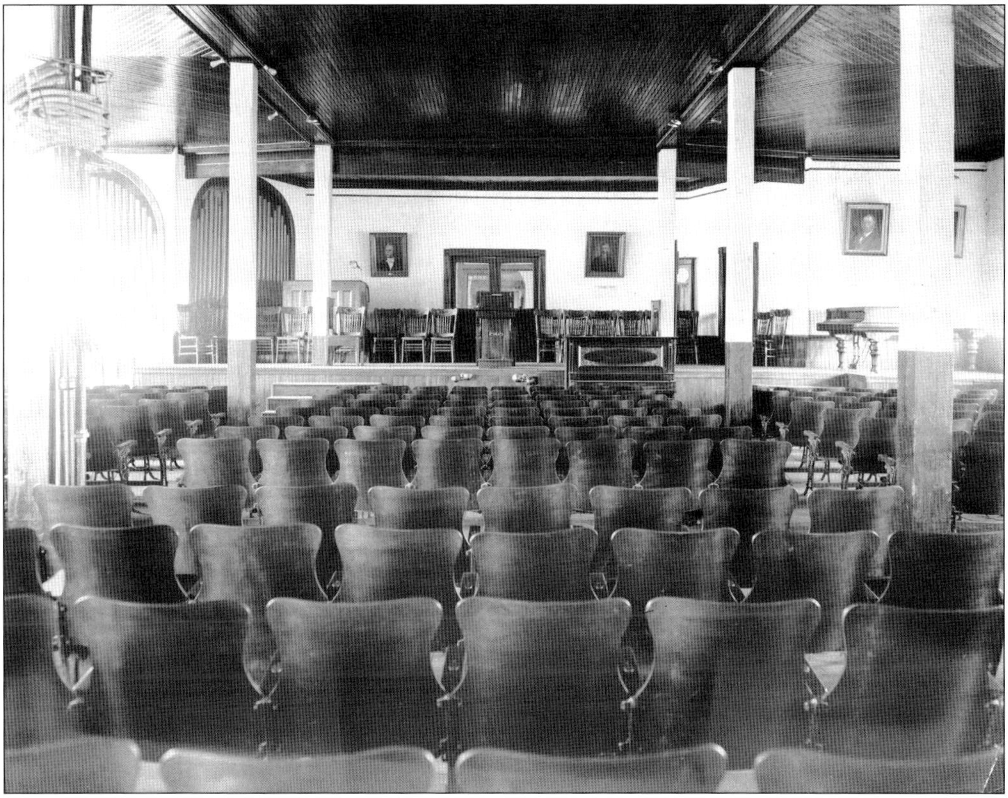

As the college transitioned to a Methodist women's college, chapel services became an increasingly central part of the educational program. This pre-1923 photograph of the chapel features class gifts from the classes of 1907 (clock), 1908 (platform seating), and 1909 (center podium). A portrait of Rev. John O. Willson hangs on the wall to the left of the podium, and a portrait of Rev. Samuel Lander hangs to the right. The portrait to the far right is believed to be Capt. Creswell A.C. Waller, a prominent member of the Greenwood community who was instrumental in securing the resources for the move from Williamston to Greenwood. The 1934 *Naiad* includes a photograph of the chapel with a description of the purpose of the Lander College Christian Association on page 72: "The association endeavors to create an understanding interest in world-fellowship, to know social problems and to study their solution, to enlarge our capacity through music and literature, and, above all, to develop our spiritual life."

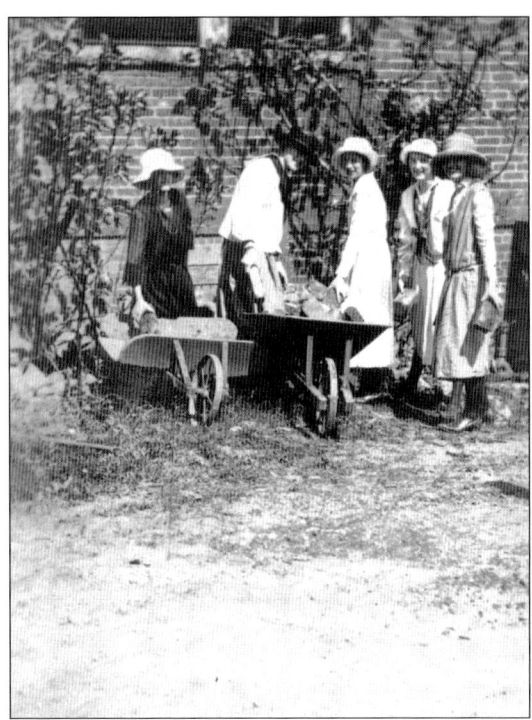

Members of the class of 1912 gather bricks made from the clay earth on campus to be used in the construction of the steps leading down to the Dingle, a gathering space for academic ceremonies and social events. Students worked to transform the Dingle into an inviting place for campus activities. In her essay "The Plants of the Lander Campus," Kathleen Lander Willson describes the Dingle in the early days of the campus as "a tangled jungle almost impenetrable. Blackberries were there in great abundance but it was only a brave soul who would risk going for them, — the place looked too snaky."

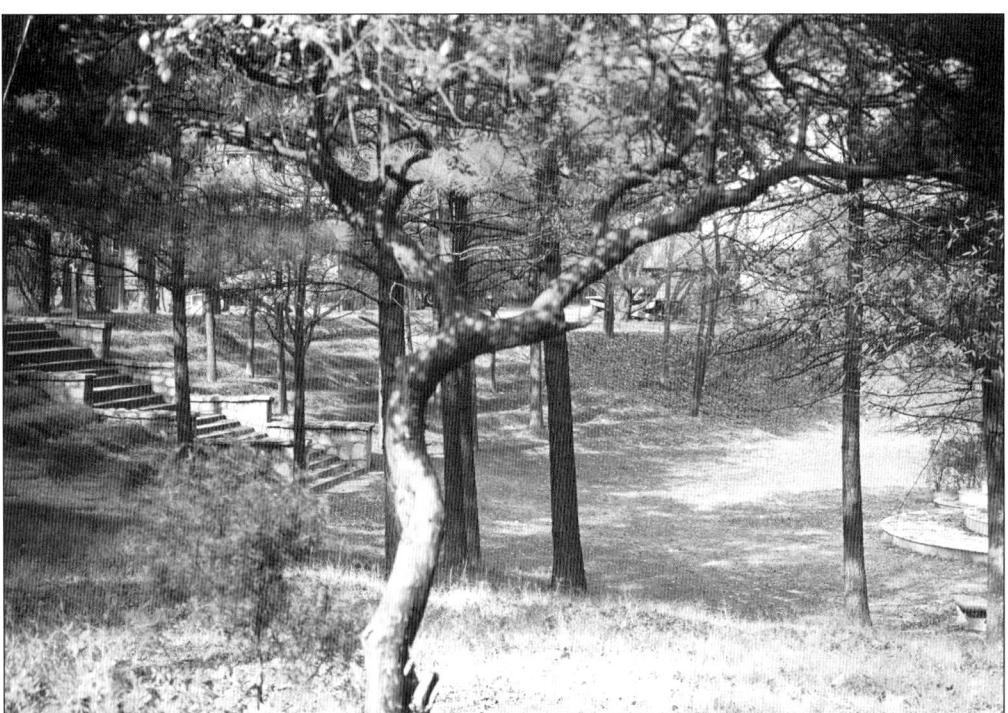

This is a view of the completed steps at the Dingle. The term "dingle" is defined by the Oxford English Dictionary as a small, deep valley or hollow that is shaded or surrounded by trees. The Dingle remains a prominent feature of the campus, still nestled on the edge of a beautiful tree-shaded hollow.

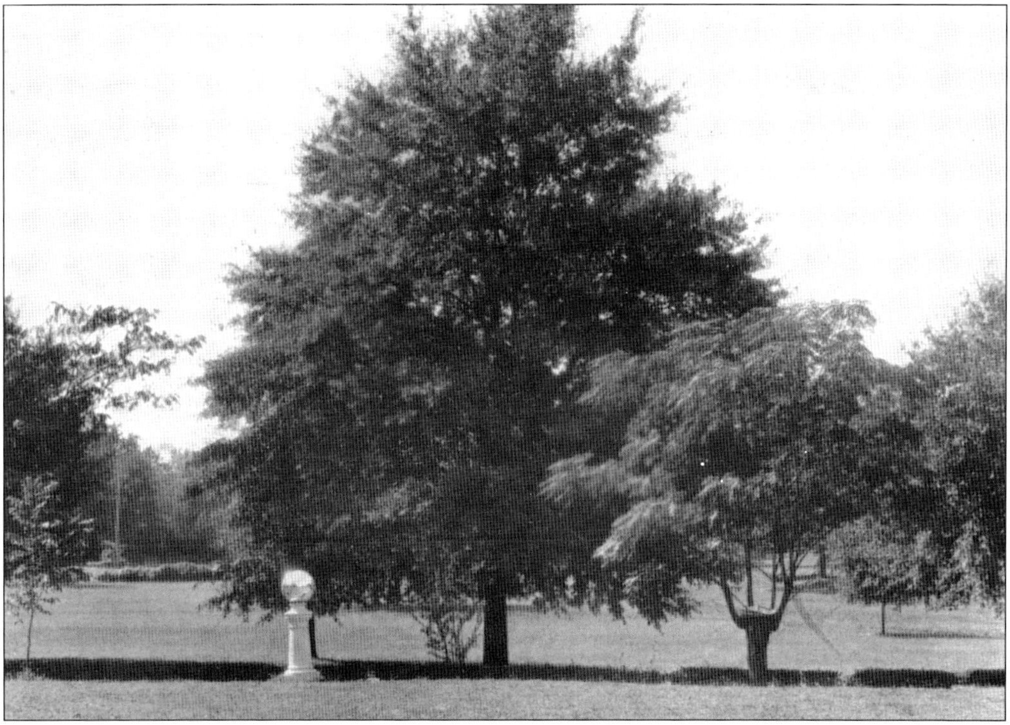

The first 18 acres of land purchased for the Greenwood campus was an abandoned cotton field with two lone trees: one pine and one black gum. Landscaping the property was an early priority, led by Laura Lander. Numerous initiatives through the years, including asking students to bring a tree native to their county to plant on campus, transformed the campus into an award-winning tree campus with the Arbor Day Foundation. Also pictured in this 1926 photograph is a glass-gazing globe. According to the 1932 *Naiad*, the globe was erected in response to a special wish of Laura Lander who loved to see the "reflected beauty of the campus." Her disciplined attention to the quality of the spaces where education occurred was a hallmark of her contribution to the college.

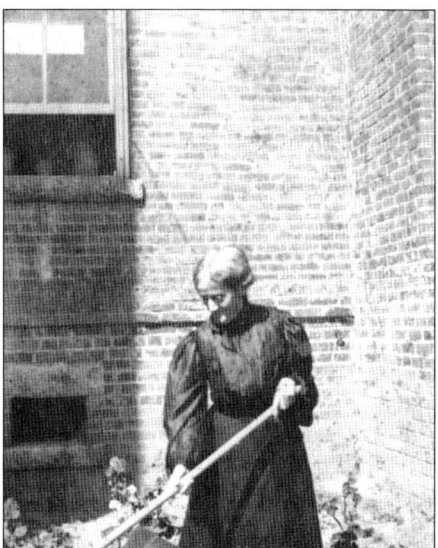

This undated photograph shows Laura Lander working in a garden on the Greenwood campus. From the 1927 *Naiad*, "Mrs. Lander was pre-eminently a homemaker. How many remain today living witnesses of her precious influence in the home—the word here the smile there, the helping hand everywhere—the open door where one might drop in for a cup of tea, a game or a chat—always welcome—just the thing that transforms an institution into a home."

25

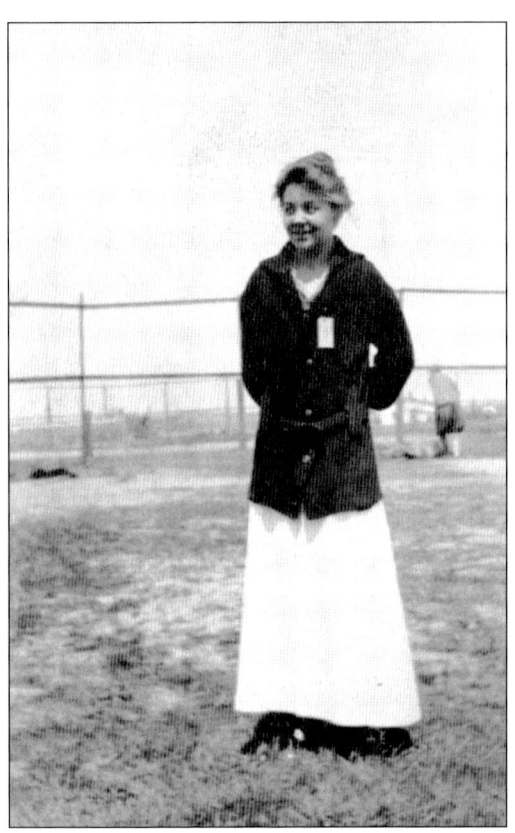

Before yearbooks were published, students created personalized memory books of their Lander experience, which sometimes included photographs of faculty members as well as a message from them. When she wrote in the memory book of student Aileen Hammond, assistant teacher Frances Ryan Lockman, borrowed from the words of writer George Eliot, "More helpful than all wisdom is one draught of simple human kindness that will not forsake us."

When he wrote in the memory book of student Ethel Anderson, Rev. Robert O. Lawton, professor of history and Bible, quoted Shakespeare, "To thine own self be true, and it must follow, as the night the day. Thou canst not then be false to any man." Photographs of Reverend Lawton and his family, who were deeply woven into the fabric of Lander life, appear in numerous student memory books. He served briefly as acting president upon the death of Rev. John O. Willson. His daughter Mary Lawton was selected as senior class mascot for the class of 1922, and his son R.O. Lawton Jr. was senior class mascot for the class of 1926.

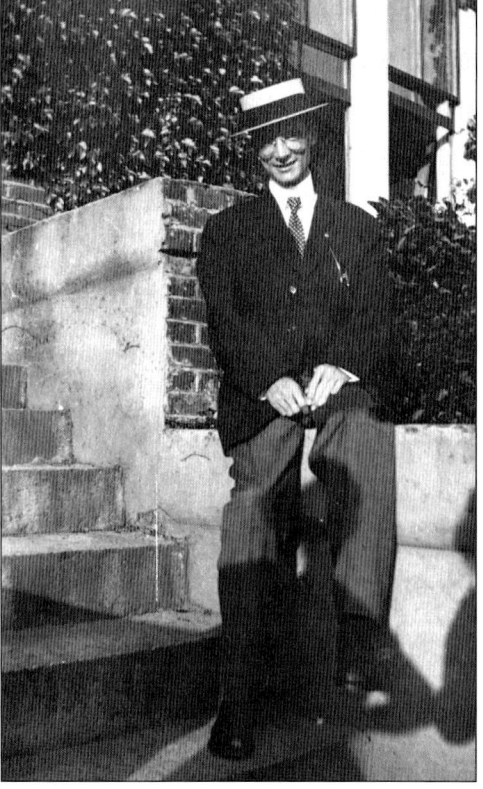

Student Ethel Anderson's memory book contains a photograph of science faculty member Roxana Clark, who quoted William Wordsworth: "May thy mind be a mansion for all lovely forms, thy memory be as a dwelling place for all sweet sounds and harmonies." In 1914, Clark taught courses in astronomy, chemistry, geology, household chemistry, zoology, and physiology.

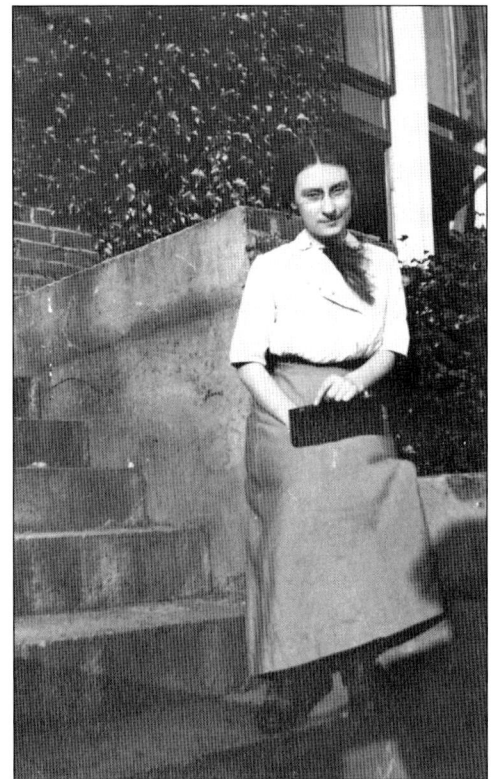

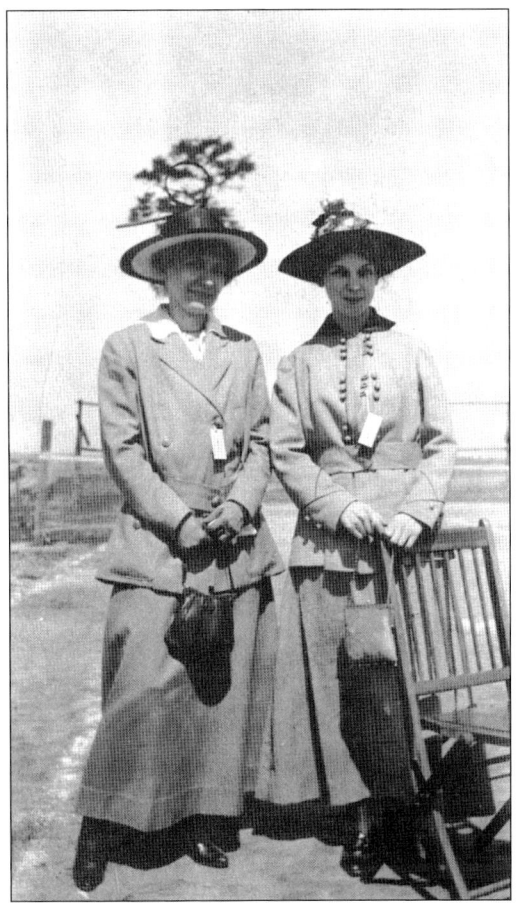

A Lord Byron quote, "All who joy would win must share it—happiness was born a twin," was penned in the memory book of Aileen Hammond by violin and piano teacher Annie Elizabeth Aunspaugh. In this photograph, Aunspaugh stands on the left. She graduated from Agnes Scott College and did graduate work at the American Institute of Applied Music in New York and the Cincinnati Conservatory. She taught at Lander from 1905 to 1941. She married Joel Aiken, was a member of the First Presbyterian Church, died in 1970, and is buried in Greenwood's historic Magnolia Cemetery.

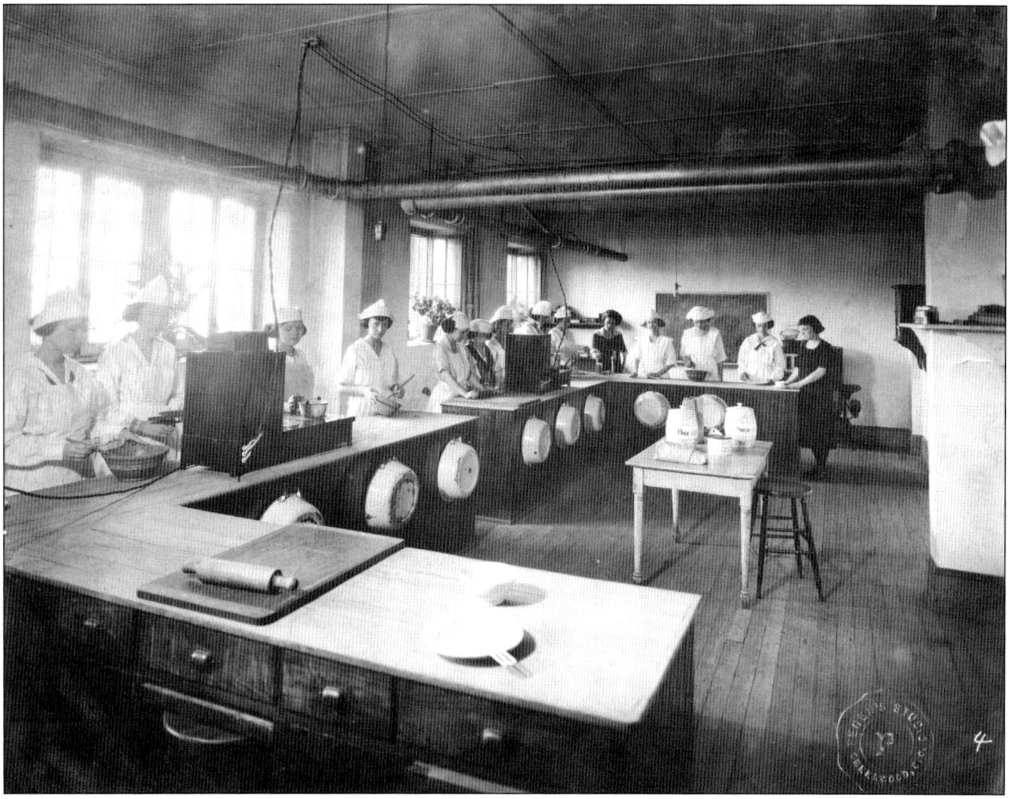

For many years, Lander College offered courses in Domestic Science and then Home Economics. Topics described in the 1915 catalog include food preservation, human nutrition, food groups and principles of balanced meal preparation, kitchen sanitation, household chemistry, and the study of textiles and the manufacture of fabrics. This undated photograph shows a lab featuring various utensils and two electrical appliances, each with a cooking surface and oven.

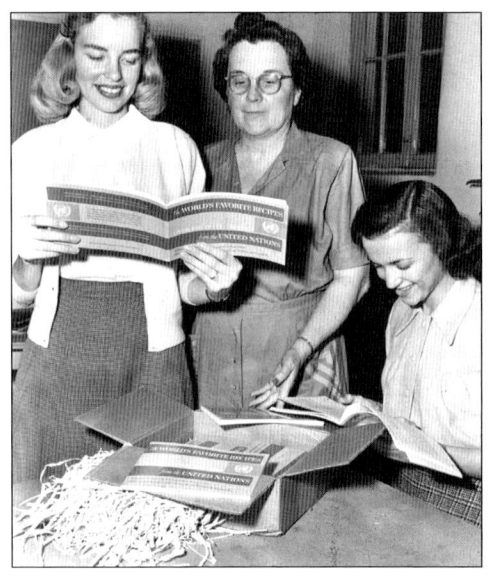

Students in the home economics program sold United Nations cookbooks to raise scholarship funds, 1952. Pictured left to right are Ray Crowder, Rennie Hook (home economics instructor), and Carolyn Hendrix. An International Relations Club was also active on campus during this period, and international students from Cuba, Greece, and South Korea were hosted on the campus. This may have sparked an interest in international cuisine.

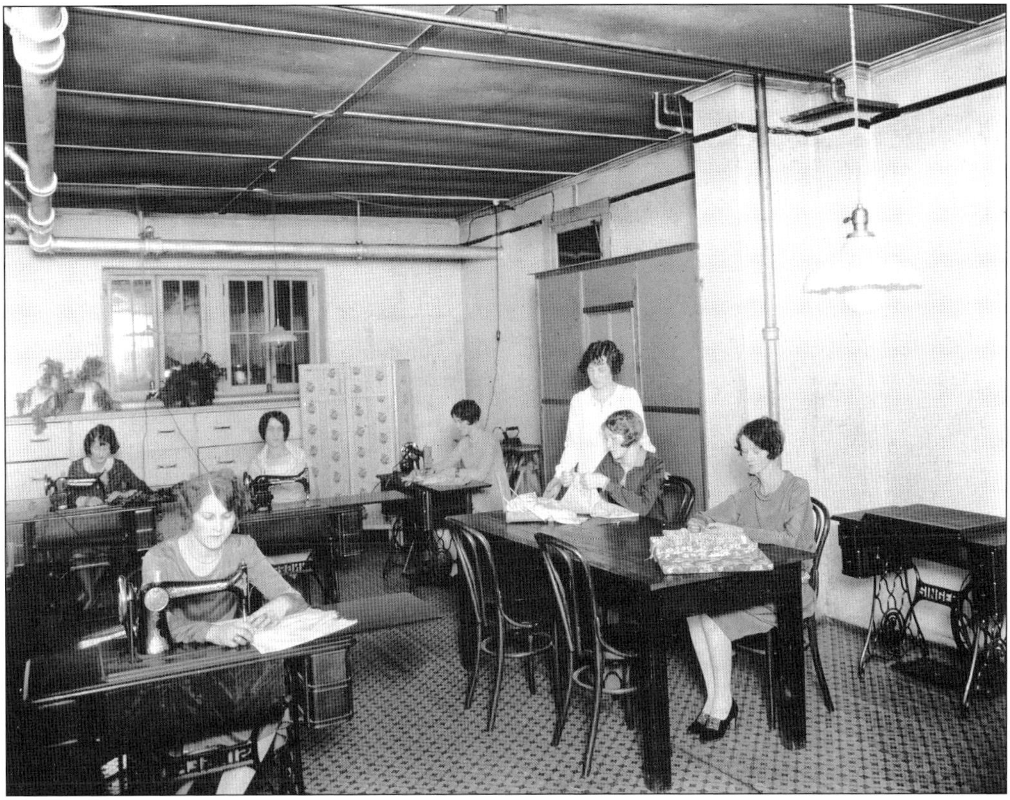

A course offering in clothing selection and construction was included in the home economics program and was taught by Rennie Hook and Miss Heuser. The course was described as "planning, selecting, and constructing clothing to meet the needs of the college girl." This undated photograph features electric sewing machines and, in the far corner, an electric iron.

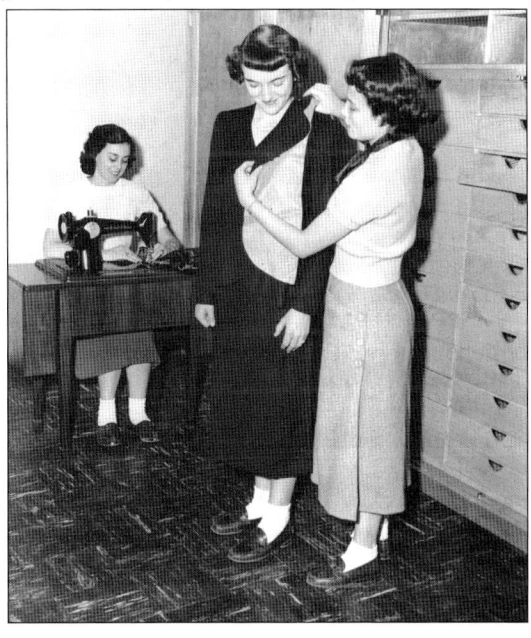

In 1941, Lander students used their tailoring skills to make more than 500 garments and sweaters for the Greenwood Red Cross Chapter for British War Relief. Students in the 1950s could take a course in advanced clothing design, in which they were taught principles of clothing design, study of the basic pattern, and simple garments design as well as the construction of tailored suits, coats, and party dresses. This photograph from the *Naiad* yearbook is described as a new sewing room.

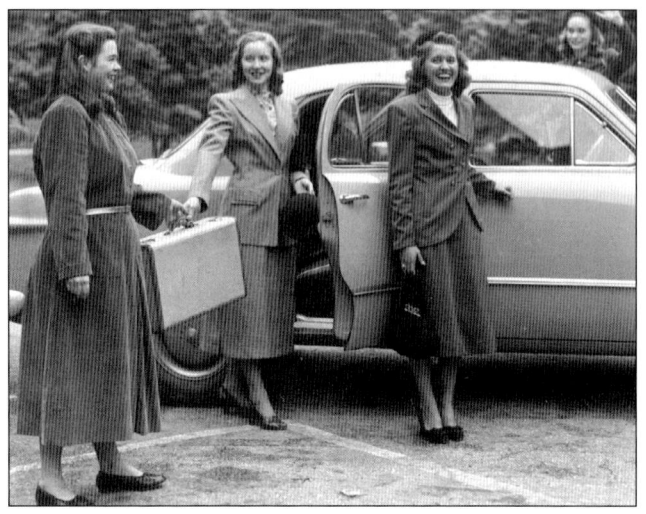

Members of the Rennie L. Hook Home Economics Club depart to attend a state convention. The club was composed of home economics majors and was a member of the National Home Economics Association. In 1950, the club met monthly to carry out the theme "Modern Trends in Family Living" in its programs. Pictured from left to right are Margaret Watson, vice president; Gloria Glymph, state officer; Carolyn Daniel, president; and Iris Wanda Miller, secretary-treasurer.

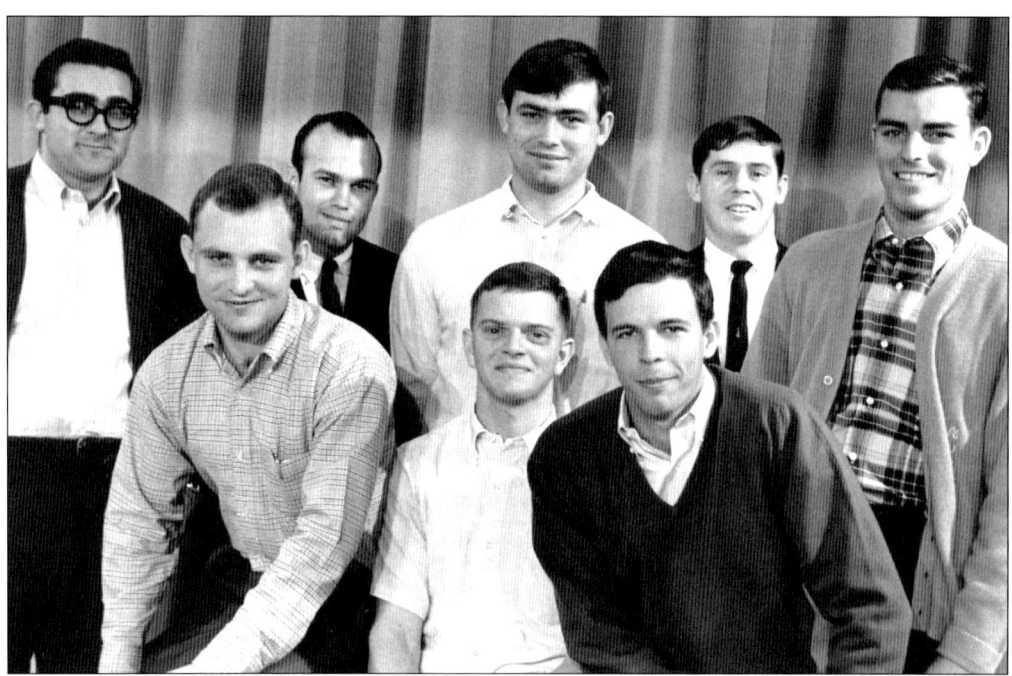

Lander became coeducational in 1948. At first, male enrollment was limited to local day students since it was not possible to adjust campus housing accommodations. Included in this 1966 photograph are newly inducted members of the Koinonia Club, a men's honor society. Pictured from left to right are (sitting) Charles Long, Terry Cann, and Ray Drummond; (standing) Carroll Clem, Rev. Dan Compton (speaker at the induction ceremony), Larry Lawson, Lincoln Privette (president), and Harold Clayton.

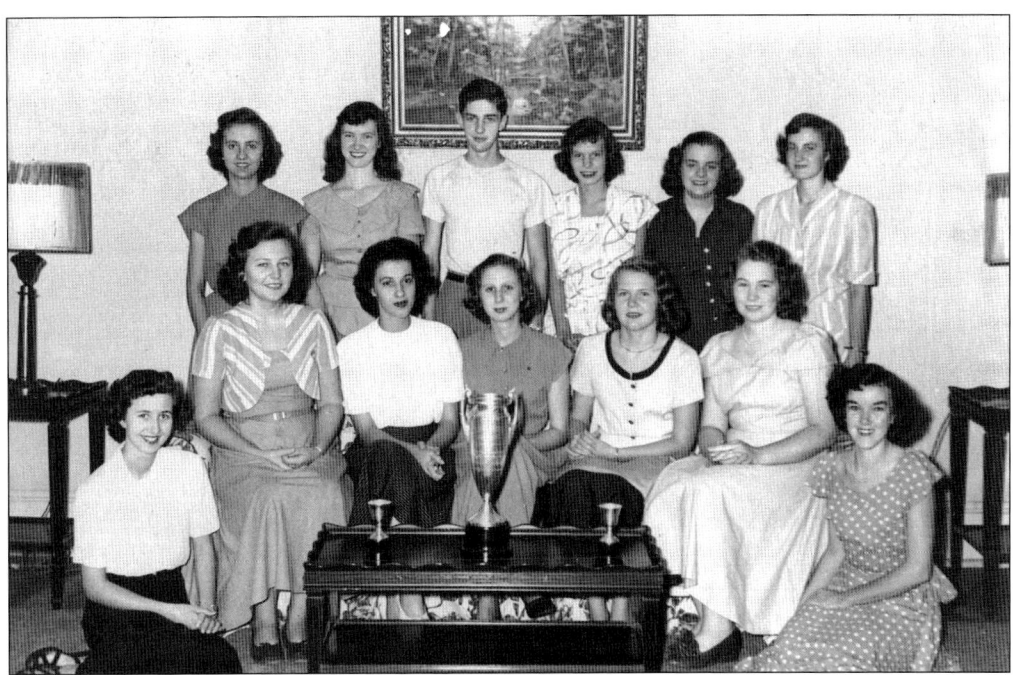

Student staff members of Lander's literary magazine, the *Erothesian*, pose with the Ben M. Robertson Jr. Cup for best South Carolina college publication. The *Erothesian* won this prestigious award in 1940, 1942, and 1948. The smaller cups pictured are believed to be the Anna Rena Blake Poetry Cup and the Maybelle Coleman Essay Cup. The magazine's title is a combination of the names of two former literary societies of old Williamston Female College, the Erosophic and the Mathesian. Pictured from left to right (first row) Ruth Botts, Betty Lomas, Mary Erneston, Tweedie Ann Durst, Gwen Laramore, Frankie Sue Dickerson, and Joyce Sample; (second row) Callie Self Coker, Sara Chandler, Charles Henderson, Ruth Burnett, Holly Coker, and Eleanor Boland.

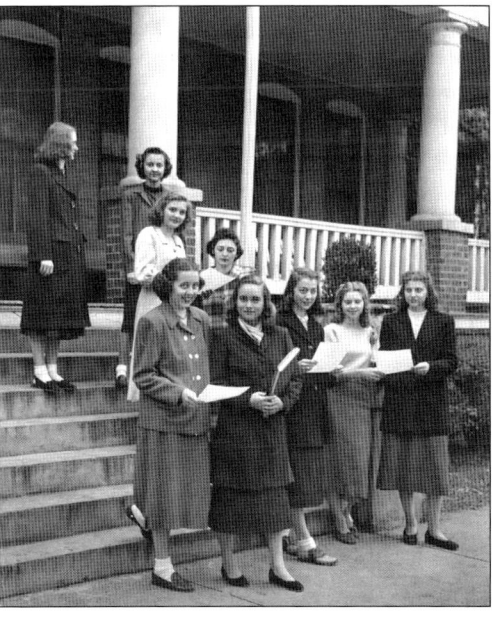

Naiad yearbook staff are pictured in 1949. Work on the *Naiad* offered an opportunity to apply skills learned in the classroom, such as writing, project management, and group decision-making. Pictured from left to right are (first row) Betty Coleman, Iris Wanda Miller, Martha Ann Wiggins, Frankie Lusk, and Jimmie Rhode; (second row) Leona Rush, Mamie Link; third row Peggy Miller, and Callie Self Coker.

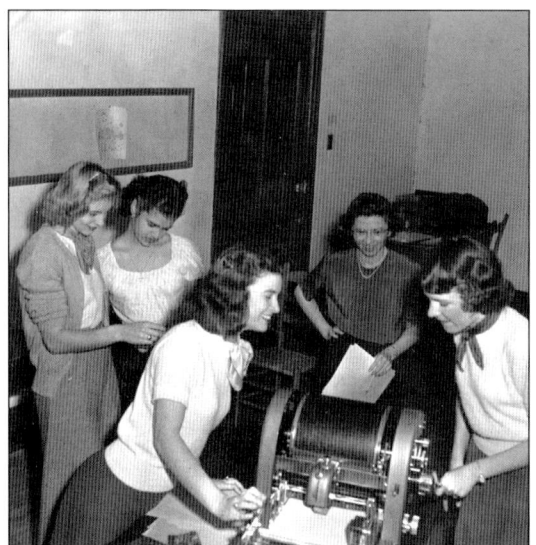

During the 1940s and 1950s, Lander students could earn a commercial certificate by completing a series of courses that prepared them for employment in a business setting. Classes in the series included accounting, commercial law, business personality, and office practice. In this undated photograph, students practice using a mimeograph machine.

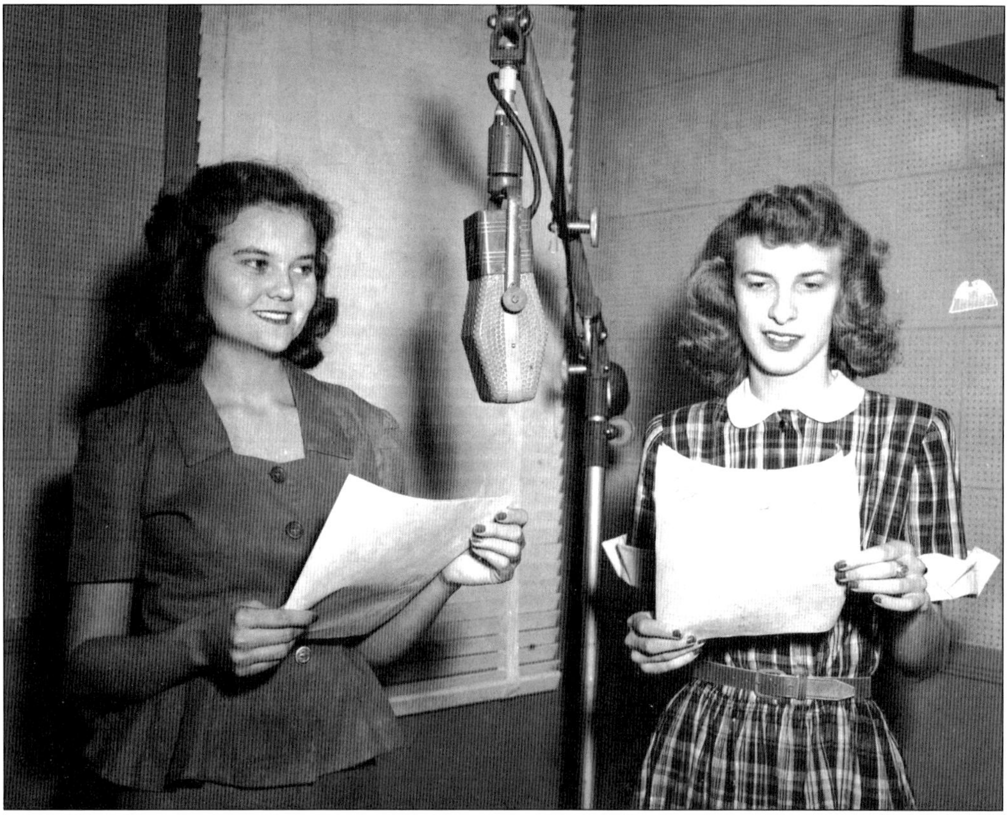

From the *Index-Journal* newspaper (March 7, 1944), "Lander College news items will be broadcast tomorrow afternoon at 2:45 o'clock over WCRS. The program is the second of a series of bi-weekly broadcasts by Lander students. The series features student, faculty, and general campus activities and news items of general interest. Listen to the broadcasts. They are both entertaining and informative." Other broadcasts included musical performances by Lander students and faculty.

Students earning a commercial certificate were required to learn how to type. The course description in the 1949 catalog describes the class, taught by Mary Frances Lide as "Instruction in the use and care of the typewriter, including straight copy, business forms, letter arrangements, tabulation." If a student had previous experience using a typewriter, they would be placed in an intermediate or advanced course.

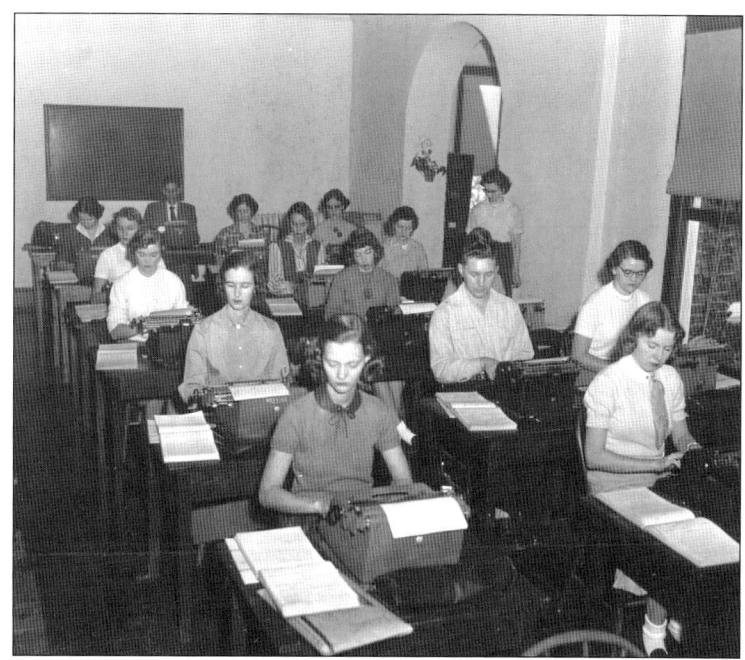

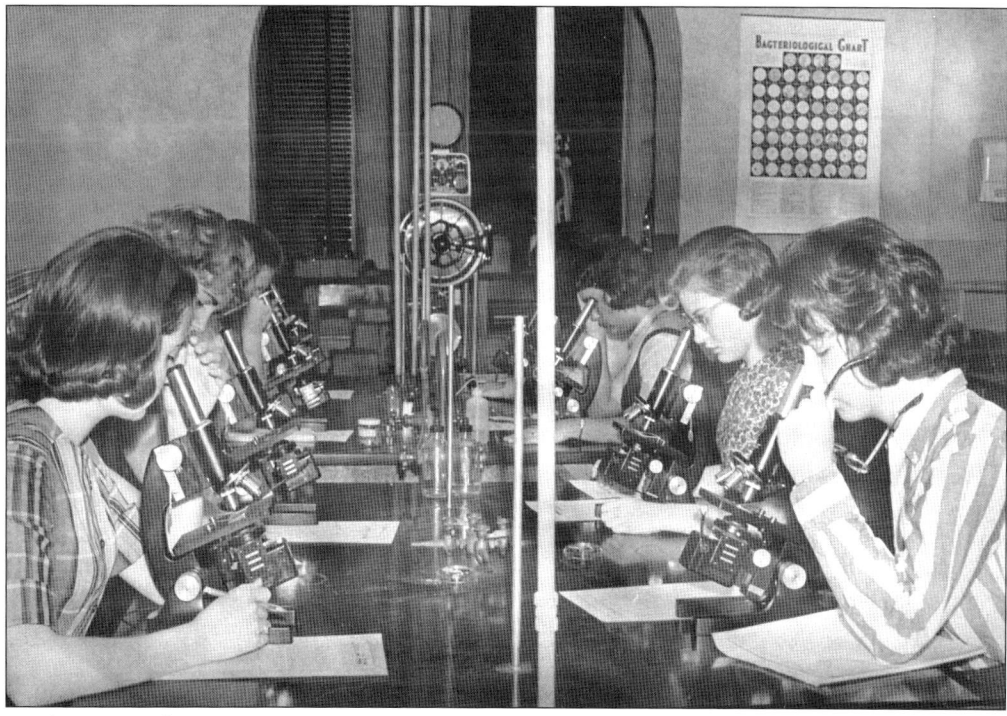

Students use their microscopes to examine slides in an early-1960s biology lab. The object in the center to the back is an autoclave, which is a machine that uses steam under pressure to kill harmful bacteria, viruses, fungi, and spores on items that are placed inside it. A bacteriological chart hangs on the wall to the right.

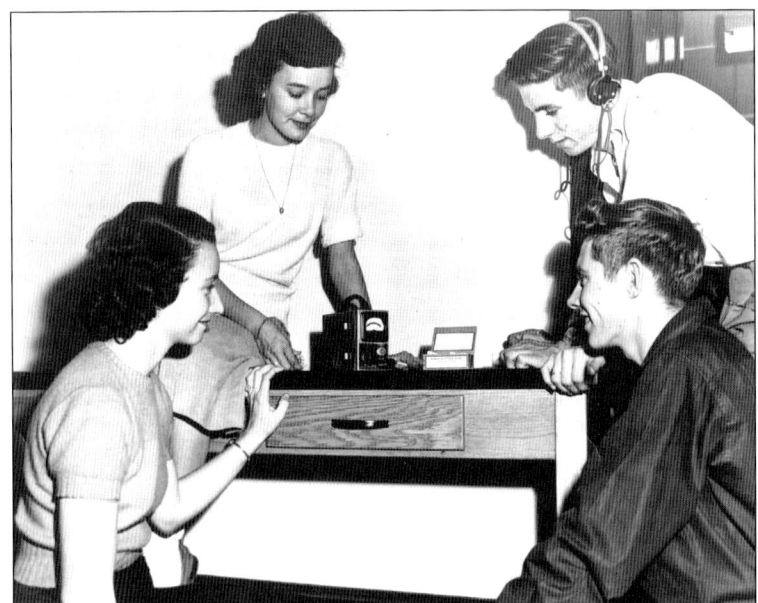

In this 1951 photograph, students try out a Geiger counter, an instrument used to detect ionizing radiation, in the physics lab. The label on the box to the right reads, "Radioactive Ore Collections." The student sitting on the table appears to be holding a piece of ore in her right hand.

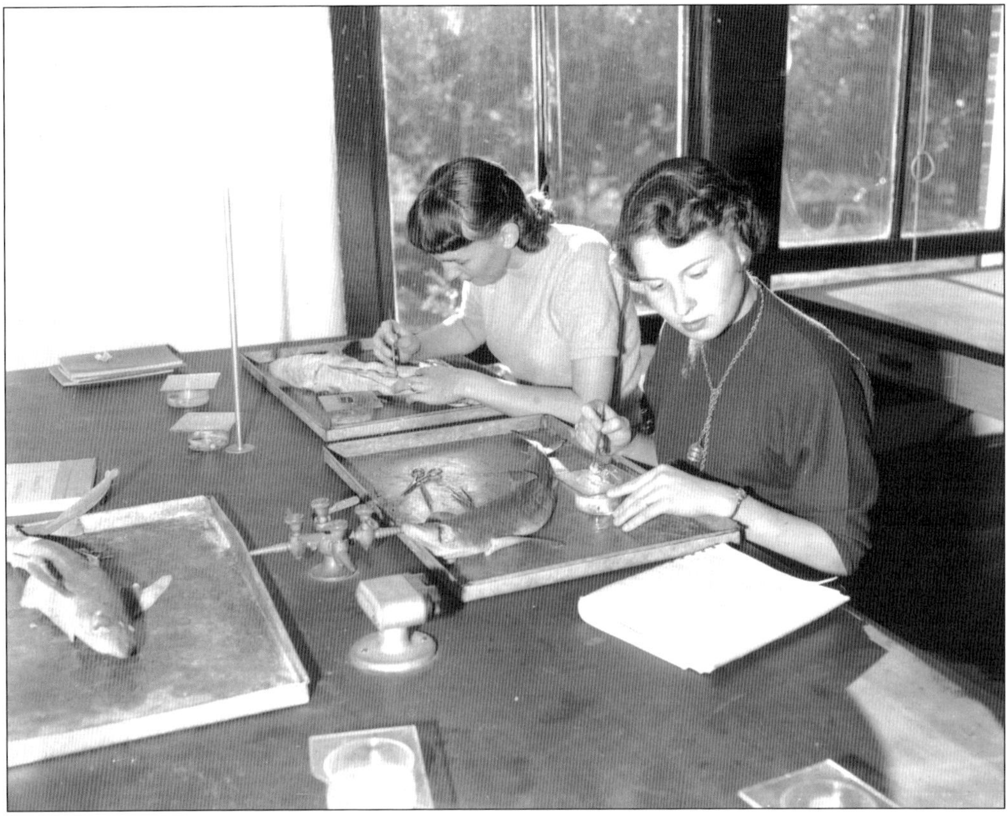

A student consults her notes as she begins to dissect a dogfish shark to gain a better understanding of vertebrae and fish anatomy in this 1950s biology lab. This was likely done in the class of science faculty member Nell Q. Henry, whose faculty portrait in the 1954 *Naiad* shows her with a partially dissected shark.

In 1956, Lander opened the first associate degree nursing program in South Carolina. The program was generously supported through training opportunities at Self Memorial Hospital and financial gifts from the Self Family Foundation. The official title of the new program was the Self Memorial Nursing Department of Lander College. This undated photograph shows student nurses gathering in the hospital cafeteria.

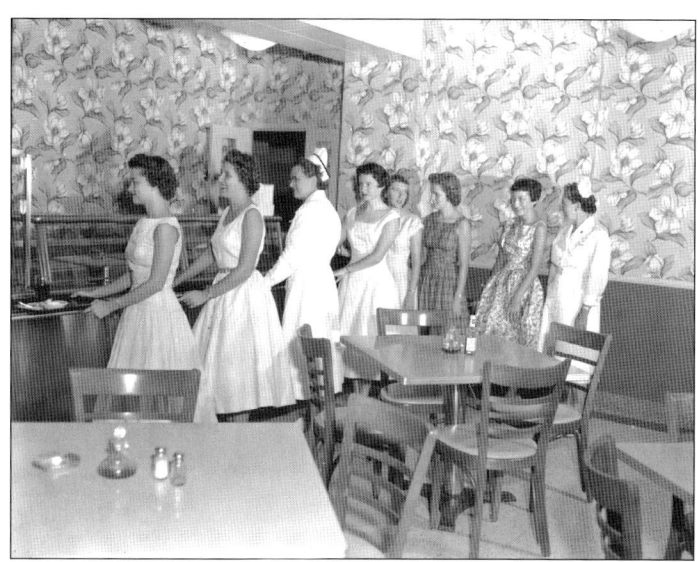

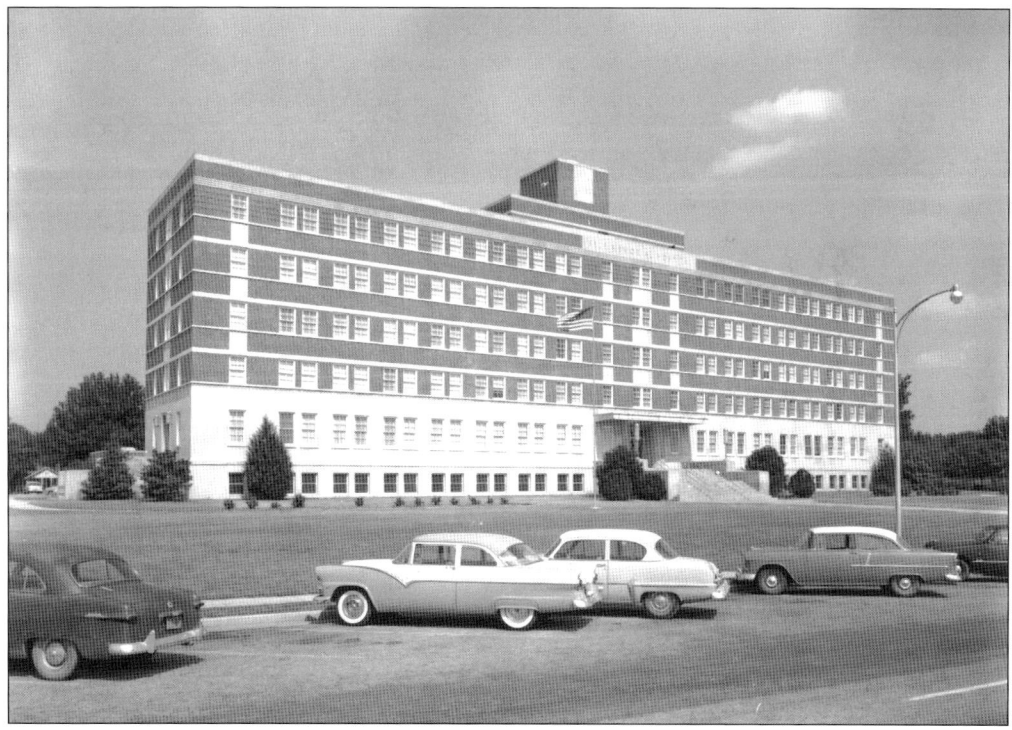

This is an exterior view of the Self Memorial Hospital where Lander nursing students worked on their clinical training over the years. The 179-bed hospital was completed in 1951 and was described in the *Index-Journal* as "ultra-modern in every respect of equipment and construction from the basement through the five main floors." The building was constructed by Greenwood Mills from architectural designs drawn by James C. Hemphill and associates of Greenwood and was funded by the Self Foundation, with James C. Self as president.

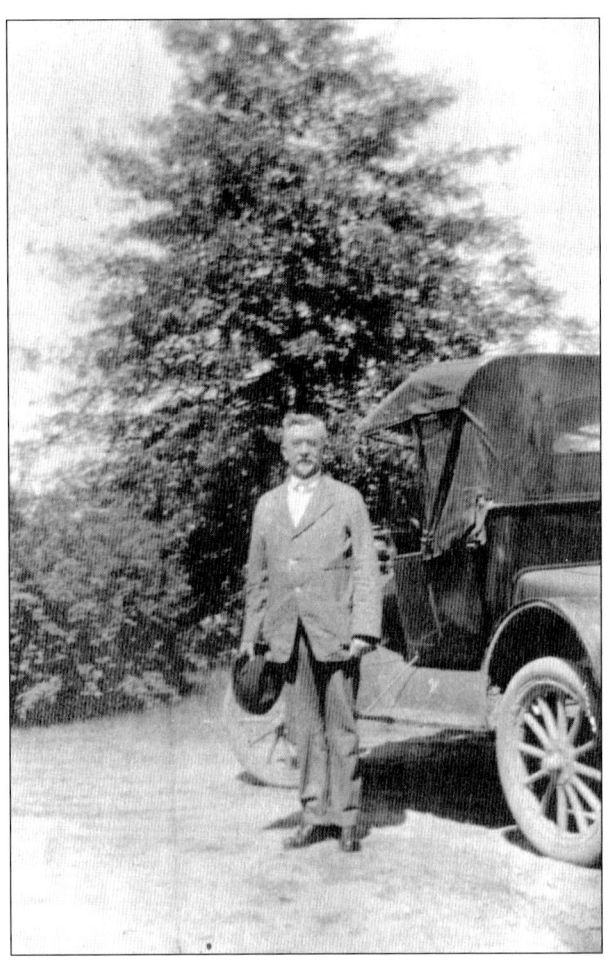

Dr. R.B. Epting was the college physician from 1904 until his death in 1923. He received his medical training from the College of Charleston and the University of Maryland. Born in Pomaria, South Carolina, Epting moved to Greenwood in 1890 to practice medicine and was hired by the college in 1904 when it opened in Greenwood the same year. Dr. Epting's leadership during the 1918 flu pandemic is credited with Lander's successful weathering of that time.

Seen here is a campus infirmary bed around 1914. The 1914 academic catalog states that "the infirmary is well arranged and equipped, containing all the appliances found in a regular city hospital." The infirmary suite included a waiting room, consulting room, eight beds (two private), a kitchen, bathroom, and bedroom for a resident "trained nurse."

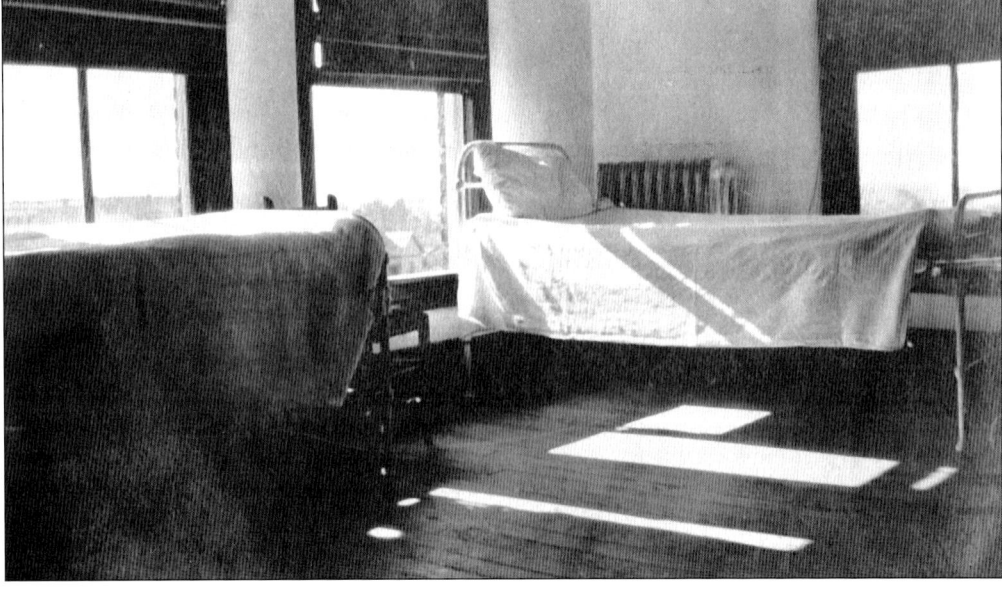

A Lander College nurse administers an injection of the Salk polio vaccine to freshman Dicksie Thornton as fellow student Janet Butler looks on in the late 1950s. Dr. Jonas Salk developed this version of the polio vaccine to combat the virus that caused the crippling disease of polio. The first injections were given to children in Pittsburgh, Pennsylvania, in 1954.

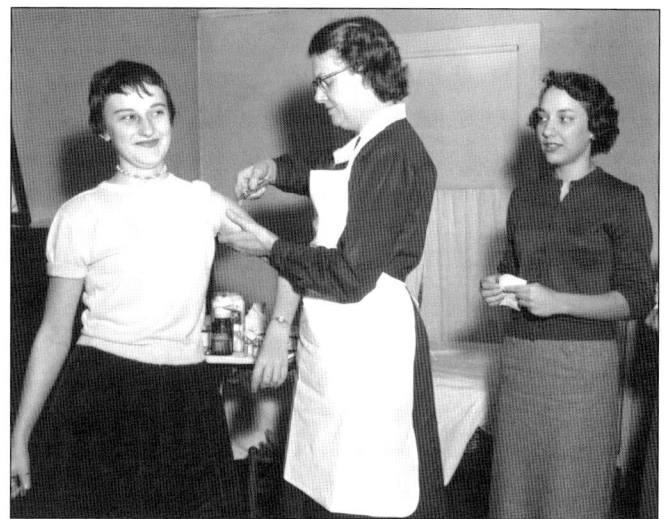

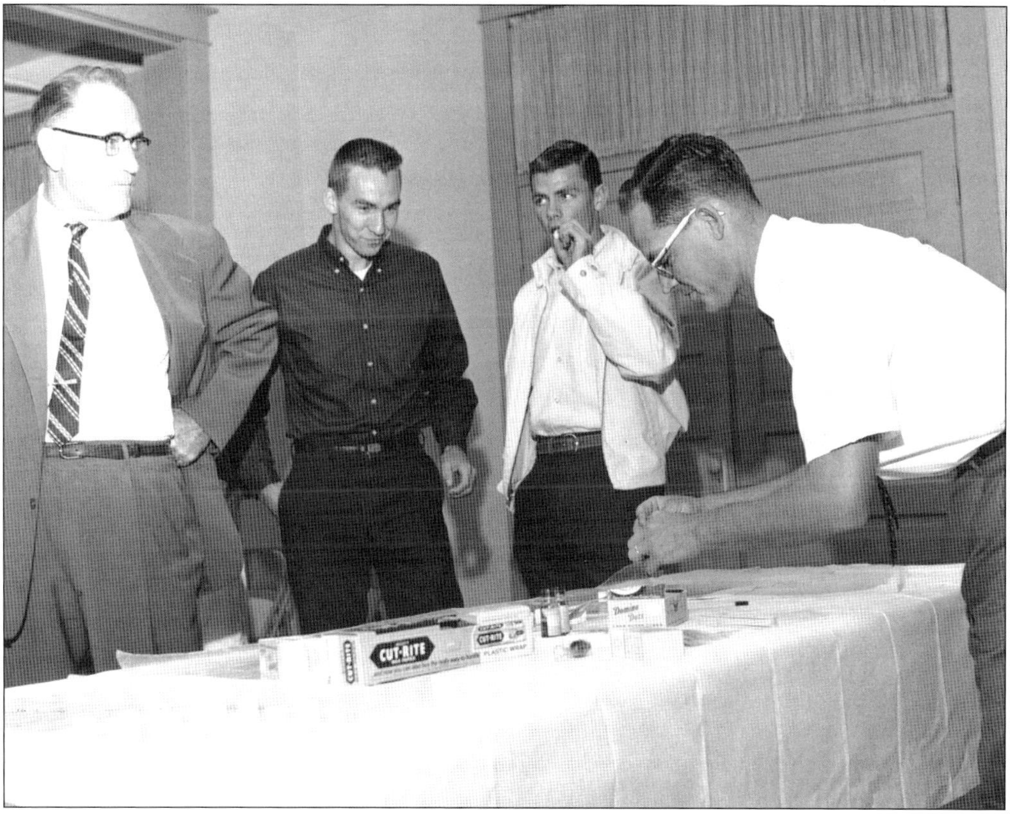

In 1963, Greenwood County participated in a "Stop Polio Sundays" campaign as part of a statewide campaign aimed at immunizing over two million people. According to *Index-Journal* reports, it was "necessary for the three different types of vaccine to be given on different Sundays to form complete immunization against the three strains of the polio virus." In this photograph, Lander students take the Sabin polio vaccine, which was added to a sugar cube and then eaten. The Sabin vaccine differed from the Salk vaccine in that it was a live version of the virus that could be taken orally.

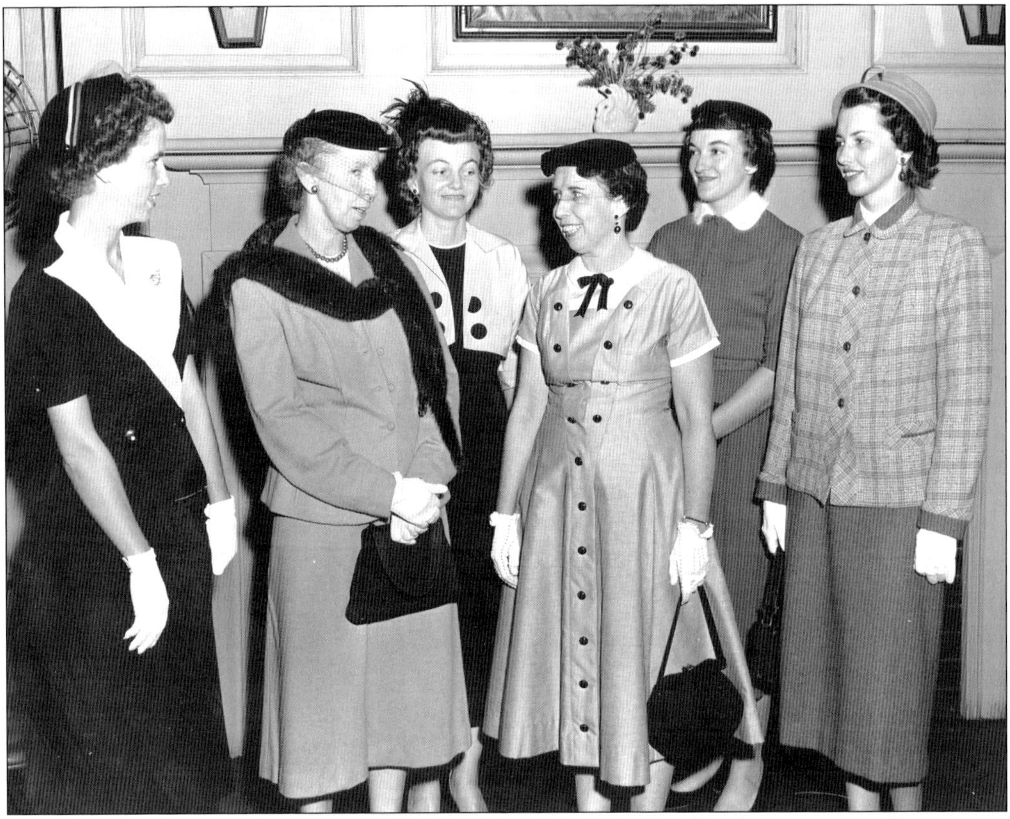

Dr. Maybelle Coleman (second from left) attended many social gatherings over the years in support of Lander. Dr. Coleman was a 1909 Lander graduate and then a faculty member for 36 years. She served as dean of the school from 1943 to 1950. Lander named Coleman Hall dormitory in her honor. She was the 1988 recipient of Lander's Medallion of Honor. Her contributions to the school were numerous earning her a special place in Lander's history. Mary Major (fourth from the left), president of the alumni association, is also pictured.

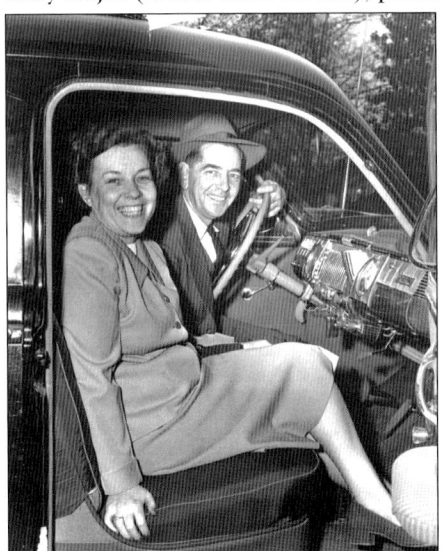

Katie Hagan Hollingsworth was a 1927 graduate of Lander College and did graduate study at the University of Tennessee and the University of Chicago. She served as the registrar at Lander from 1945 until her death in 1969. Between 1951 and 1963, she also served as dean of students. Prior to becoming registrar, she was alumni secretary and secretary to Lander president Marvin J. Rast. She is pictured here with her husband, Robert.

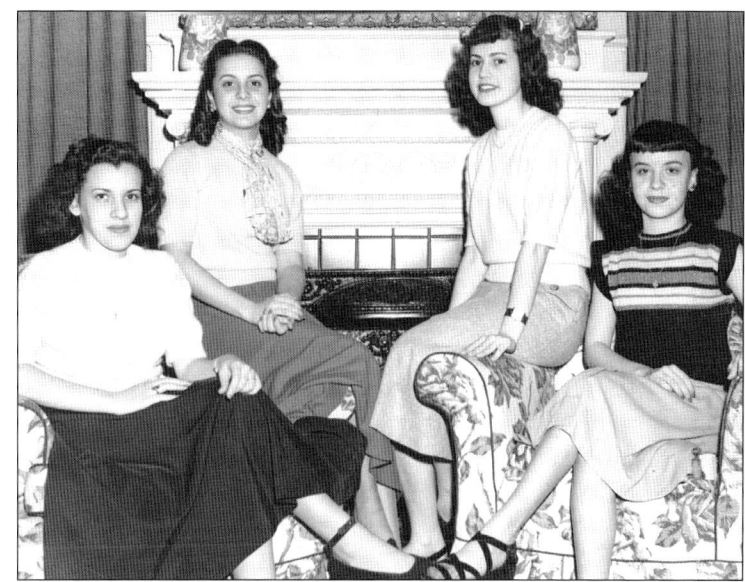

Between 1945 and 1951, nineteen students from Cuba attended Lander. Dozens of local news stories show that these students were warmly embraced by the Lander and Greenwood communities. Pictured in 1949, from left to right are Elsa Vasquez, Raquel Canosa (voted Miss Lander, 1948), Juanita Cerda (voted "Sophomore Class Beauty," 1950), and Lydia Canosa.

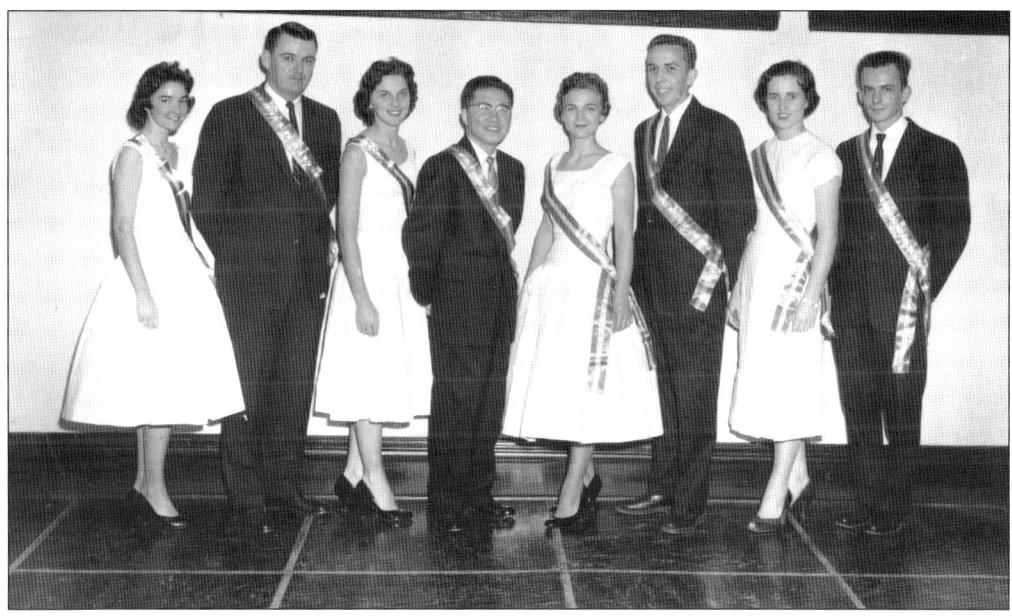

This 1956 photograph shows the student commencement marshals for that year. Featured fourth from the left is Chin Sae Jhung, the first Asian student to graduate from Lander. He attended Lander on a full scholarship, jointly sponsored by the Rotary Club of Greenwood and Lander College. Rotary supplied room, board, and books, and Lander College supplied tuition. His father had been a university professor but was kidnapped during the 1951 communist invasion of Korea. Chin fled with his mother to rebuild their lives. He never saw his father again. Dozens of local newspaper stories demonstrate that he was very active on campus and a sought-after speaker in town. Pictured from left to right are Frances Bolton, Roy Wilson, Joanne Guerry, Chin Sae Jhung, Mary Cameron Shealy, Sammy McQuerns, Beverly Keadle, and Richard Shaffer.

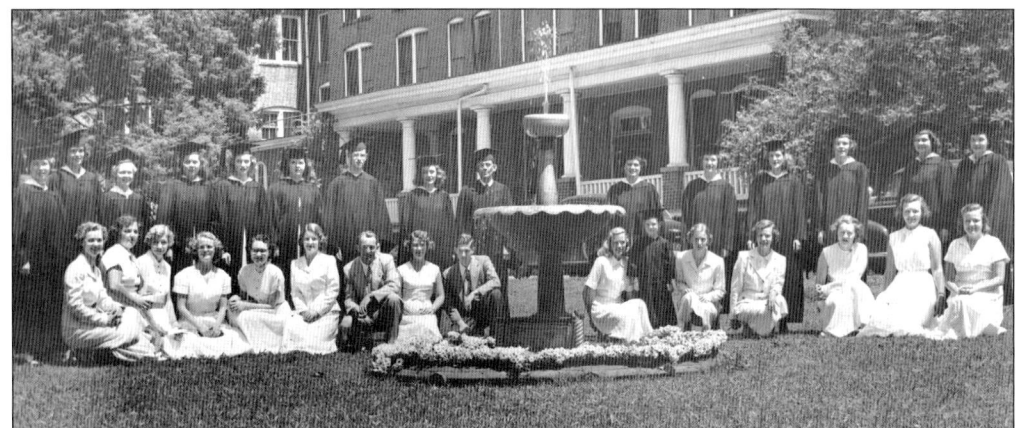

Seniors pose by the front lawn fountain on Class Day in 1950. Note the small child in the photograph dressed in academic regalia. Each year, the senior class would select one child to serve as class mascot, the French term for "good-luck charm." Mascots would participate in academic ceremonies, athletic, and social events throughout the school year. This tradition at Lander can be documented from 1922 to 1968.

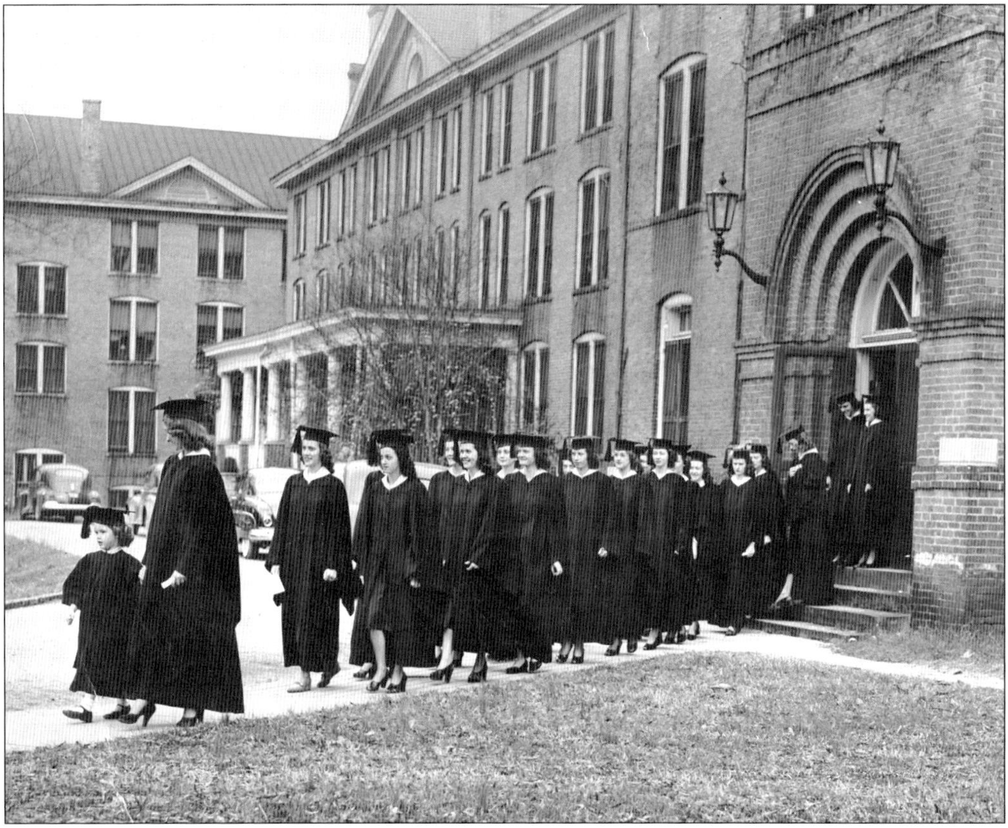

Seniors in their caps and gowns file out of Laura Lander Hall on commencement day and are led by their class mascot down to the Dingle for graduation exercises in the late 1940s. The large bronze lanterns above the doorway to Laura Lander Hall were a gift of the class of 1911.

Three

THE SOCIAL STREAM OF LEARNING

During the early years at Williamston and Greenwood, social opportunities for Lander students were limited by today's standards. Cultural values and physical circumstances—Williamston had fewer than 1,000 residents—were strikingly different from the 21st-century college environment. Yet, within the setting of the day, Rev. Samuel Lander was committed to a healthy social life—in the context of intellectual cultivation, as an adjunct to the mental stream—for the women under his charge.

Extracurricular opportunities are mentioned in the first catalogs of Williamston Female College. A weekly meeting of the Young Ladies' Christian Association was available when the school opened in 1872. Subsequent catalogs highlight the gradual addition of other opportunities: the Erosophic Literary Society and twice-daily outings to the town spring (1873); the construction of a "large society hall" (1874); the Mendelssohn Society and the Sue Kirkland Missionary Society (1887); and the Mathesian Literary Society (1895).

Upon moving to Greenwood in 1904, the college added the Bonheur Art Club and an annual lecture and concert series, named the Lyceum in 1905 that offered 21 events during the 1905–1906 school year; from the catalog that year: "We support a regular Lyceum—with the kind assistance of friends in Greenwood—and through this we enjoy the benefit of a series of lectures and entertainments of high grade." In 1906, there was a music festival on campus, and in 1917, music students had two clubs: the Lyric Club and the B Sharp Club.

Social opportunities expanded well beyond purely intellectual cultivation in the 1920s with the formation of an athletic club and the annual field day. The indoor gymnasium was open for free-time sports. An Epworth League was formed as well as a chapter of the YWCA with its own space: "The YWCA hall is one of the beautiful things in the college. It is a pleasant recreation room when it is not in use otherwise" (according to the 1920 academic catalog). The year 1923 saw the formation of the first student government association as well as the first issue of the *Naiad* yearbook. That publication year included full features on numerous clubs on campus: the Press Club, the Glee Club, the Lotus Eaters Club, the Sisters' Club, the Happy Bunca Club, the Preachers' Daughters Club, the Rat-Hole Rowdies, the Pirates, the Long Distance Club, clubs for each county represented in the student body, and the Loafers Club, whose motto was "Loaf and the world loafs with you, work and you work alone." Alas, the 1925 *Naiad* features a short-lived organization called the DMC (Do More Courting) Club. Finally, the first sororities at Lander appear in the 1926 *Naiad*: Beta Lambda Kappa and Tau Chi. By 1930, there were 10 sororities.

As reflected in the photograph selections for this chapter, social life at Lander came into effulgent bloom in the post–World War II years. The postwar boom enabled a context for fun with others just for the sake of fun in amount and variety not previously seen on campus.

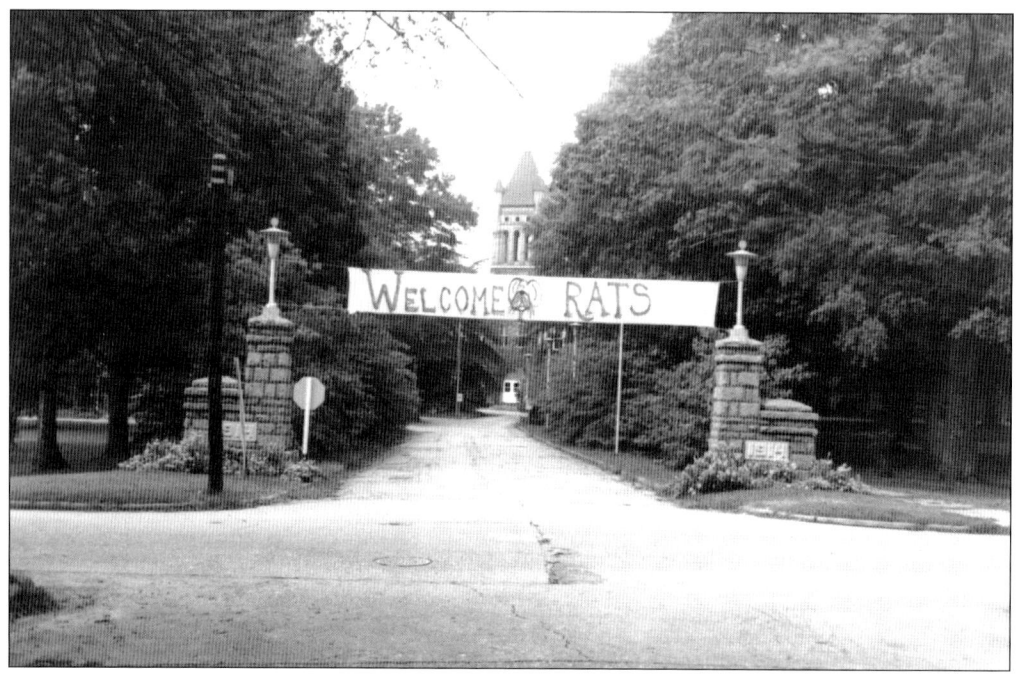

A banner hanging from the stone columns (a gift of the class of 1914) in front of Laura Lander Hall welcomes new freshmen to campus. From as early as the 1920s through the 1970s, Lander freshmen were referred to as "rats" during their first few weeks of school. The term was common at numerous universities. New students went through a "ratting" period, where they participated in a variety of campus social activities.

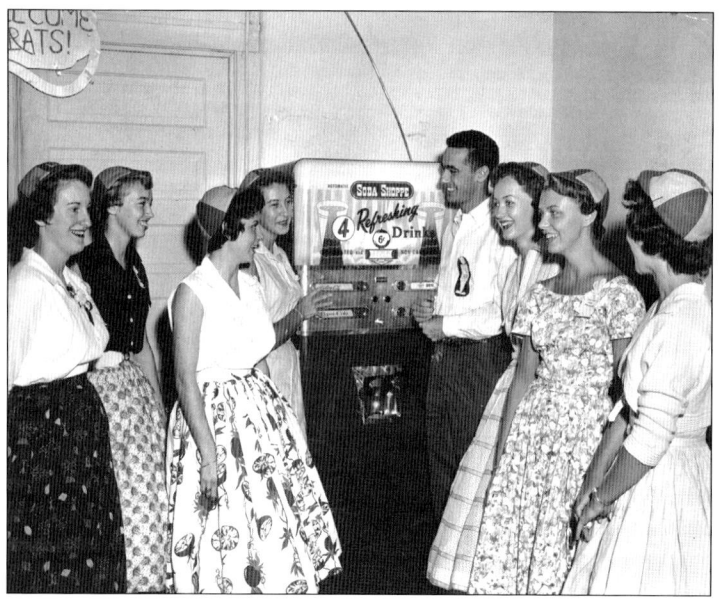

During their first weeks at Lander, the freshmen wore rat caps to distinguish them from upperclassmen. The beanie-style caps were very eye-catching in the school colors of blue and gold. Pictured while visiting the campus canteen during 1957 orientation week are Ann Harris, Peggy Clyburn, Nancy Hand, Glenda Garvin, Steve Byrd, Jo Ellen Roberts, Bettye Sue Browne, and Lillian Holman.

These Lander rats receive a friendly welcome on a visit to the local movie theater in the 1950s. Students got to know all the local hotspots in Greenwood in addition to becoming familiar with the campus as part of their orientation process. The ratting process was intended to be a helpful way to welcome new students to Lander life.

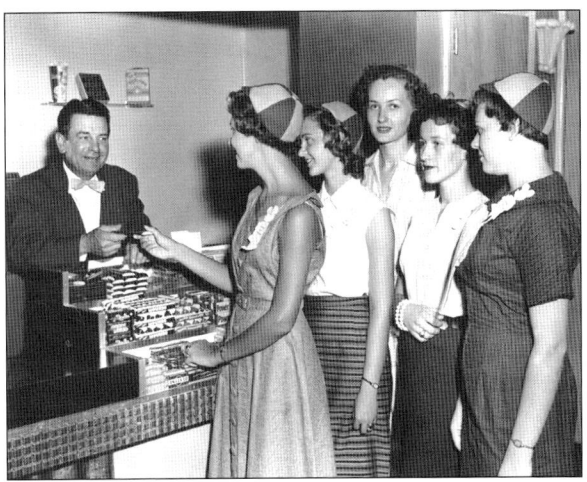

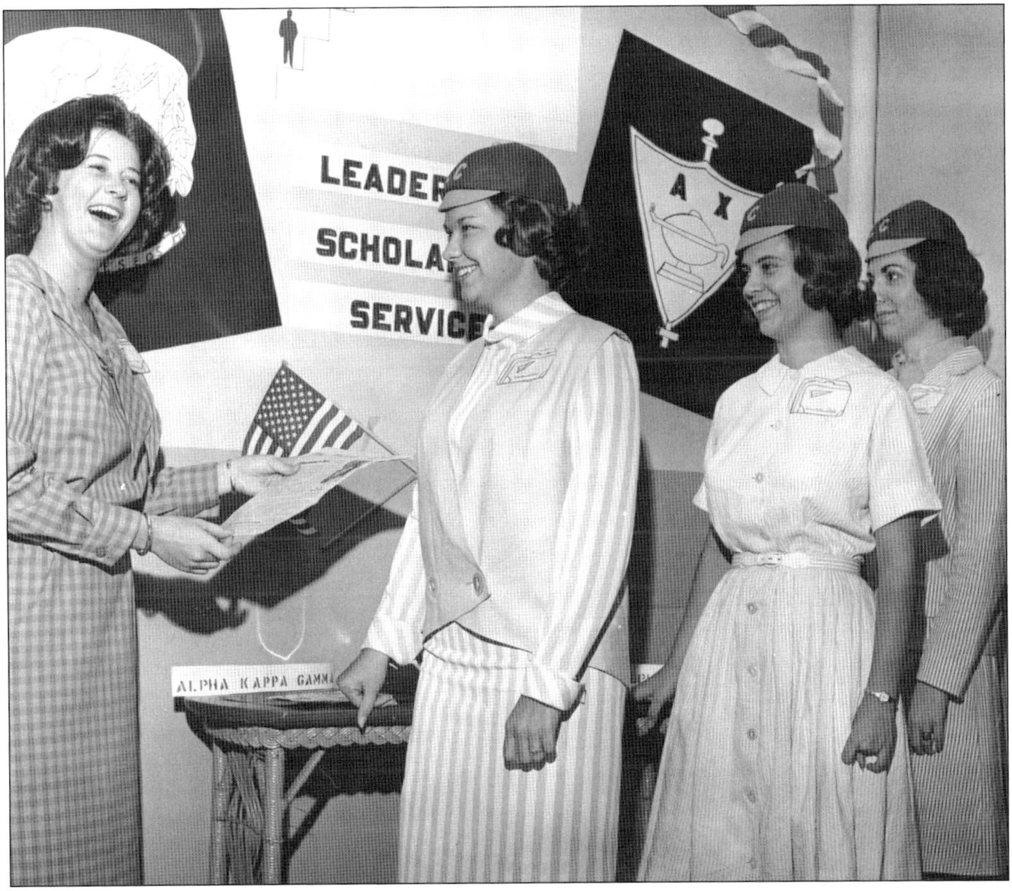

Freshmen rats are shown attending an organizational fair during orientation week to learn more about campus clubs and leadership opportunities. The students in this 1960s-era photograph are making a stop at the Alpha Kappa Gamma National Honorary Fraternity table. The Lander Chapter, Sister Kenney Circle, was composed of those who had shown themselves to be constructive leaders on the campus. Their advisors at the time this photograph was taken were Dr. Maybelle Coleman, Katie Hollingsworth, and Mary Frances Lide.

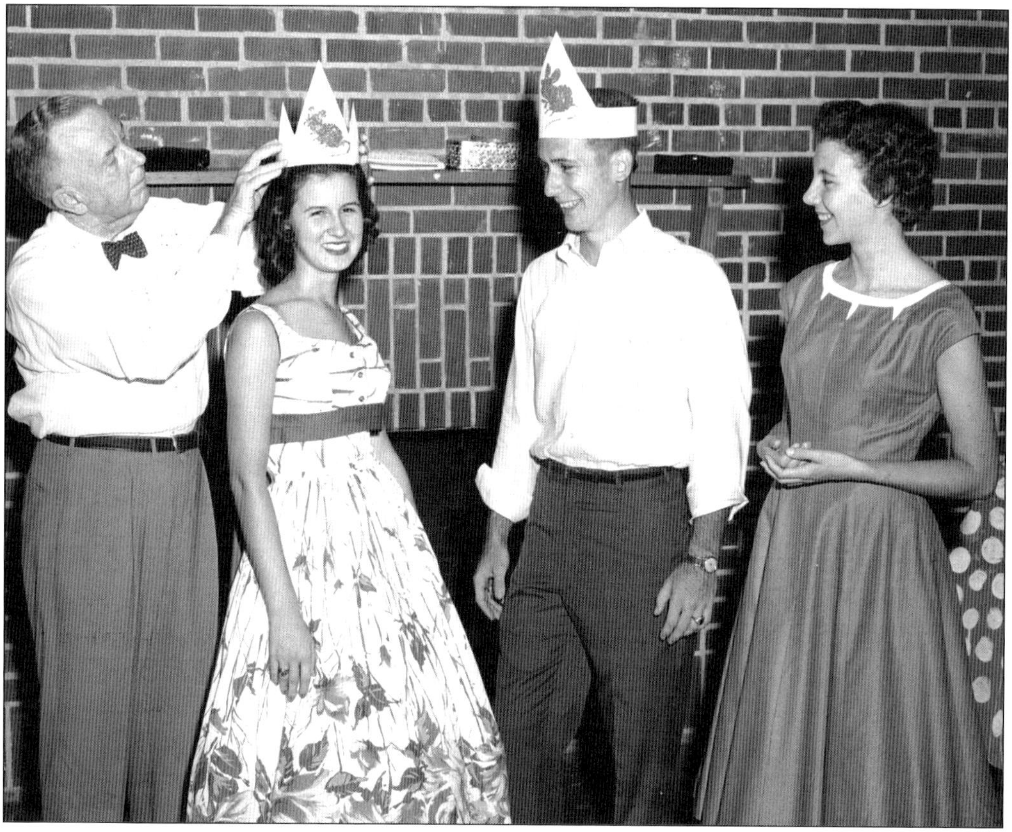

At the end of orientation week, a dance called the "Rat Hop" was held in honor of the new freshmen. A queen and king of the hop were selected by the students. In this photograph from 1958, Dr. Boyce Grier, Lander president, crowns Sabra Grice "rat queen" and Tommy Anderson "rat king." Both queen and king are wearing paper crowns decorated with illustrations of rats.

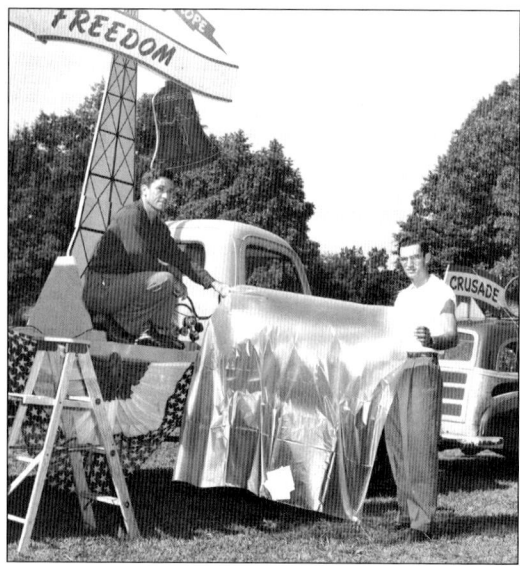

Socially active students belonging to Lander's International Relations Club sponsored this Crusade for Freedom demonstration on the college campus. The two men in this image are holding a balloon used to carry messages of hope to people in countries behind the Iron Curtain. The balloons were filled with helium and carried by Europe's westerly winds, bursting at 30,000 feet and releasing printed messages over a wide area. The Crusade for Freedom was an American campaign conducted by the National Committee for a Free Europe. *Index-Journal* headlines reported that Greenwood County had the distinction of being the first in the nation to complete a fundraising drive for the cause in 1951.

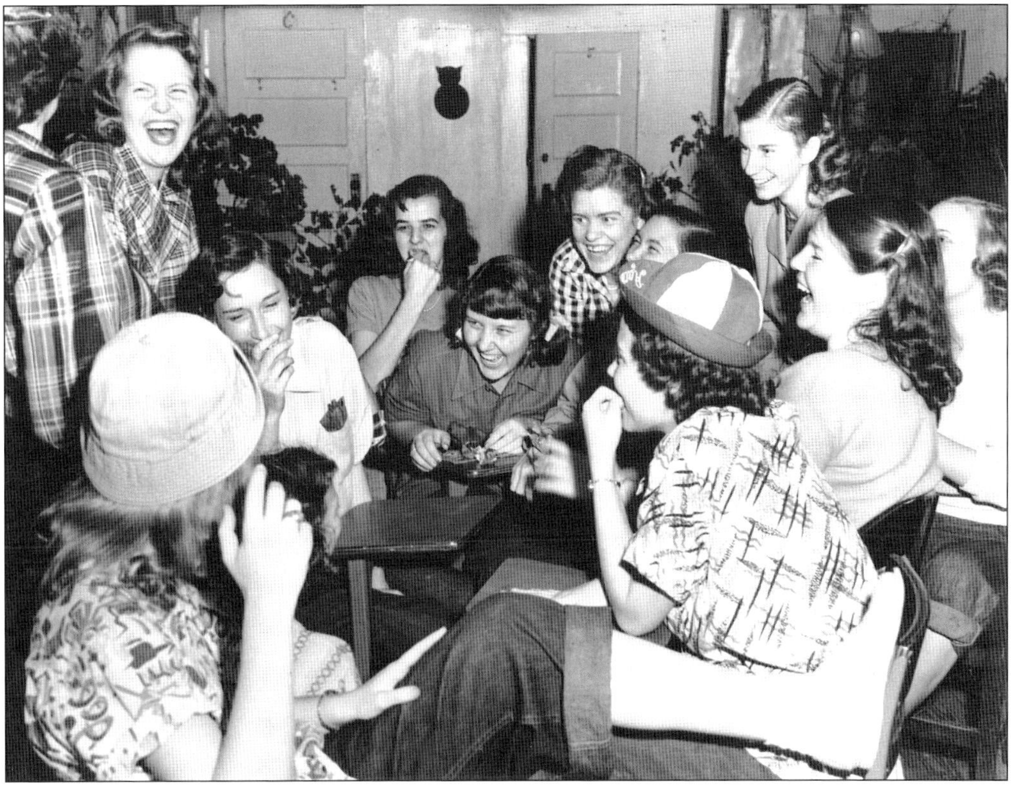

Lander students have a great time during a Halloween party held in their dormitory in 1950. The evening included bobbing for apples and pumpkin carving. The Greenwood Recreation Committee sponsored a carnival and parade that year for young people in the community so there were opportunities for Lander day students to get into the spirit of the season as well.

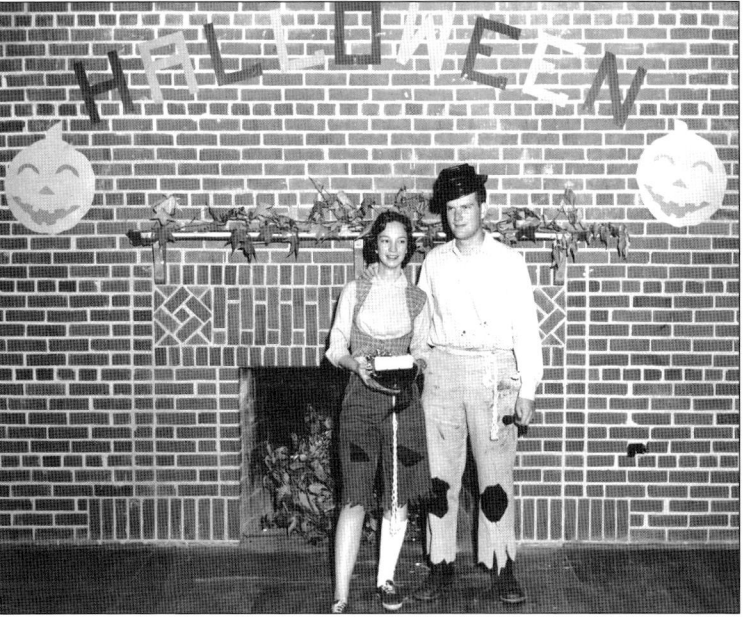

Lander students Mary Jo Garrett and David Boswell wear festive attire at the annual Lander College Halloween dance held in the Sproles recreation building in the late 1950s. In an *Index-Journal* gossip column called "the Chatterbox," it was announced that several Greenwood High School students also attended and "danced their way through a wonderful evening."

45

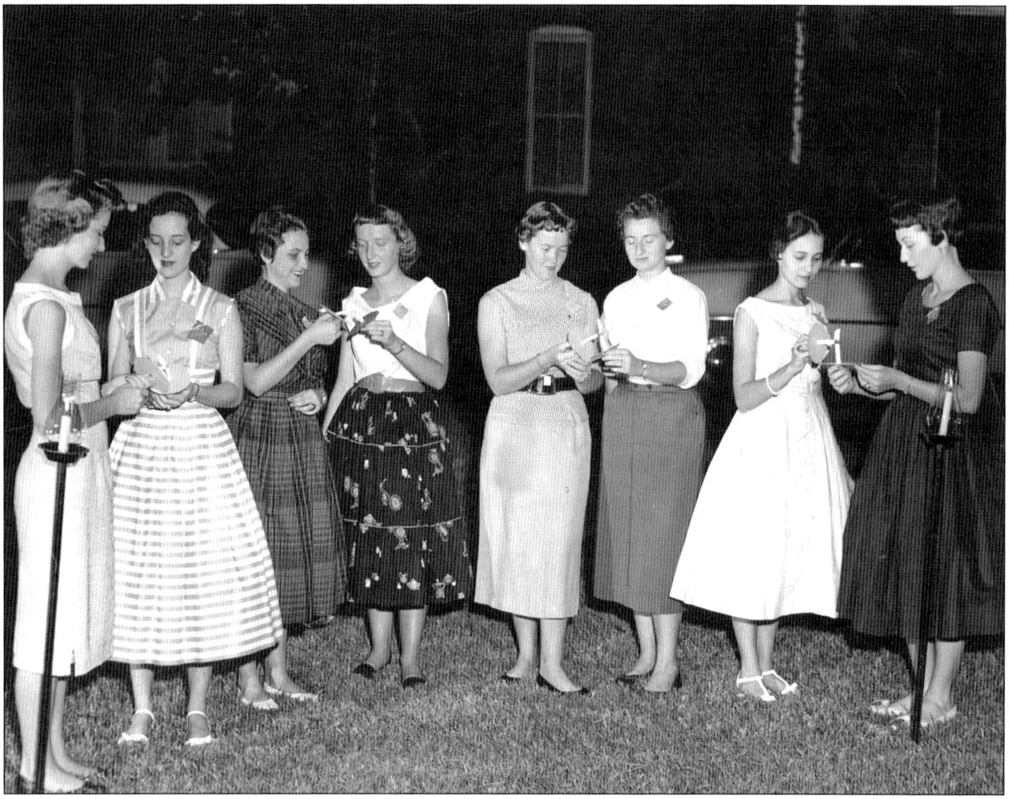

Lander freshmen and upperclassmen used to conduct a candlelight ceremony at the fountain in front of the main building on campus. The event was described in a September 1953 issue of the *Index-Journal* and was reportedly called the Big Sister-Little Sister, Big Brother-Little Brother candlelight ceremony. It was designed to draw all students into a close bond as each new student was placed in the care of an upperclassman who would aid the little sister or brother in becoming acquainted with the college's traditions and regulations. From left to right are Peggy Knight, Cathy McCain, Ruth Tisdale, Sylvia Boozer, Joyce McDonald, Dolores Johnson, Kay Hazel, and Mary Jo Harris.

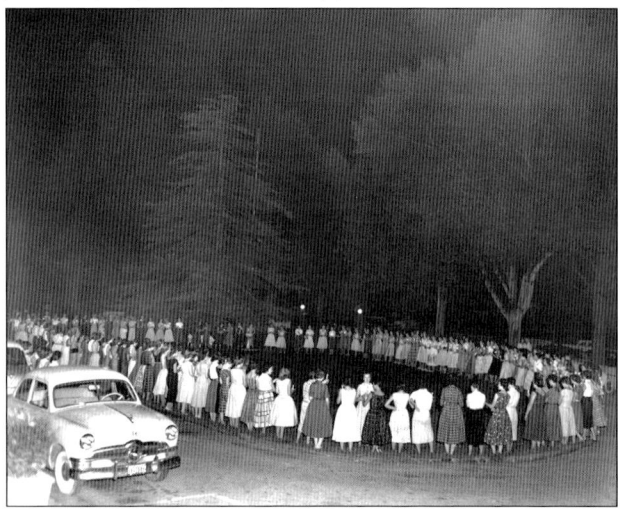

Students encircle the front lawn fountain to exchange vows of friendship at the 1957 Big Sister- Little Sister, Big Brother- Little Brother candlelight ceremony. As the big sisters and brothers light the candles of the new students, the ceremony becomes symbolic of the upperclassmen's desire to "light the way" of the freshmen.

Members of the Pamican Club, an organization for physical education majors, gather around a campfire in 1958. Pictured from left to right are Carolyn Farmer, Peggy Davis, Lal Minus, Nancy Gantt, Gayle Overby, Linda Kemp, Jackie Crowder, Jessie Finucan, Joyce McDonald, Gloria Strother, Susan Way, Patsy Floyd Brown, Mary Frank Gantt, Pat Whitten, Peggy Carter, Verna Cooper, Bobbie Myers, and Betty Ann McFadden.

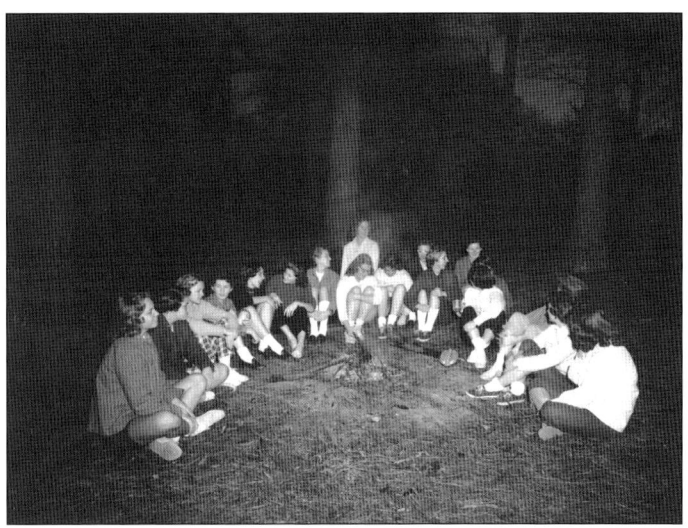

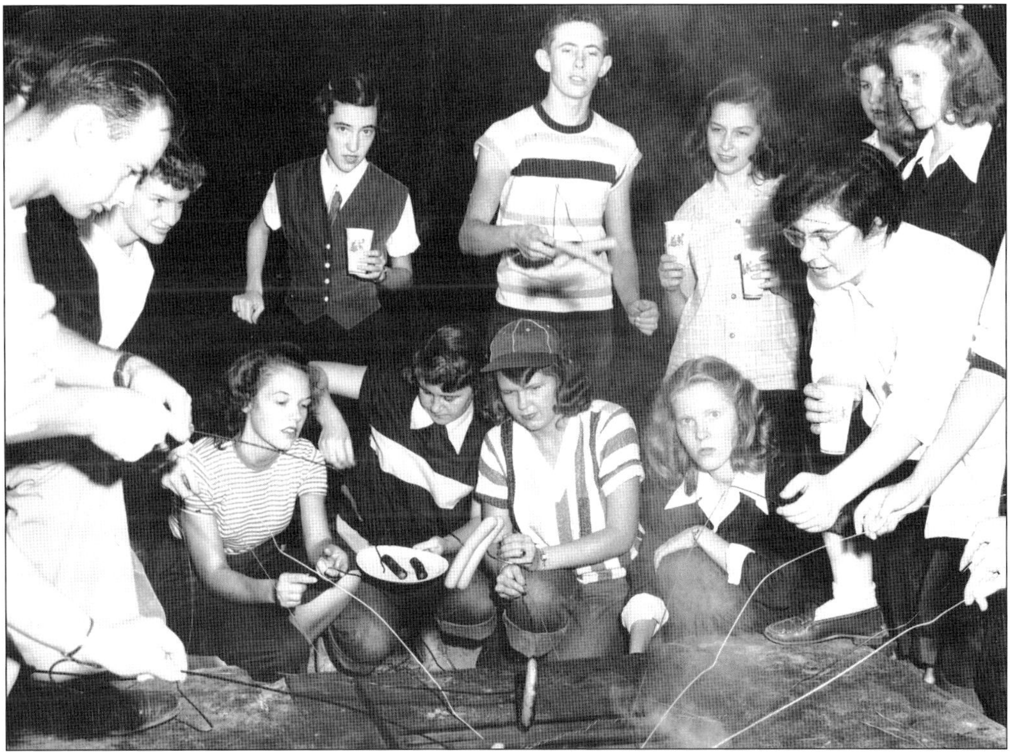

This photograph from the 1951 *Naiad* shows a hot-dog roast sponsored by the student government association for new students. The student wearing glasses on the right side of the image is Sotiria Liori, from Athens, Greece. Liori was a child during the Nazi occupation of Greece and came to Lander to study psychology so that she could "return to her native Greece, and do all in her power to help the children of the country live a normal life" (according to the *Index-Journal* on January 25, 1951). Her story of life under the Nazis, as movingly recounted in the *Index-Journal*, is heart-rending. Liori's ability to study at Lander was made possible through the generosity of the Rotary Club of Greenwood.

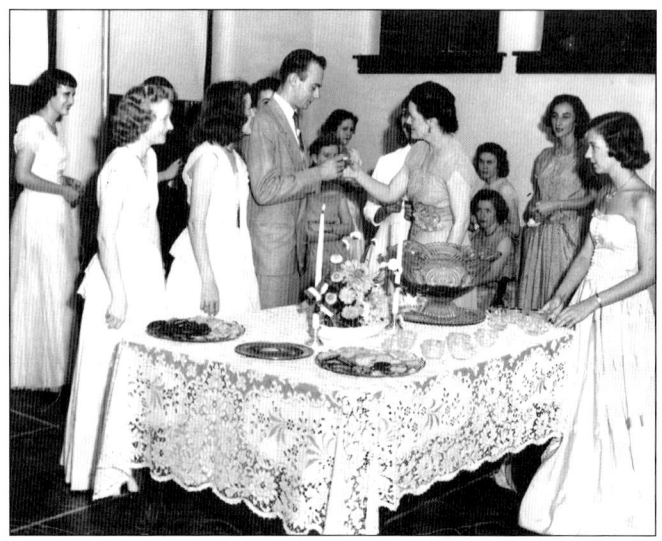

The man in the center of this photograph is Bill Willson of Greenwood, who enrolled that day in 1950 as a Lander freshman. Surrounded by other incoming students, Bill received a cup of punch from Azile Fletcher, Lander's field representative. The reception had been given for the incoming class by the dean of students, Annette Crickard. Faculty and staff greeted the new students in a receiving line. A dance followed the reception. The following day, the freshmen went to Lake Greenwood for an outing.

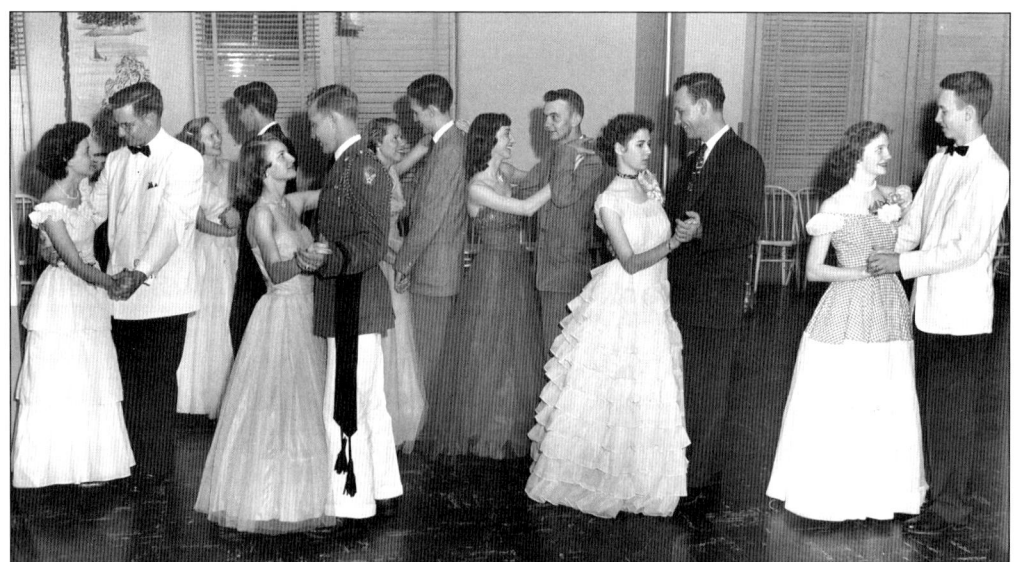

Both formal and informal dances were an important part of Lander social life year-round. This photograph appeared in the 1953 *Naiad*, and the dance appears to be held in a dining hall. Note the eye-catching military dress uniform of one of the attendees. Upon enlargement, it appears the shoulder sleeve insignia on his coat is the Hap Arnold Wings patch worn by Army Air Forces personnel.

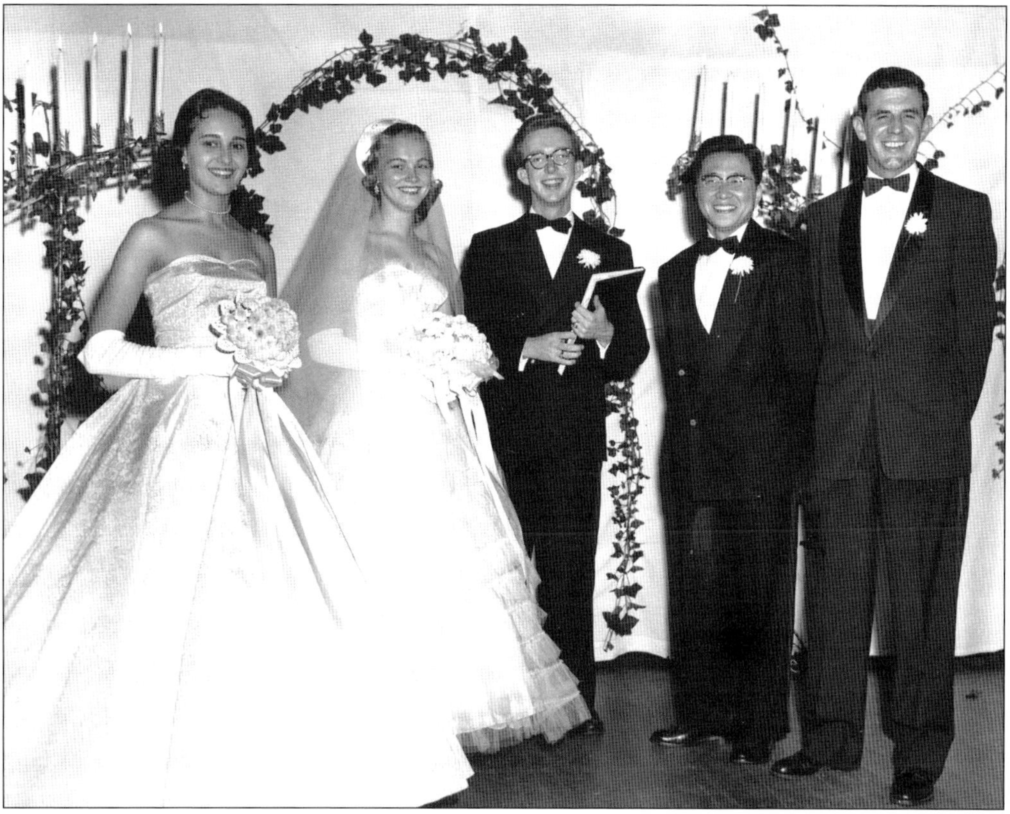

The annual freshman-junior wedding was a symbolic union of friendship between the two classes. Although not an actual wedding, the ceremony was acted out on stage and at times in chapel to look like one. These ceremonies had student actors from each class playing the roles of preacher, bride, groom, maid of honor, best man, and father of the bride. After the ceremony, a formal reception complete with a receiving line, fancy food, flowers, and decorations was held. The vibrant celebration rivaled any real wedding, and students, faculty, and the college president were always in attendance. Pictured from left to right in 1956 are Kay Hazel, Carol Smith, Conrad Sprouse, Chin Sae Jhung, and Ben Cook.

Students get ready to attend the 1955 junior-senior dance. The graduating senior class was honored that year by the junior class at an annual banquet in the college dining hall. Following the banquet was a formal dance held in the recreation center. All Lander classes had a hand in preparing for the event with the freshman class in charge of decorations, the sophomore class with invitations, and the junior class with refreshments. From left to right are Vera McMillan, Betty Stone, Janice Curran, Ernestine Ivester, Billy Garrison, Sara Nell Bishop, and Joan Bonnette.

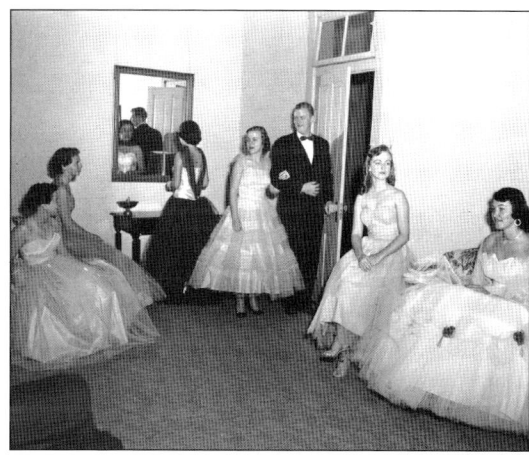

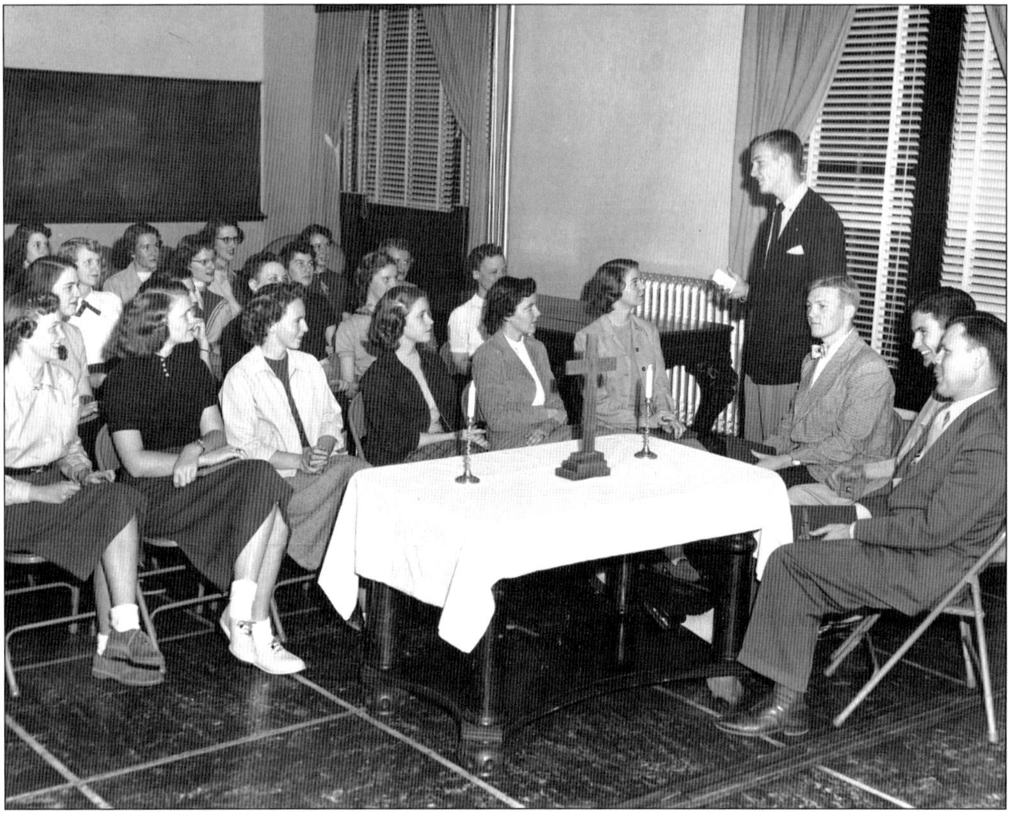

From 1904 until 1948, Lander College was operated as a Methodist institution. The Lander College Christian Association was an interdenominational group with several subcommittees including worship, social welfare, world student service, and recreation. In this 1953 photograph, Lander students attend a vespers service led by students visiting from Wofford (also a Methodist college).

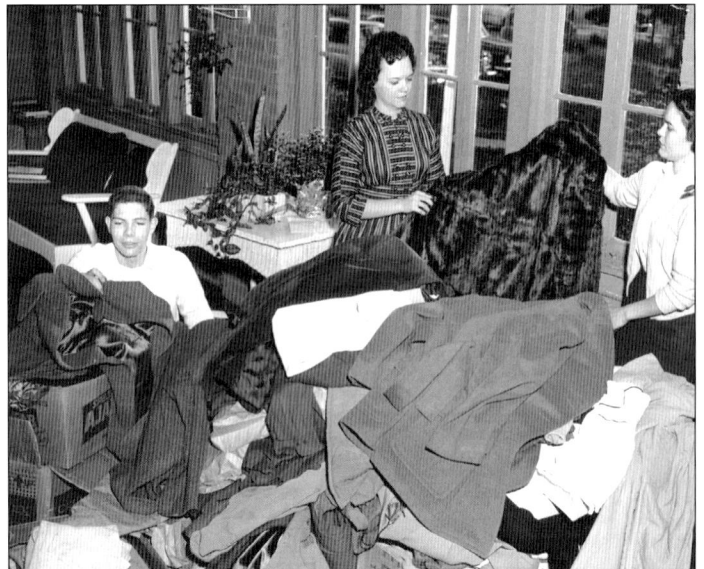

Social service has always been an integral part of Lander student life. This photograph shows members of the Lander College Christian Association gathering clothes to send to Hungarian refugees from the 1956 Hungarian revolution and invasion by the Soviet Union. From left to right are Phillip Robuck, Mary Lou Aultman, and Marguerite Rogers.

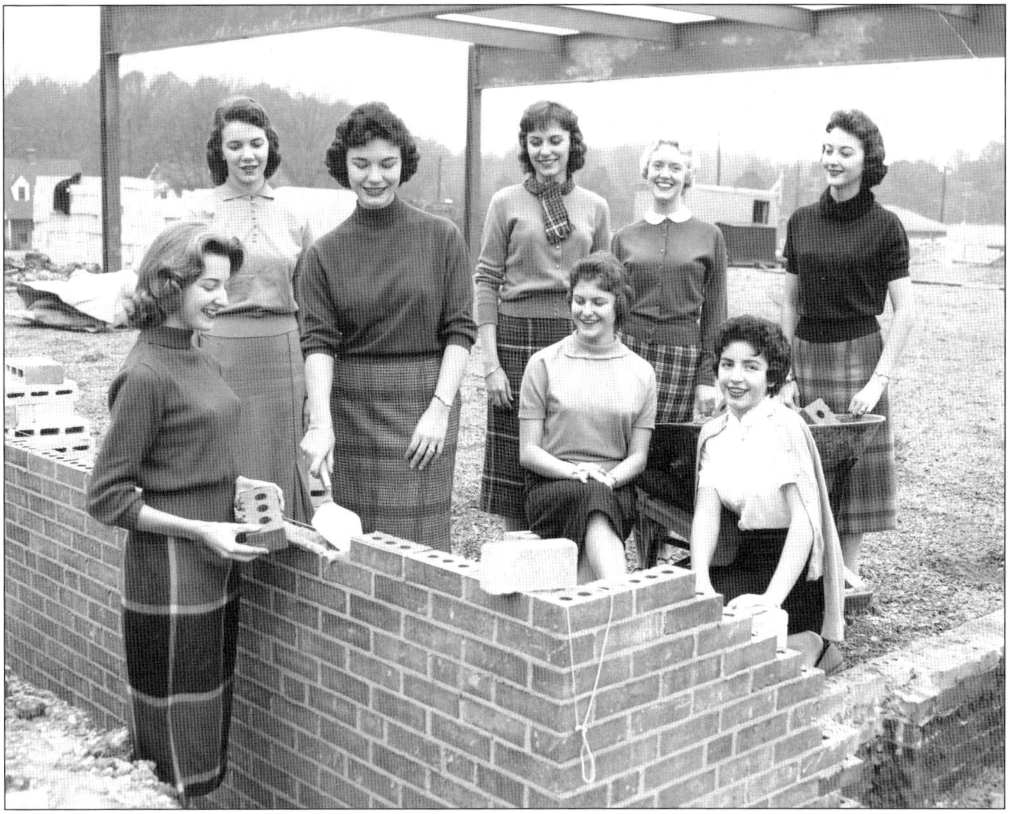

In 1958, Lander began construction on a new student center. It housed a dining hall, canteen, bookstore, day student rooms, locker rooms, lounges, student organization meeting rooms, an office for student publications, a post office, and a main lobby with a television. Pictured from left to right in this promotional picture are Wilhelmina Pate ("Freshman Class Beauty"), Lunette Anderson ("Sophomore Class Beauty"), Betty Ann McFadden ("Senior Class Beauty"), Mary Alice White ("Junior Class Cutie"), Jackie Anderson ("Freshman Class Cutie"), Gwen Herring ("Senior Class Cutie"), Nancy Leonard ("Junior Class Beauty"), and Darlene Newell ("Sophomore Class Cutie").

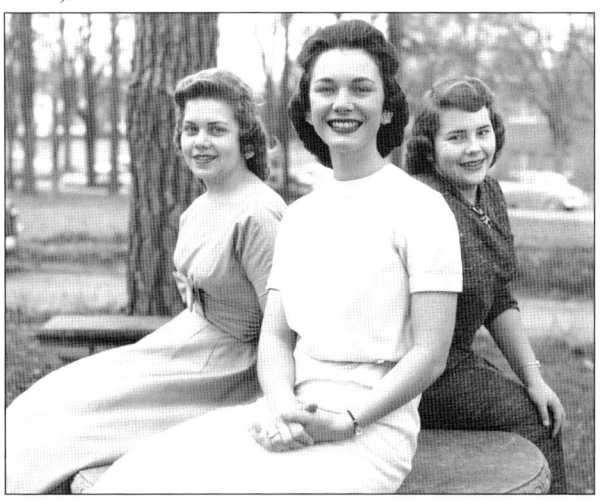

These education majors were members of the Future Teachers of America Club at Lander in the late 1950s. In addition, cumulatively the three were members of over three dozen social organizations on campus during their time at Lander. Pictured from left to right are Peggy Page, Betty Ann McFadden, and Peggy Davis.

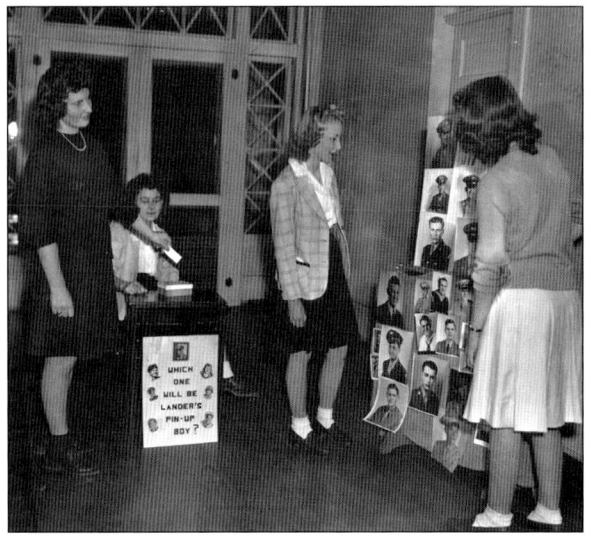

In this 1945 photograph, Lander students do their "civic duty" by voting for "Which One Will Be Lander's Pin-Up Boy?" The portraits on the "candidate" display show men in a variety of different military uniforms, a reminder of the importance of service during this time. The contest was part of a fundraising effort by the Naiad staff to raise money for the yearbook. The names of the men, described as "Don Juans and Beau Brummels to the poets," chosen by popular vote as the "College Pin-Up Men" were, Bill Hammett, Herbie Francis Jr., Buddy Lesesne, Joe S. Isgett, Cody Livingston, and Carlisle Wharton.

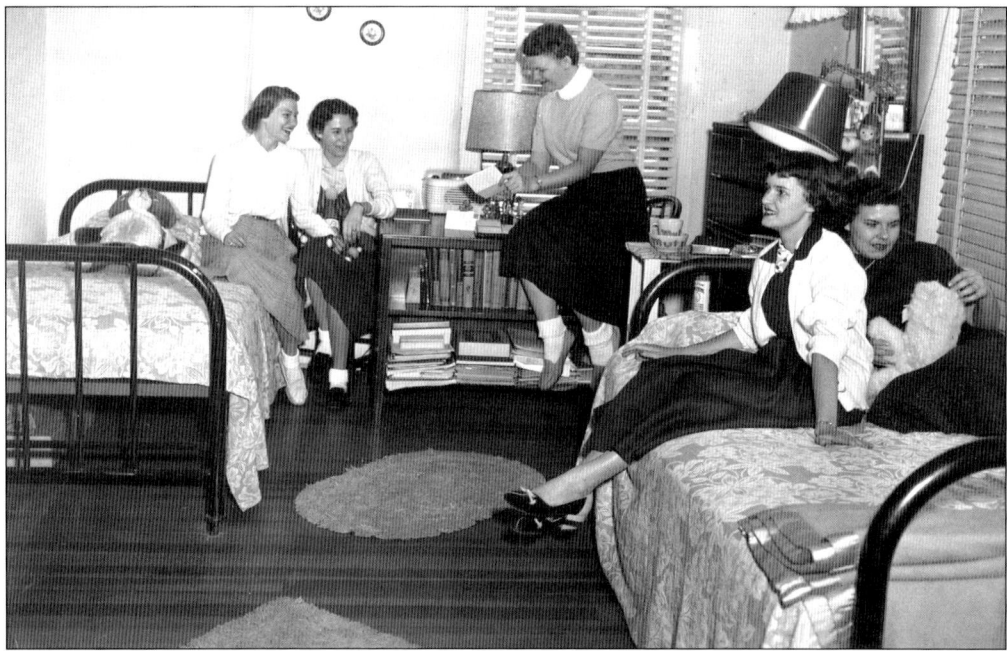

This is a dormitory room in 1955. The college catalog described the dormitories to students during this period: "The two dormitories, Main and Chipley, are modern and homelike. The Chipley rooms are divided into suites, each suite containing two bedrooms, two large closets, and a connecting bath, the two rooms being designed for four occupants. The suites are furnished in steel mission furniture, contain lavatories and baths. Main dormitory, recently renovated, is furnished with heavy hardwood furniture of latest design, has clothes closet and lavatory with hot and cold water. Adequate bath facilities are provided on each floor." Pictured left to right are Diana Belk, Jane McTeer, Patsy Butler, Marian Lawhorn, and Helen Bales.

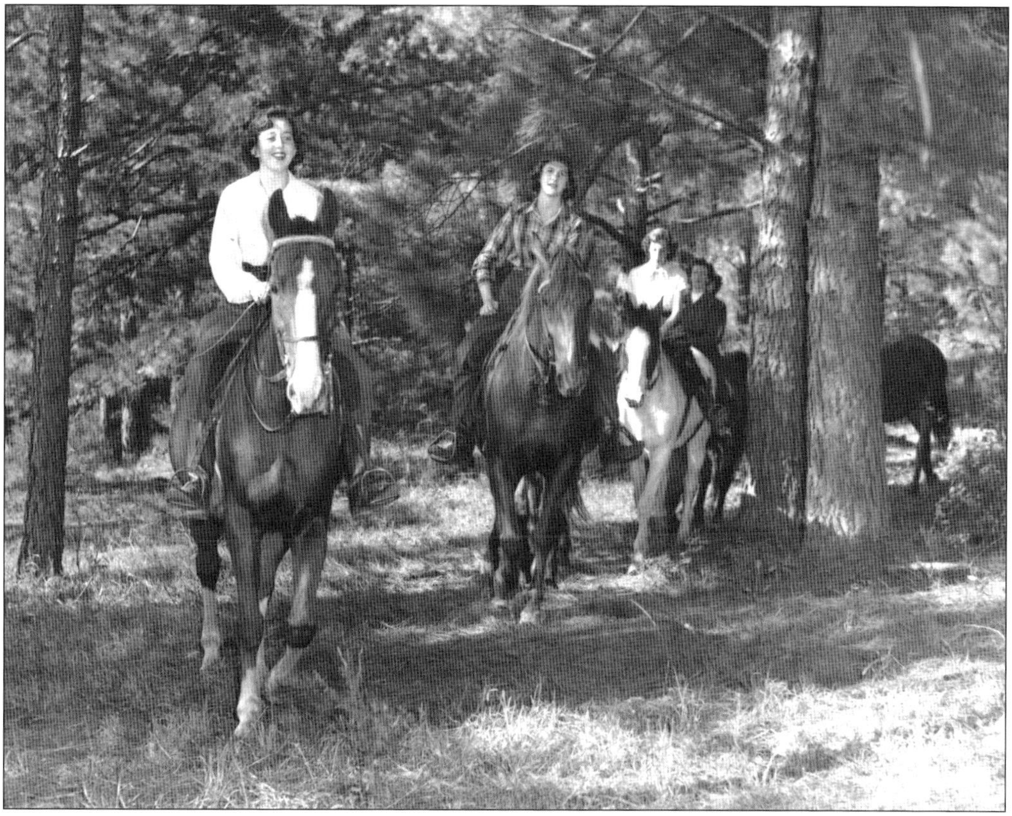

First rider Betty Coleman leads other equestrians down a campus bridle path. Stables, a riding ring, and paths on campus for equestrian activities gave students a chance to spend time with their favorite horses, which are described in the 1952 *Naiad:* "Thunder's dapple grey, Slow Joe's familiar creep, Heigh Ho's sudden limp and Star's statuesque beauty—all are remembered with affection by the students."

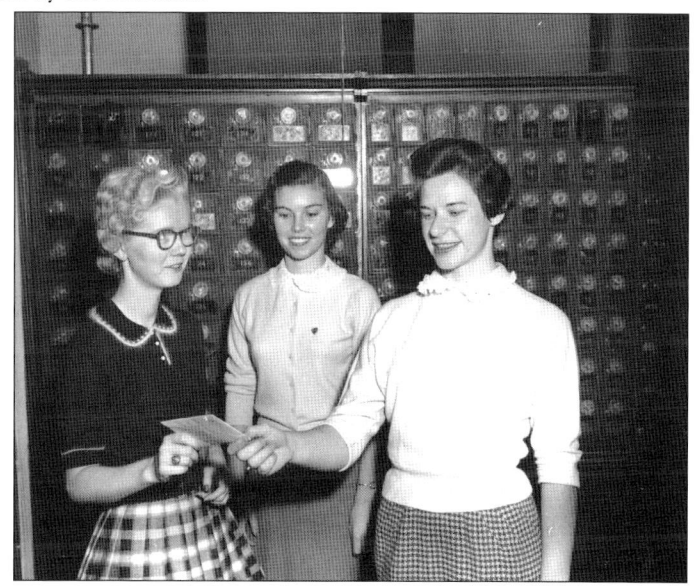

The students in this 1957 *Naiad* photograph stand in front of the student mailboxes located in the campus mailroom. Receiving a care package or letter was surely something to look forward to, since mail was a way for boarding students to maintain connections with friends and family from home. From left to right are June Cromer, Charlise Hughes, and Faye Mitchell.

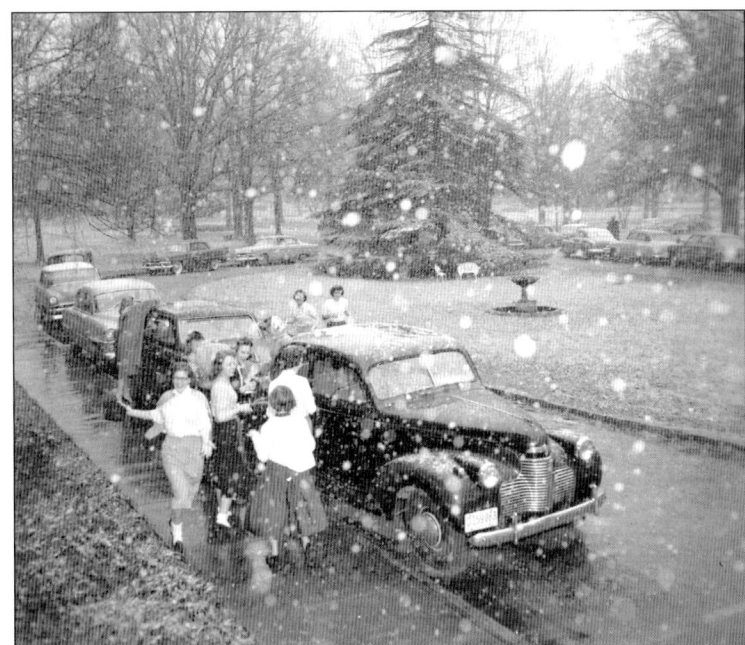

Were classes canceled on this snowy day in 1955? Exuberant students rushed outside without their jackets on to play among the snowflakes and enjoy the winter wonder. Now-vintage automobiles lined the drive outside of Laura Lander Hall. The fountain on the lawn at center-right in the photograph was a gift of the class of 1912.

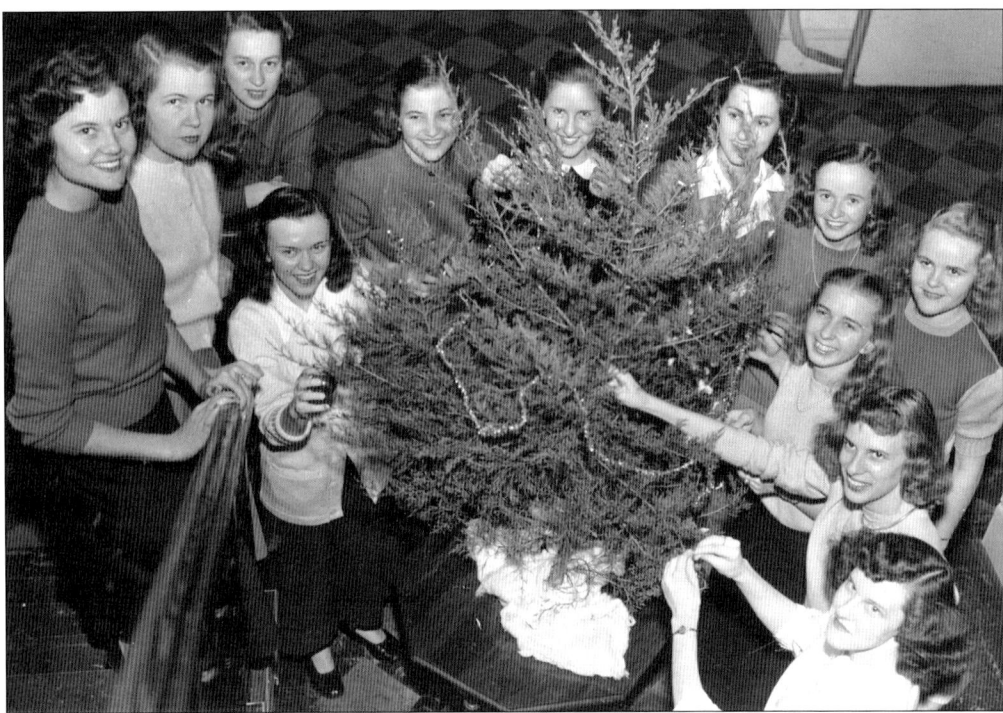

Student government council members decorate a tree for a Christmas party in 1948. The council was busy that year helping to plan a Christmas banquet as well as several formal dances that were held in the Greenwood Armory "under soft lights." The armory was the site of many Greenwood parties and balls. Pictured from left to right are Geneva Moore, Gwen Laramore, Wilma Duckett, Betty Turner, Blanche Gilstrap, Mary Bryan, Marjorie Hipp, Martha Anderson, Willene Barnett, Martha Gravely, Mary Elizabeth Bodie, and Hilda Creed.

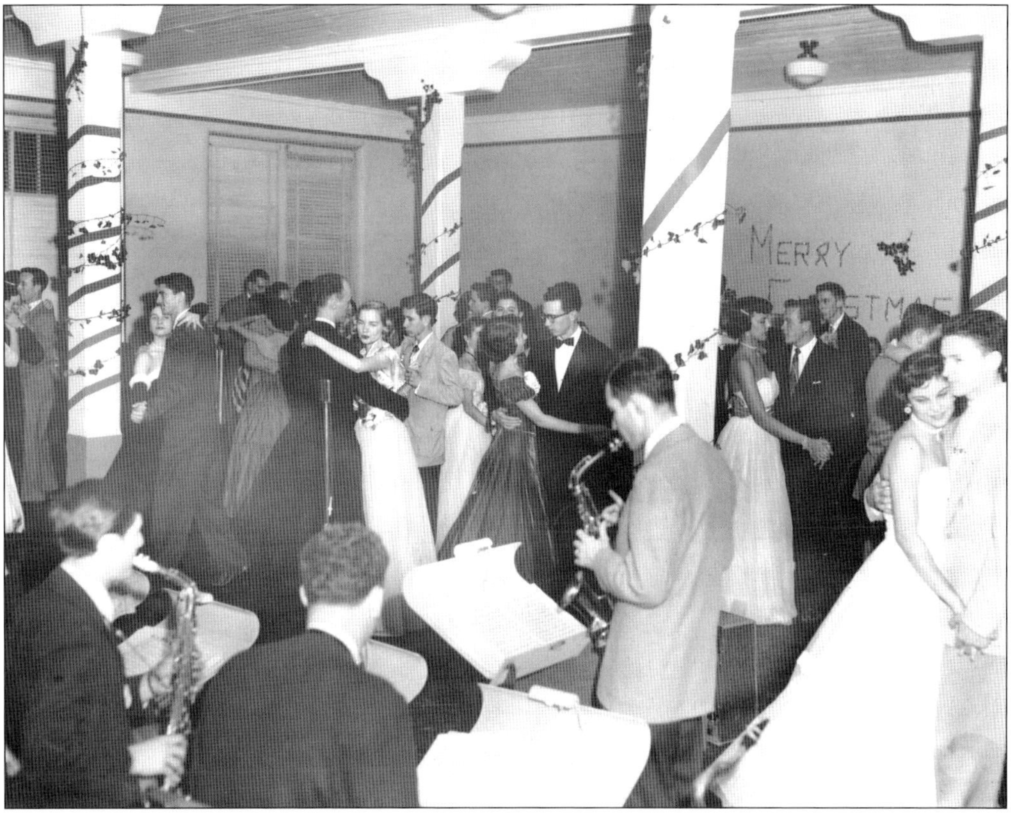

This dance held in 1950 in the college dining room was part of "Christmas Week" at Lander, which featured a formal dance, tea, Christmas dinner, and a program of entertainment. The dance was sponsored by the Student Government Association, and the musical entertainment was provided by Harry Fraser's Rhythm Masters. Special invitations were sent from the dean of students office to students at Clemson, Erskine, and Presbyterian College. Invitations were also sent to several outstanding high school seniors who had indicated an interest in attending Lander.

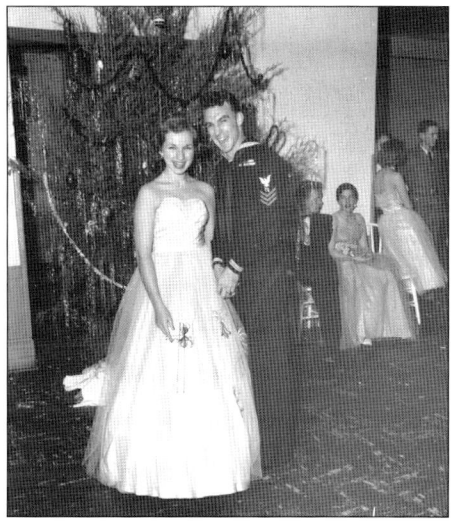

Ann Martin and her escort were enthusiastic attendees of Lander's annual Christmas dinner and dance. Students and faculty were first invited to a formal dinner before attending a dance, where the highlight was the crowning of "Miss Merry Christmas." The event was planned by the Lander Dance Committee appointed by the Student Government Association. Per the 1958 yearbook, the committee had the duty of planning the Halloween dance, the Christmas dance, the Valentine dance, and the Commencement dance.

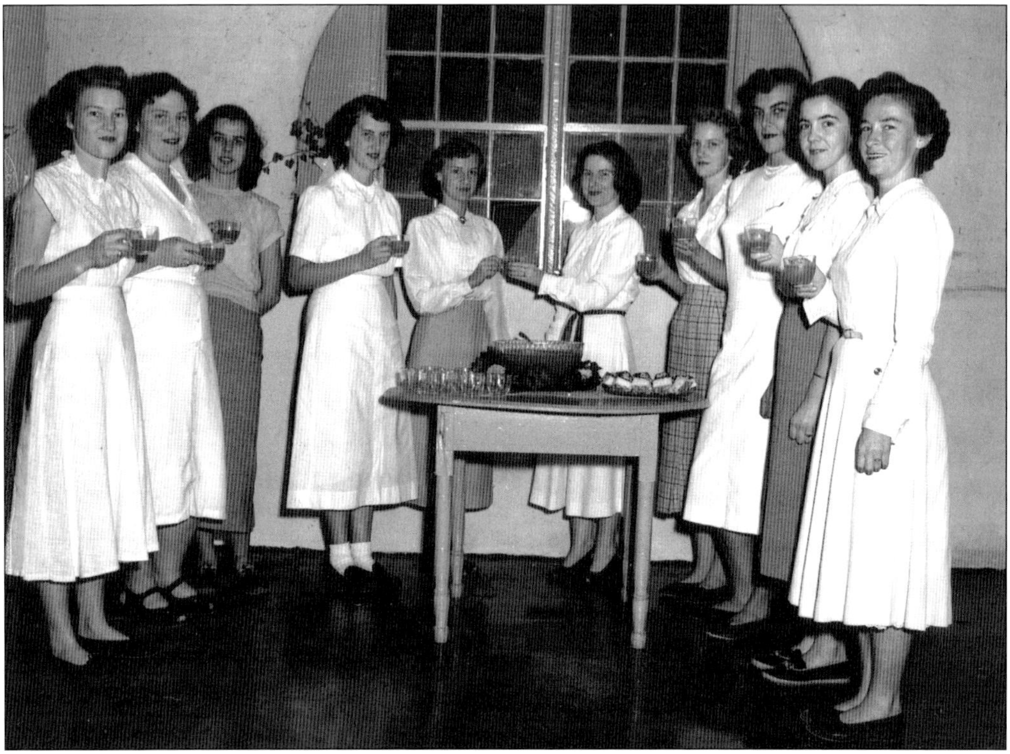

This 1951 photograph of students enjoying a reception with punch and cake was taken in the campus canteen. The installation of the canteen was a project of the Home Economics Club in 1946. This club also built a towering outdoor fireplace near the president's home with a grill for campus cookouts.

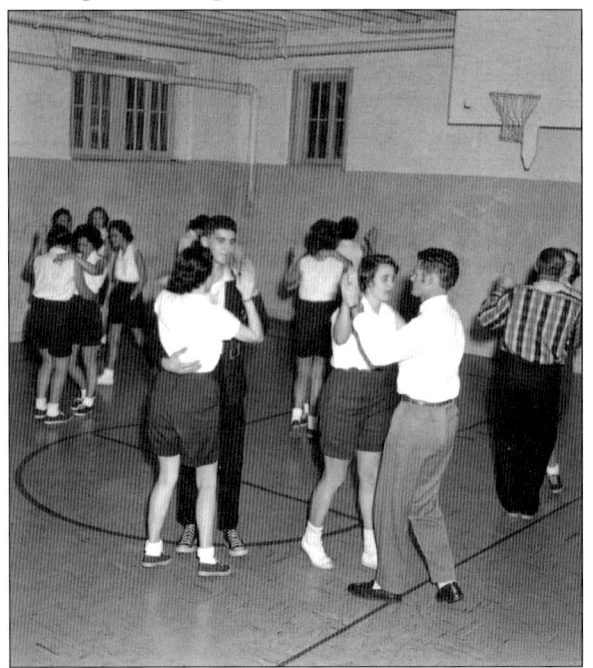

Lander students were well prepared for social functions after taking dance classes, which were described in the 1950 *Naiad*: "Gymnasium classes at Lander include instruction in dance. The fundamental steps of the waltz, fox trot, polka, and schottische provide the students with an ideal means of relaxation, as well as the opportunity to express themselves in the oldest of fine arts. Students who find hidden talents during participation in preliminary classes have an opportunity to learn the folk dances of many nations, such as the French *Minuet,* the *Norwegian Mountain March*, and the Irish *Blarney."*

Faculty and students enjoy a soft drink in the campus canteen in 1954. In a section titled "Home Life," the college catalog describes the rapport between faculty and students: "A majority of faculty members take their meals in the college dormitories. This affords daily association and personal contact with the students. The kindest relationships exist between teachers and students. The college is not too large to forbid personal oversight. The atmosphere of Lander College is home-like, radiating the joy and satisfaction that come from mutual interests."

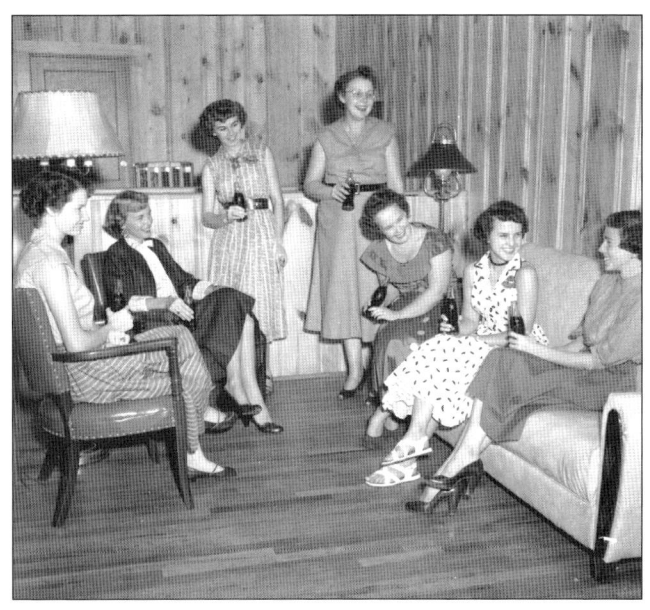

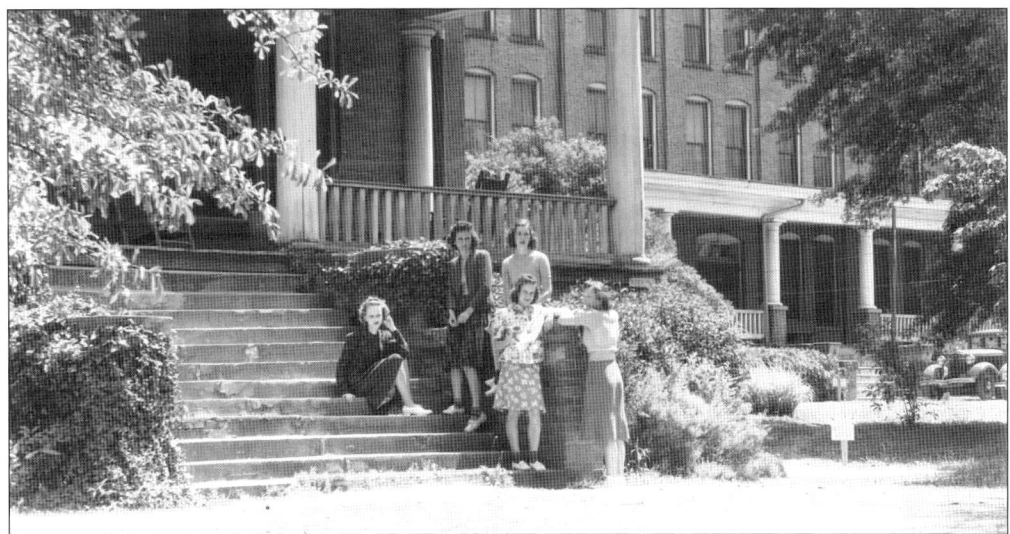

It was not uncommon for students to gather for conversation on the steps in front of Willson Hall, a former campus building named for Dr. John O. Willson, first president of the campus in Greenwood. The ground was broken for construction at commencement time in 1911 and was later demolished during a major campus building project in the early 1990s. The small sign in the lower right of this 1940s photograph says, "Keep Off Grass."

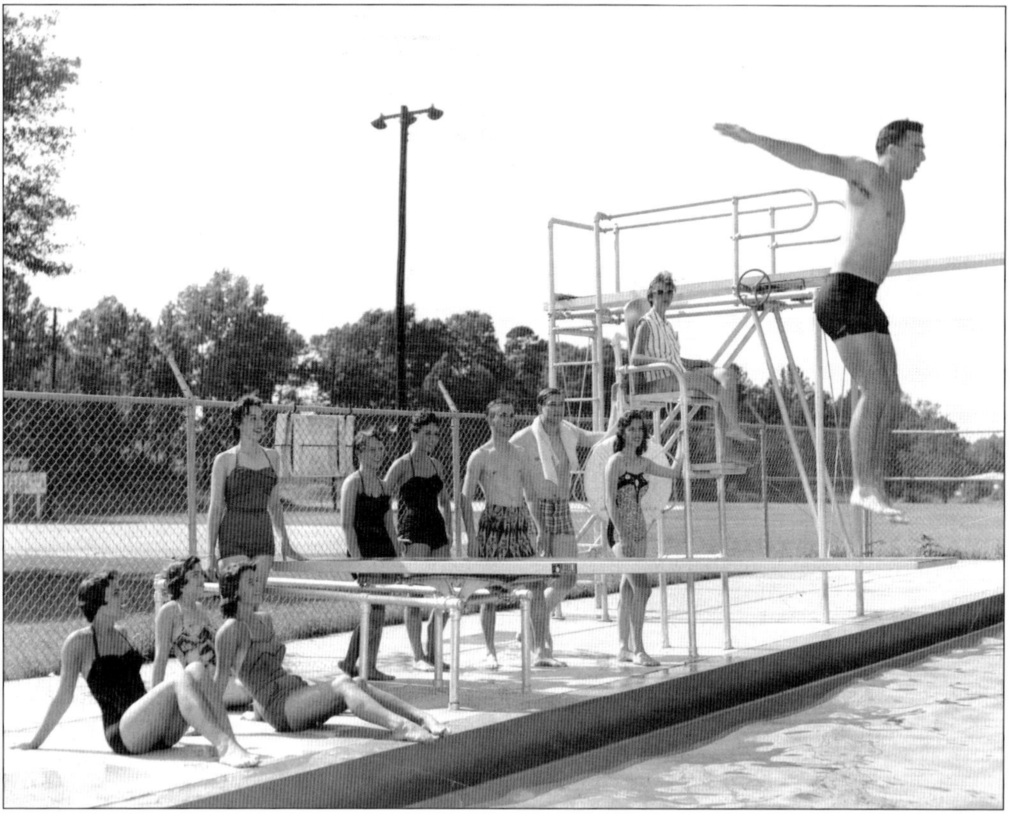

Lander students cool off at the Greenwood Recreation Center pool in the 1950s. Pictured from left to right are (seated) Emily Taylor, Melba Hughes, and Charlotte Irby; (standing) Betty Hanks, Louise Wavra, Eleanor Seel, Scoopy Polatty, Allan Goldman, and Kathy McCain. The lifeguard is Mary Frank Gant, and diving is Sonny Hall.

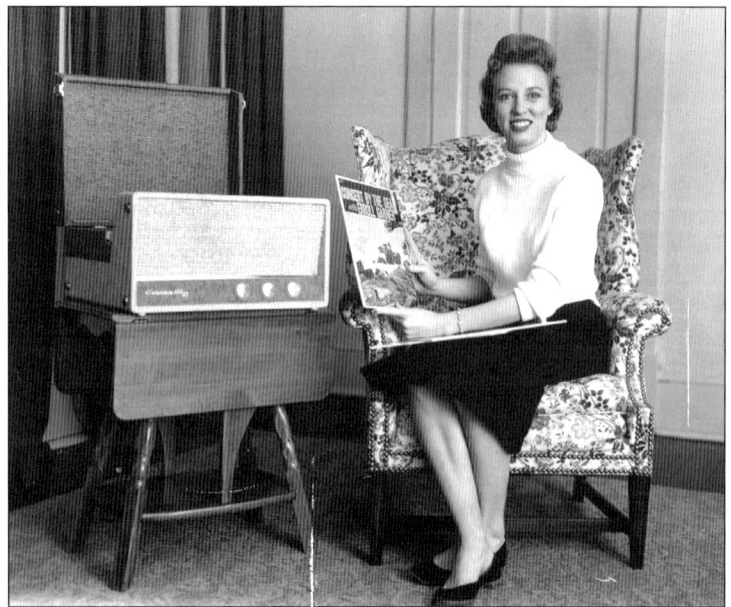

Barbara Allen, voted "Best All Around" in 1958, shows a vinyl recording of Concert by the Sea by pianist Erroll Garner. Allen was also honored that year on Class Day held in the Dingle. She presented the class poem at the ceremony and then received a certificate of membership in "Who's Who" among students in American colleges and universities as well as a key for service on the student council.

These Lander Lilies (a nickname for female Lander students) in lovely spring attire socialize on the steps outside of Chipley residence hall, an all-female dormitory. Chipley Hall was built in 1924 when the campus population grew, and there was a need for more on-campus housing. The residence hall is named after businessman and a former trustee of Lander College, Marvin Chipley, whose generous financial donation along with gifts from other friends of the school made it possible to construct. Marvin Chipley was uncle to Lander alumnus and well-known beloved citizen of Greenwood W. Marvin Chipley.

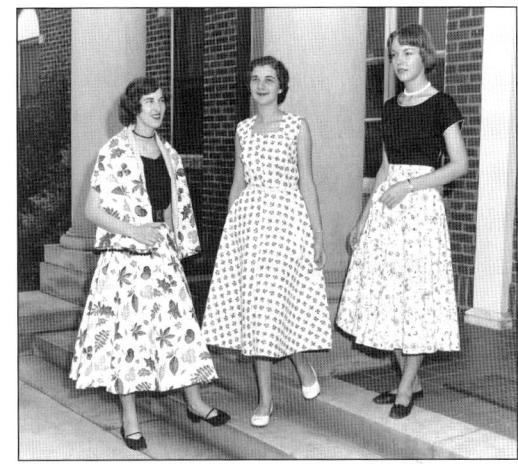

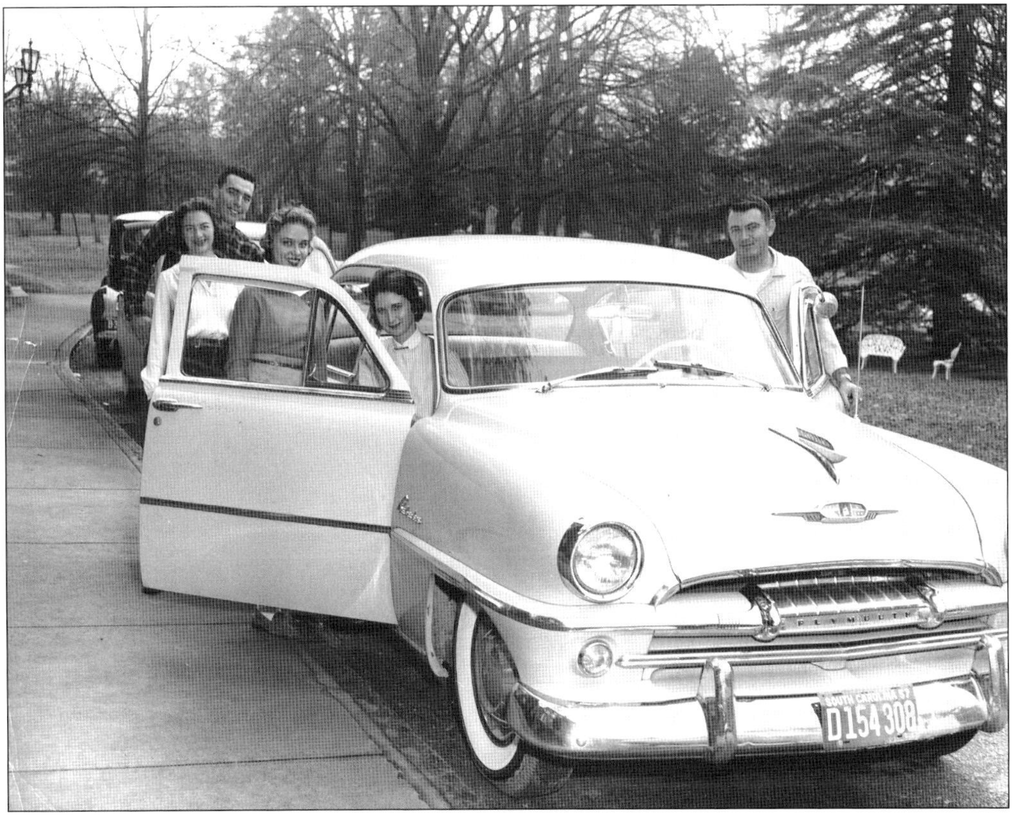

A group heads to the "Y" for bowling intramurals in 1957. While bowling was a fun social activity for male and female students, it was also the only organized intramural sport aside from basketball for the male students during this time. The men's bowling team was referred to as "Pope-Lander" because Pope's Clothing Store was the team co-sponsor. In order to launch the team, the male students solicited donations from the local merchants that they frequented. Those merchants were, Rosenberg's, the Ranch, Bob's Drive-In, Covil's Texaco Station, and the Fairway. Individuals W.H. Ehrich (music faculty) and Bob Hollingsworth (husband of Lander's registrar) also gave donations to the team. From left to right are Sonny Hall, Anne Kircus, Lillian Kirkland, Jenny Lynne Touchberry, and Roy Wilson.

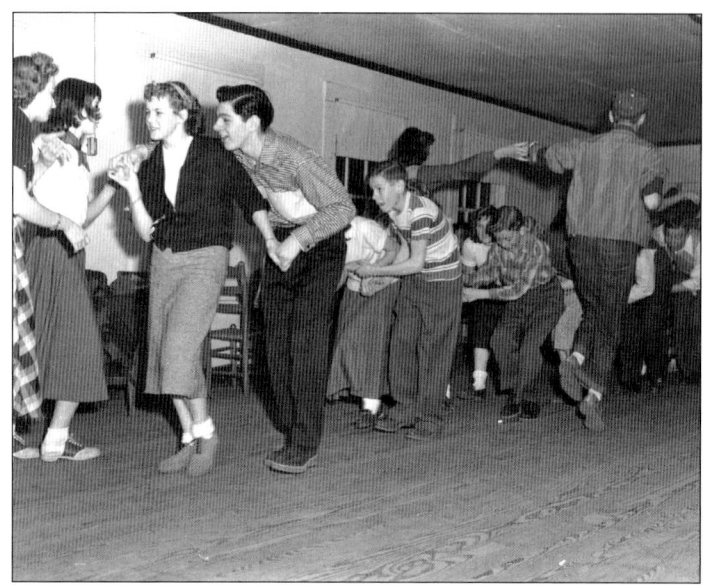

With arms in the air and feet off the ground, Lander students and young members of the local community are engaged in a high-velocity group line dance. Could this be a version of the Virginia Reel or perhaps another equally invigorating dance? The occasion of this dance is not known; however, it may have been taken at the square dance organized by Lander student government officers for area high school students.

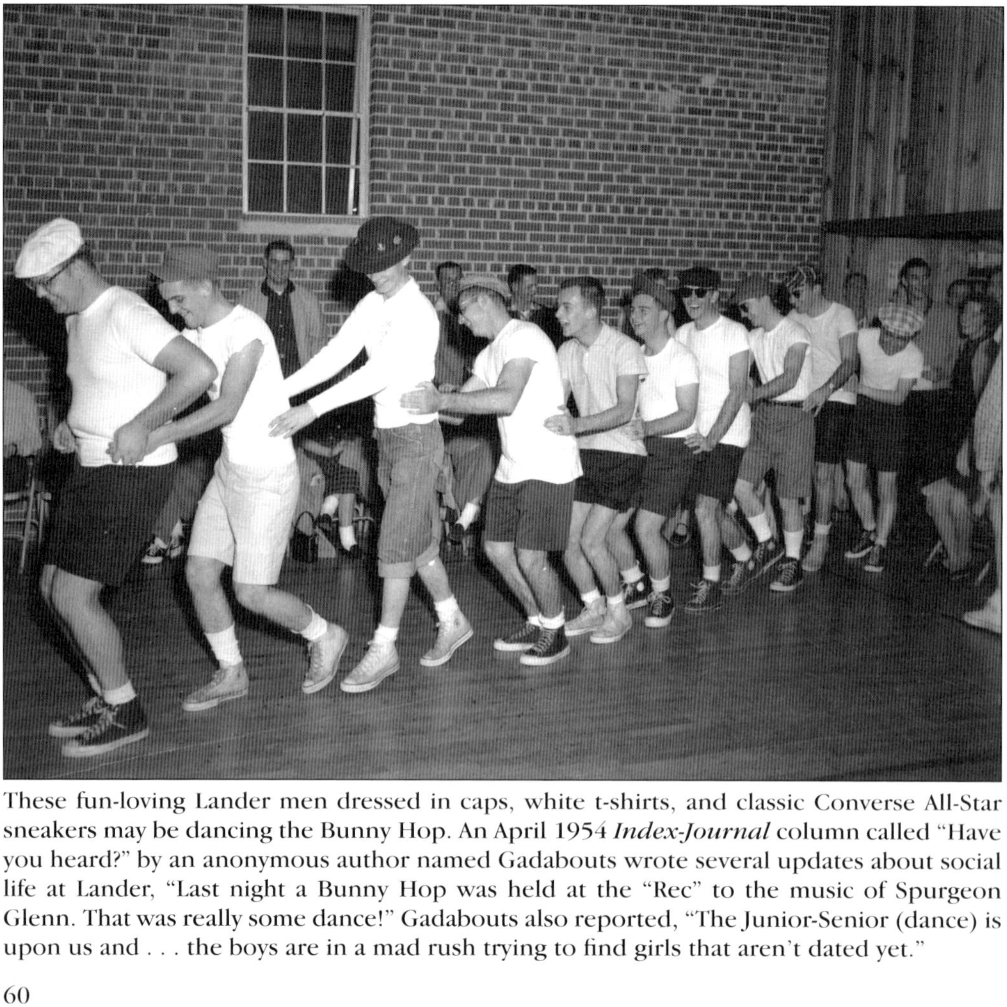

These fun-loving Lander men dressed in caps, white t-shirts, and classic Converse All-Star sneakers may be dancing the Bunny Hop. An April 1954 *Index-Journal* column called "Have you heard?" by an anonymous author named Gadabouts wrote several updates about social life at Lander, "Last night a Bunny Hop was held at the "Rec" to the music of Spurgeon Glenn. That was really some dance!" Gadabouts also reported, "The Junior-Senior (dance) is upon us and . . . the boys are in a mad rush trying to find girls that aren't dated yet."

Four

THE PHYSICAL STREAM OF LEARNING

The physical stream of learning was emphasized from the earliest days of Williamston Female College. Under a heading for "Physical Exercise," the 1874 academic catalog states, "Our boarding pupils have the opportunity of walking, for recreation, beyond the College premises, twice every day. And besides, they devote a stated portion of each day to systematic instruction and practice in light callisthenic exercises."

The 1875 academic catalog statement read, "We have found that the general health and cheerfulness of our pupils have been much improved since the introduction of systematic physical exercise." The following year brought the daily use of "Dr. Johnson's Health Lift" and "Goodyear's Pocket Gymnasia."

The *Naiad* issue of September 1884 noted that:

> A few minutes every morning and every afternoon are devoted to systematic practice in light callisthenic exercise under the inspiring stimulus of a stirring march. Stated walks to the Spring or elsewhere about the village, and occasional romps and exercises in the playground, added to the above furnish ample protection against the enervating tendency of a student's life.
>
> Our callisthenic movements are selected or devised, without reference to mere show or intricacy but simply for the healthful exercise of those parts of the body especially which are most injured by sedentary habits.

In 1889, the academic catalog announced, "We have recently introduced the graceful exercise Indian Club Swinging, which we have found highly captivating and beneficial. The Athletic Club, formed for the purpose of perpetuating an interest in the exercise, is a voluntary organization of pupils and teachers."

Daily physical exercise requirements carried over to the Greenwood campus, though without the advantage of the Williamston Spring Park. The 1905 academic catalog used the phrase "physical culture" to describe the required program of disciplined daily physical exercise.

The Lander College Athletic Association was formed in 1908 with officers, and the first-known Lander Field Day was held, with trophies awarded for intramural tennis and baseball. The first mention of an indoor gymnasium is found in the 1918 catalog.

In 1923, the physical education department was established. All students were required to take a course in gymnastics, and class intramural teams were formed for basketball, volleyball, baseball, tennis, and track. The 1927 academic catalog includes a 40-minute-per-day requirement for exercise comprised of "two periods a week in gymnastics, other exercises, and games, and four periods in out-door sports and walking."

By 1932, every resident student was automatically a member of the Athletic Association. Intramural sports that year were hockey, speedball, track, tennis, stunts, cheerleading, basketball, volleyball, and baseball. Later years brought even more variety to the options for Lander students to get regular exercise, such as archery, horsemanship, and ping-pong. Sports at Lander remained intramural until 1968.

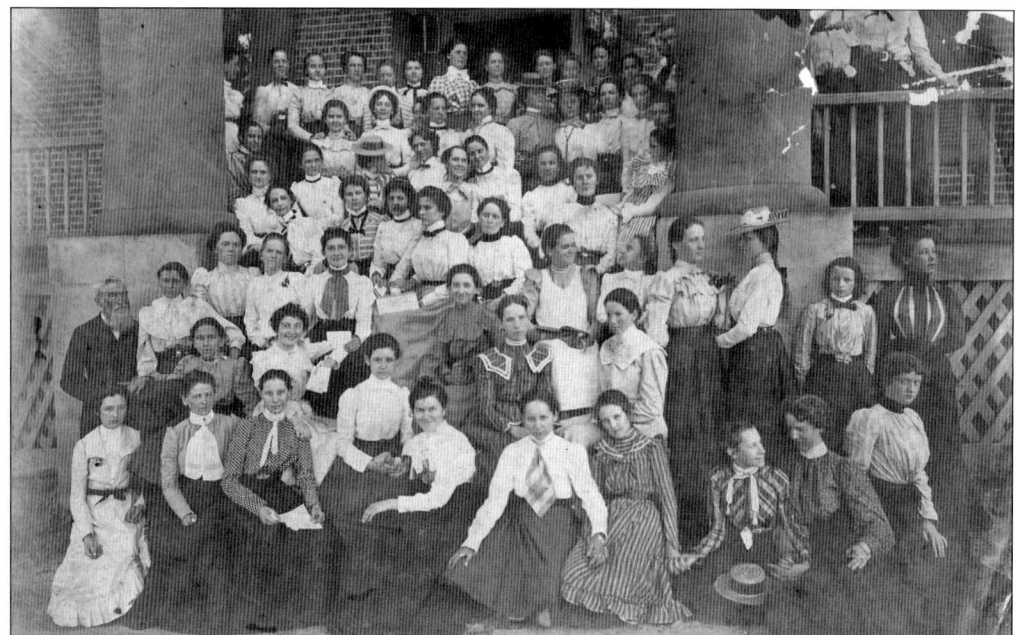

This atypical photograph shows a gathering in front of Williamston Female College. Rev. Samuel Lander stands to the far left. In contrast to most other Williamston photographs in the Lander archives, the students in this pose are wearing less uniform clothing with a beautiful variety of patterns and styles. Several are wearing fancy sun hats, an indication that the gathering was on an outdoor event or excursion.

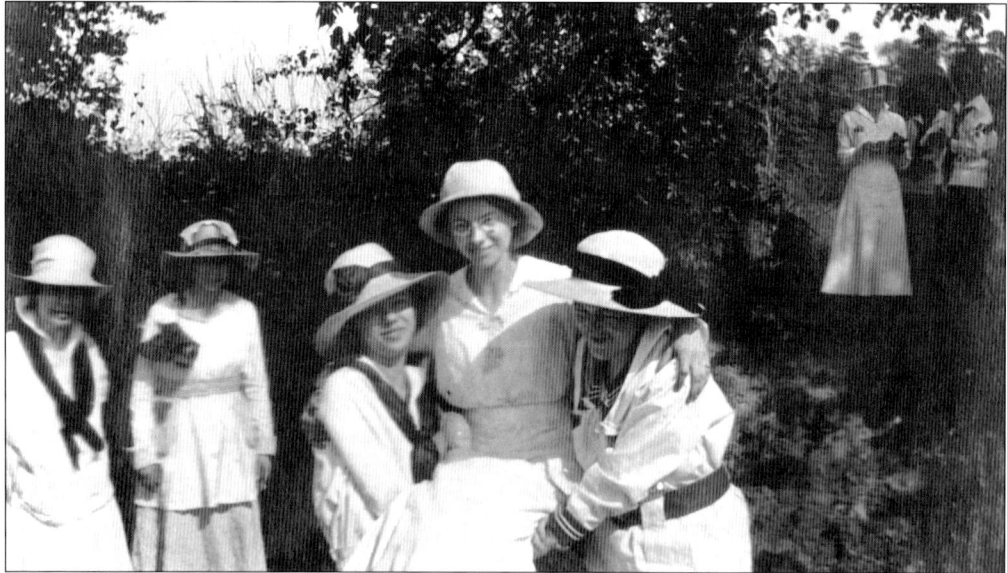

Time in nature enjoying a stroll with friends was a common pastime for students, as can be seen in this photograph, taken between 1914–1918, from the Lander memory book of student Marian Sheridan. The image calls to mind Rev. Samuel Lander's sermon No. 199, in which he observes, "The flower is beautiful. . . . We enjoy the symmetry, the color, the odor; but we commune with the human flower; and it reciprocates our love, and intensifies our joys." Dr. Lander's sermon notes are housed in the Lander University archives.

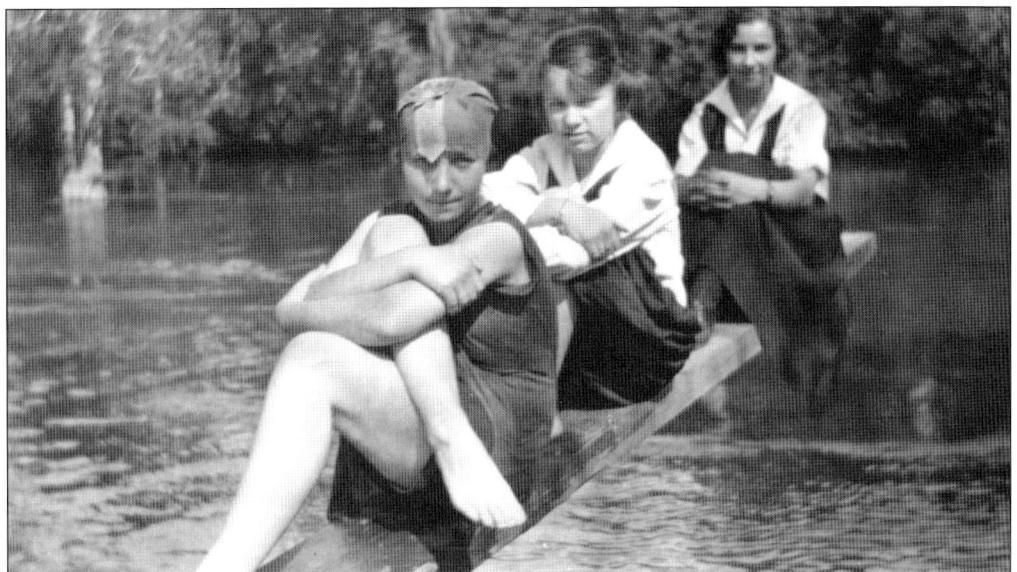

Students on break enjoying recreational time by the water as documented by Marian Sheridan in her Lander memory book. Sheridan graduated in 1918. The image is a good example of how an appreciation of outdoor time was cultivated at Lander and carried over to the lives of students when they were not on campus.

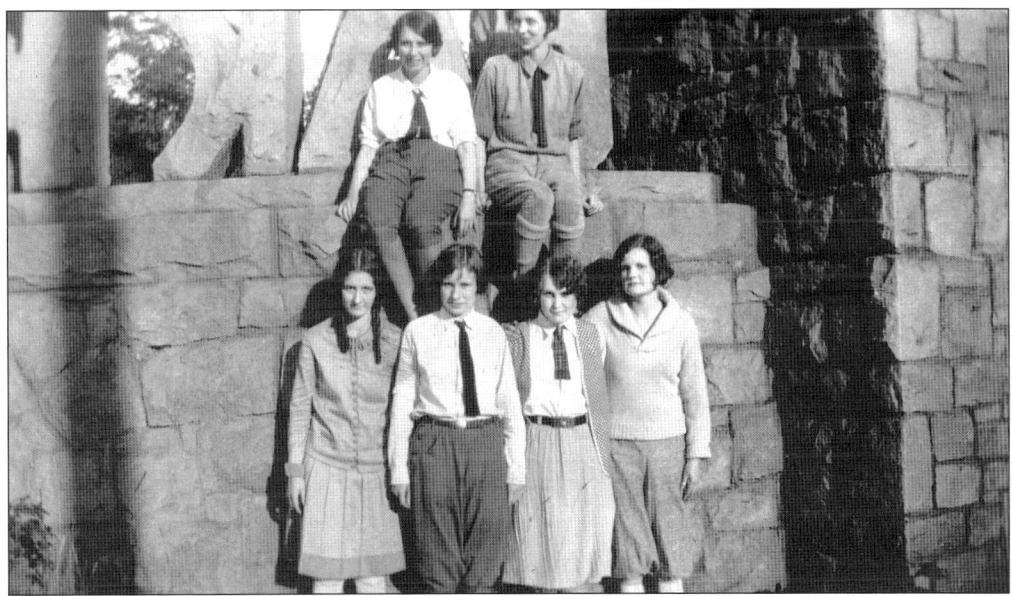

A subset of HDE social club members are pictured sometime between 1926 and 1930. The club's acronym was not documented, but the group was largely comprised of day students who enjoyed hiking and exercise. Student Mary Major describes the outing in her memory book: "In October we took pictures for the annual, then we hiked to the power-house and had a weinie [*sic*] roast." Major went on to serve as president of Lander's alumni association.

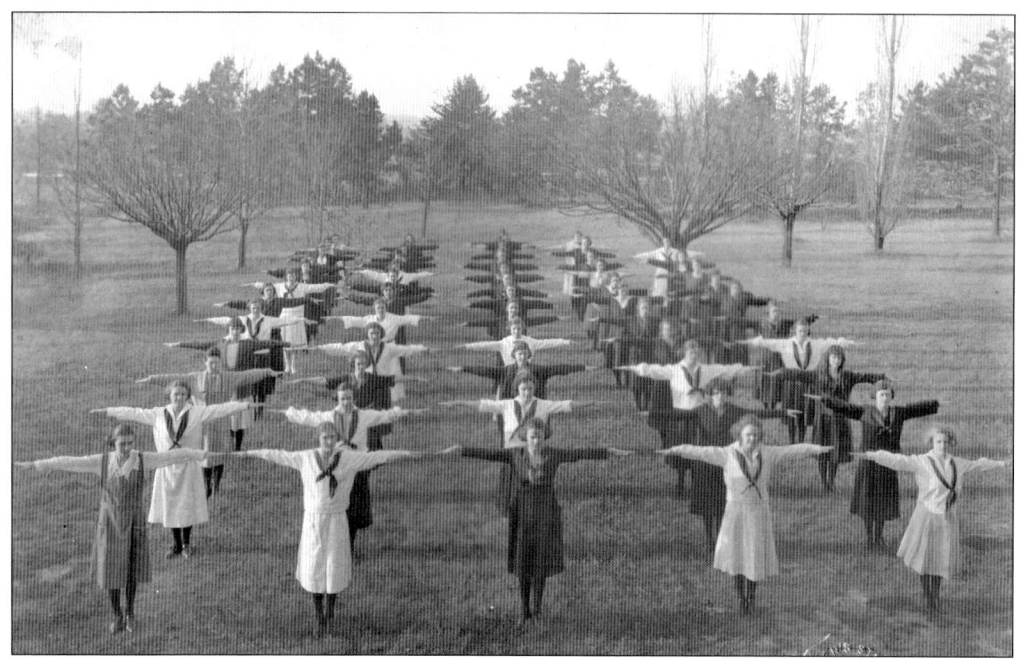

From the 1905 academic catalog: "We encourage open air games and exercises, and require a short walk every day. Then we have gymnastic practice every day, except Sunday. A few minutes are spent in light calisthenics, club swinging, setting-up exercises, and in deep breathing. We think this is more helpful than more violent efforts. The health of our student-body causes us to believe that our theory is correct."

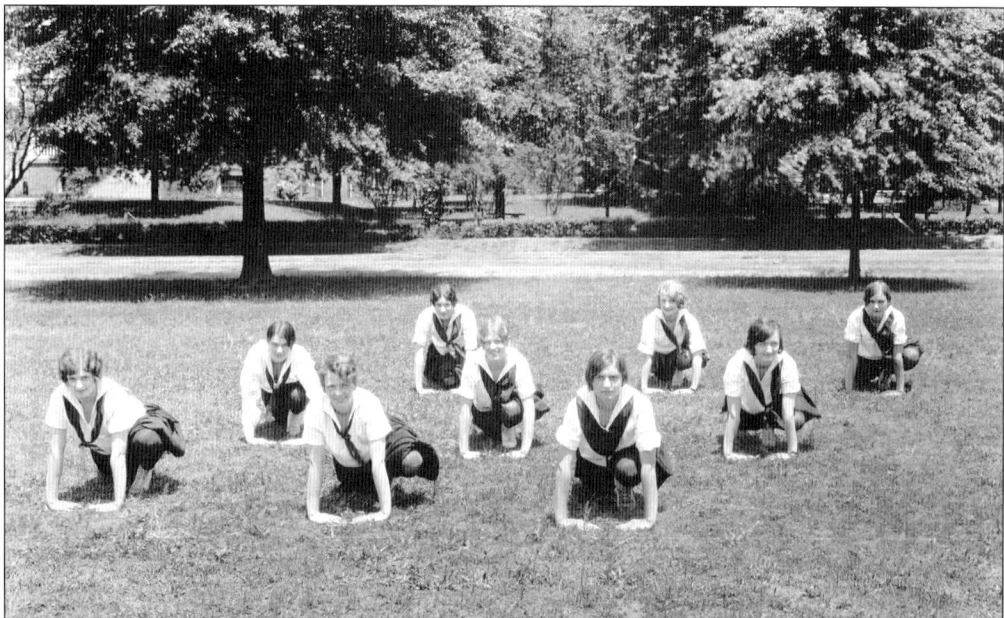

When weather permitted stretching, exercises took place on the campus lawn in the 1930s. The 1930 college catalog describes regulation dress for physical education classes: "Students must wear dark bloomers, white middy, black tie, black hose, and white tennis shoes. It is strongly urged that every student bring a tennis racket and hiking shoes to college."

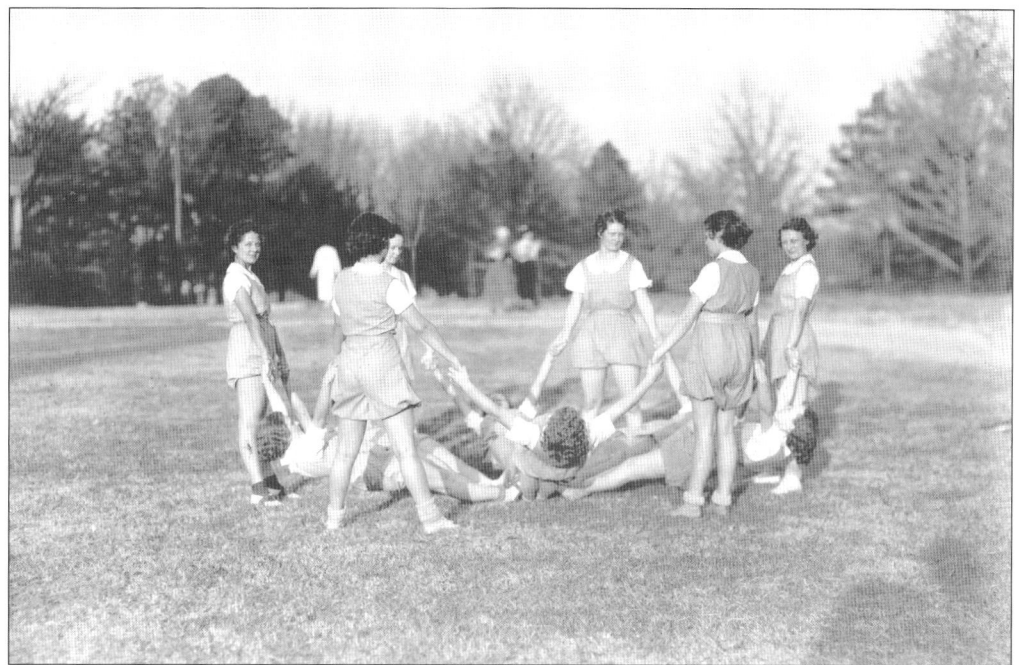

This formation in this 1934 image was a stunt called "the merry-go-round." Each student was required to take two periods a week in gymnastics. The work included gymnastics, marching, games, and stunts; indoor and outdoor sports in season; and rhythmic work. A gymnastics and stunts demonstration was given each spring. Stunts were also performed as part of the entertainment at pageants.

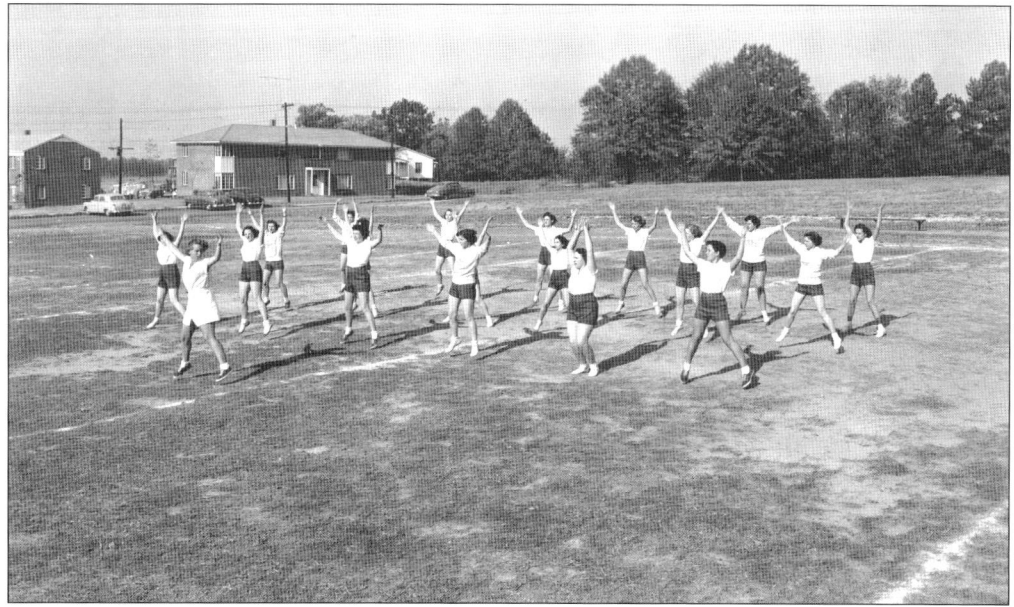

In this 1950s photograph, students perform jumping jacks. According to the 1950 college catalog in a section titled "Regular Gymnastic Costume," "Each student will be furnished a gymnasium suit. Students are required to furnish their own gym shoes and riding clothes if they wish to join the riding class."

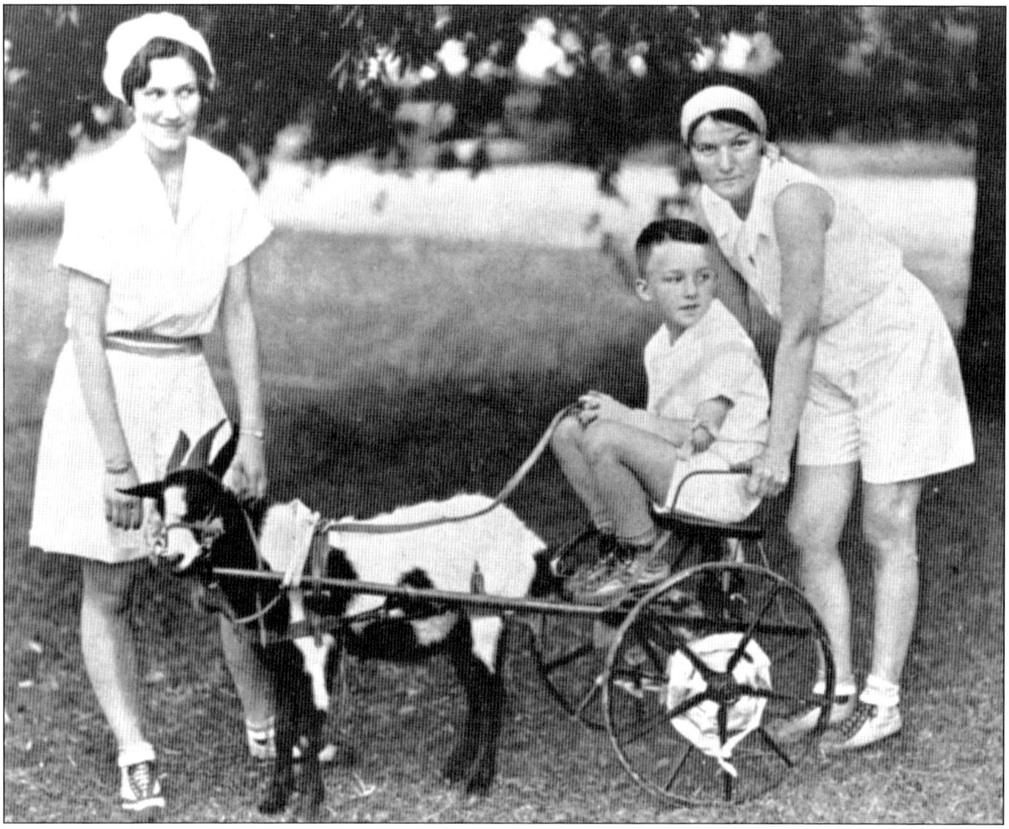

Members of the junior class pose with the young driver of this goat wagon after being declared winners in the 1932 Field Day animal races. Each class selected a young child to race their wagons. According to the *Index-Journal*, "The program opened with a section from the Bailey band (from the Bailey Military Institute in Greenwood) and little Virginia Hale Eskeridge, mascot from the Athletic association riding onto the field in a goat wagon. Six Bailey cadets were on hand for judges and were the guest of the students for luncheon."

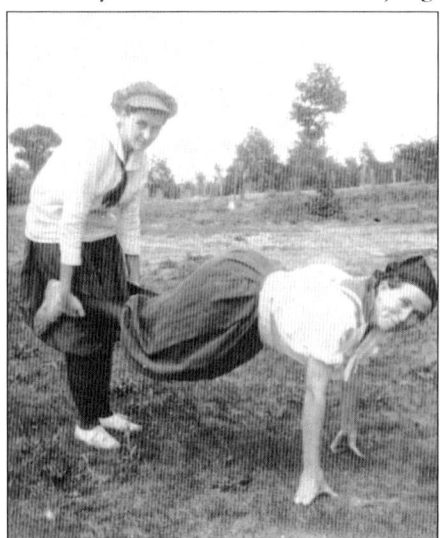

The photograph from the 1919 Lander memory book of Dorothy Rayson Stokes shows students practicing for a wheelbarrow race. The caption "Field Day" was handwritten above the photograph. Pictured here are Effie Graham (left) and Lila Peden (right). The 1919 college catalog describes the role of the Lander College Athletic Association: "The purpose of this organization is to induce its members to take more exercises in the open air. Besides, it plans and conducts a Field Day at which trophy cups in tennis and baseball are awarded."

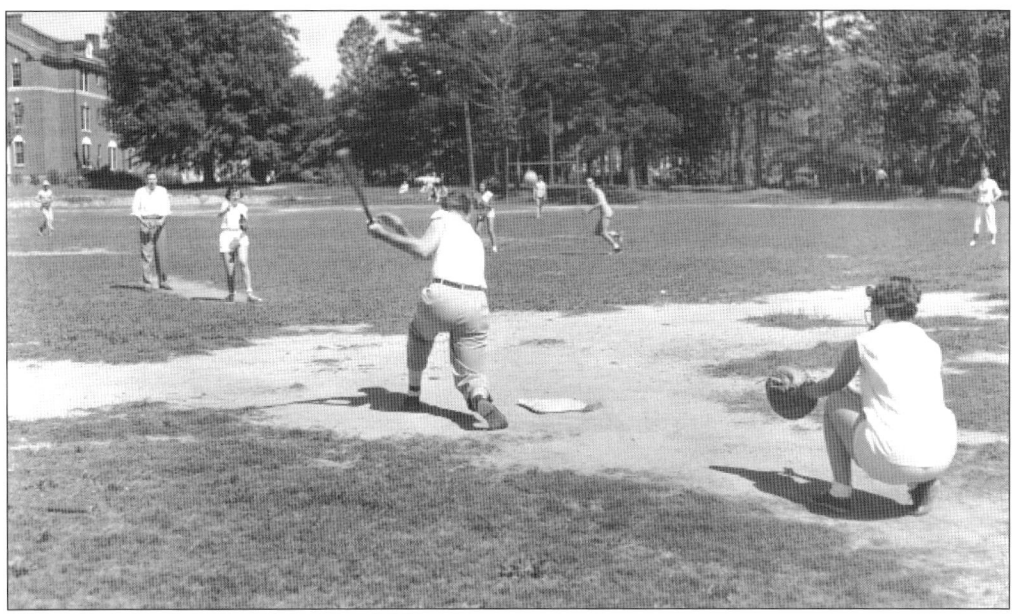

As the school year ended the Lander College Athletic Association sponsored Field Day, a time described in the *Naiad* yearbook when "students put aside their books to compete in dashes, races, high jumps, broad jumps, and skits prepared by each class." One of the highlights of the 1954 Field Day gala was this student and faculty softball game. Scores were tallied, and the class winning the most points was awarded a rotating trophy.

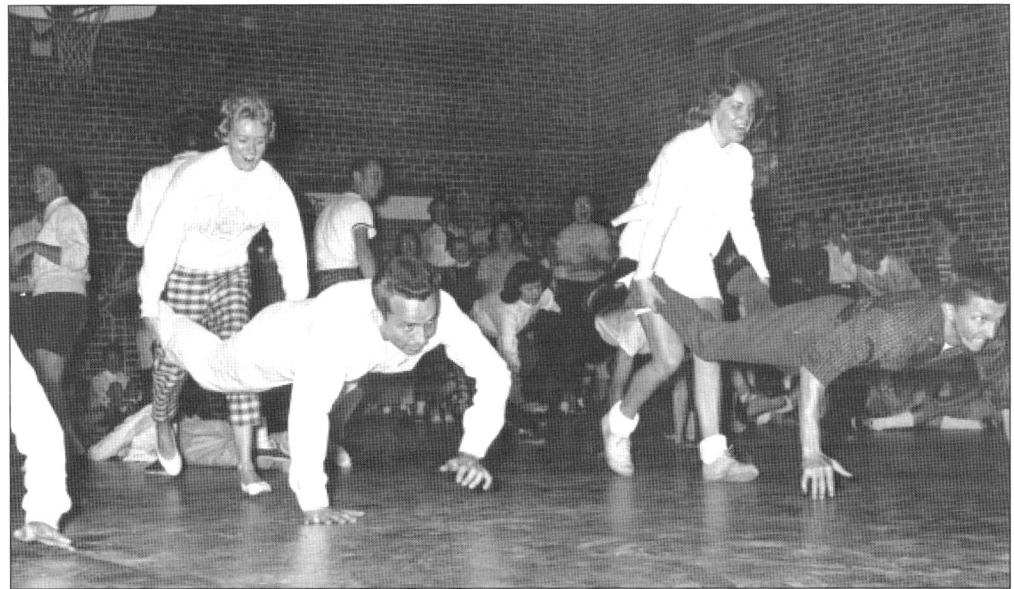

In 1958, the wheelbarrow races were held indoors as can be seen in this photograph from the *Naiad*. The location is likely the campus recreation center. From left to right are Gwen Herring, Sammy McQuerns, Carolyn Farmer, and Claude Wells.

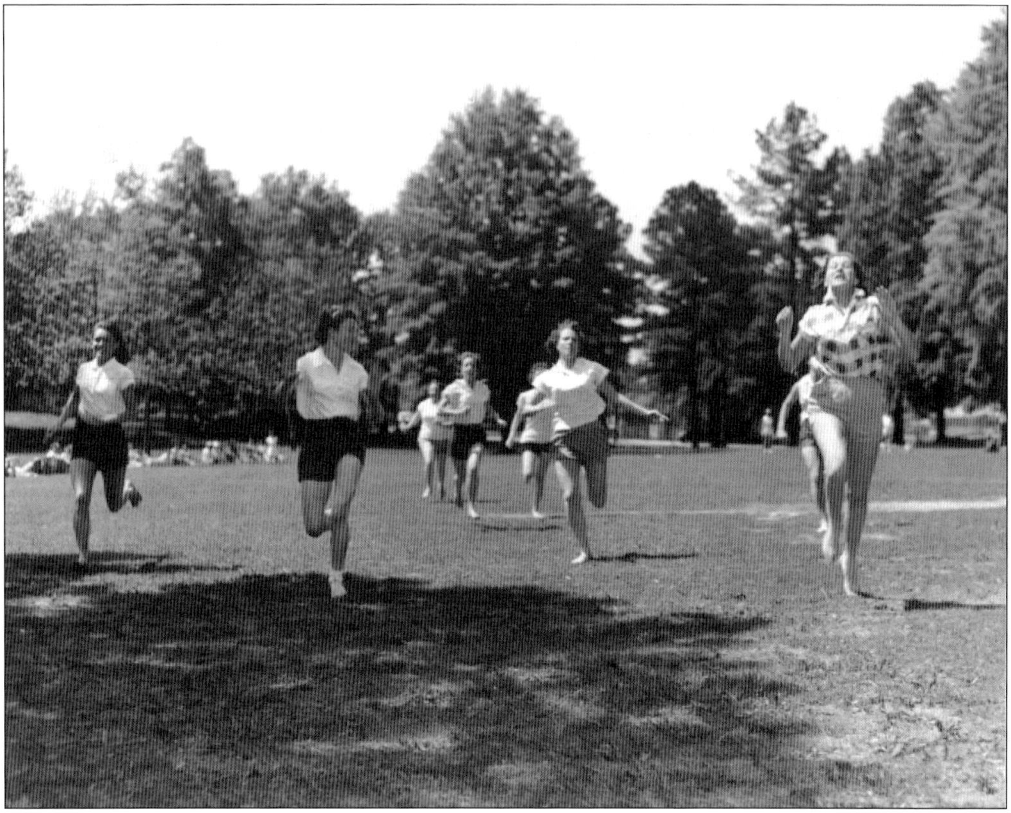

It was common to compete in a 50-yard or 75-yard dash during Field Day, as shown in this undated image. The 1953 *Naiad* provides a further description: "Classes enter students in the various races, relays, jumps, and skits and fight to the finish by cheering for their classmates as they participate in each event." Field Day typically closed out the Athletic Association's season.

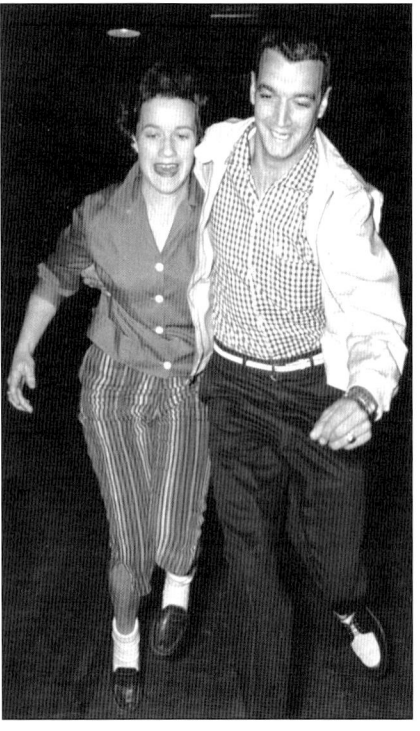

These students in the 1950s are trying their best to win a race. A typical Field Day during this era included numerous types of relay races including an egg and spoon relay, a cracker relay, a costume relay, and a pass ball relay. Field Day would be held indoors during times of poor weather.

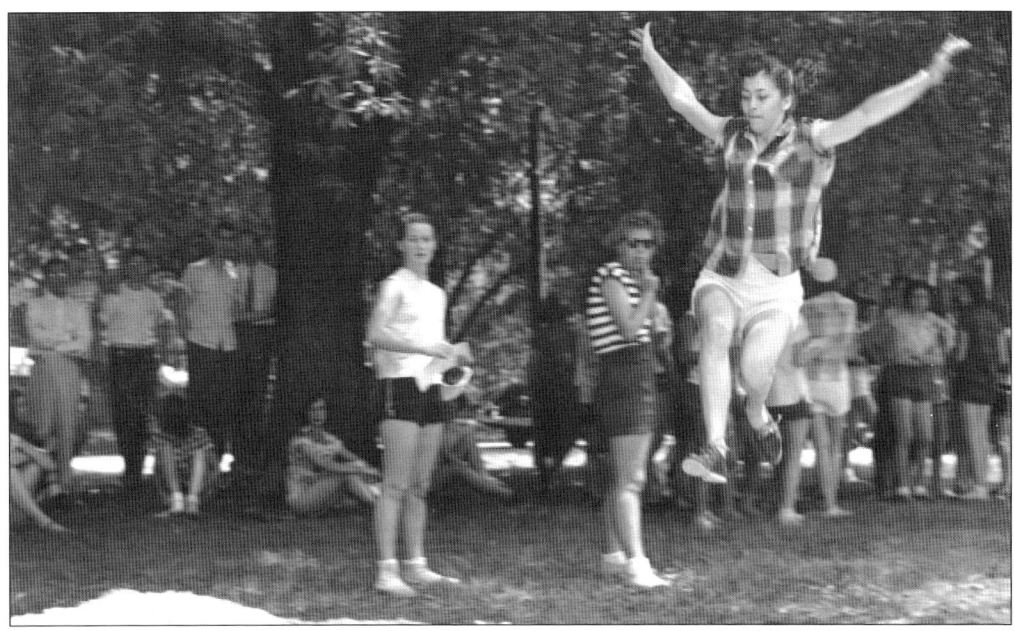

Carolyn Summer, shown mid-air as spectators look on, placed first for her broad jump in the 1952 Field Day games. The freshman from Ware Shoals was the highest individual scorer for the day, winning first place in the 50-yard dash, first place for the broad jump, and second place in the high jump.

This photograph from Field Day appears in the 1951 *Naiad* yearbook with the caption "Janie wins the race." The student pictured is Janie Patterson. According to descriptions of the day's events, one of the highlights was the student-faculty softball game, where onlookers "watched in amazement as Miss Wham slugged balls over the third baseman's head, Dr. Grier threw curve balls over the plate, and Miss Coleman tore around the baselines."

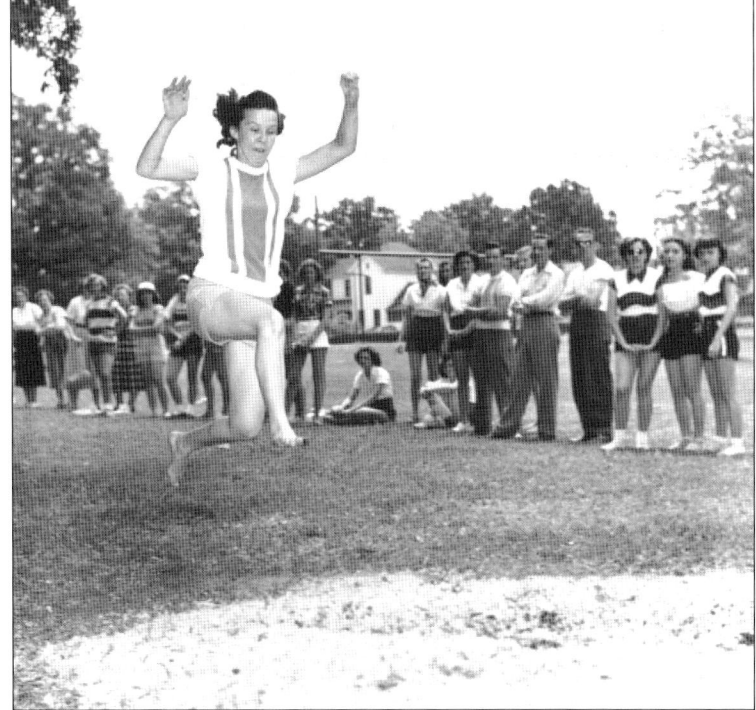

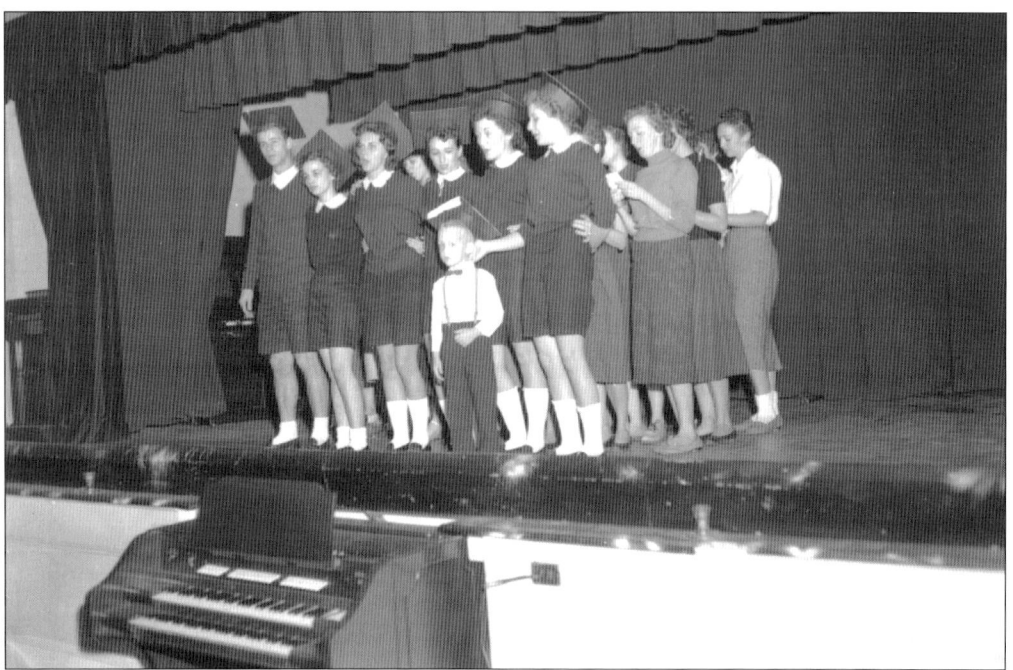

Pep night was an annual event in October sponsored by the Athletic Association of Lander. This night formally opened the athletic program for the school year. Each class made up yells, songs, decorations, and a skit. Pictured in 1957 are members of the senior class with their child mascot, four-year-old Michael Senn. Michael was the brother of senior business administration major Rebecca Senn. The senior-class child mascot attended a variety of social, athletic, and academic events and ceremonies over the course of the school year.

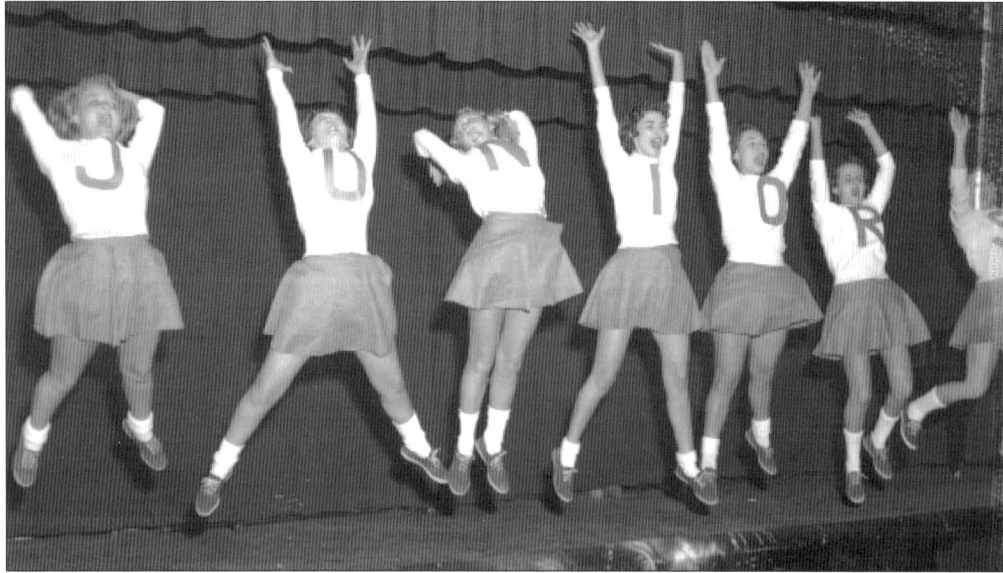

The *Naiad* yearbook offers this description of Pep Night: "At this lively affair, class songs, skit, and colors are shown, accompanied by loud cheering and keen excitement. The class receiving the most points is the acclaimed winner." In this photograph from 1957, members of the junior class are engaged in an energetic pep night cheer.

Knit caps, shawl-collared sweaters, and slacks made up the cheerleading uniforms of 1931 during cooler months. Students with a hexagon leather patch with an "L" in the center were members of the "Order of the L," an exceptionally accomplished group of student-athletes. The cheer squad consisted of one student to represent each class and then an at-large member who represented the entire student body. From left to right are Mary Good (sophomore), Eloise Klebb (at-large), Frances Leeson (freshman), Audrey Shirley (senior), and Reby Rykard (junior).

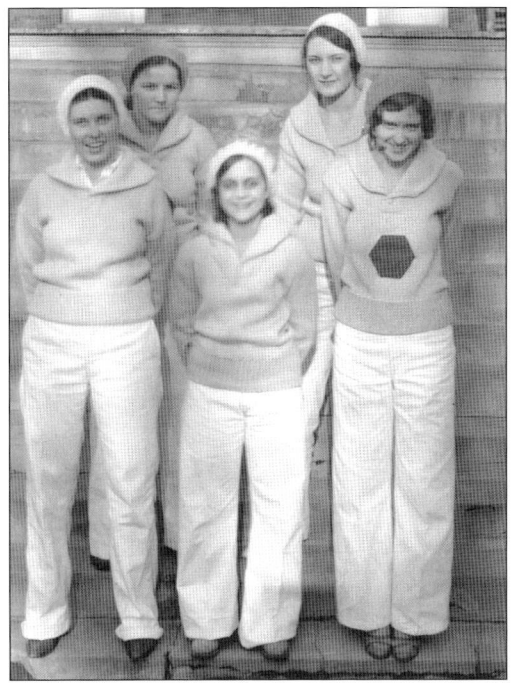

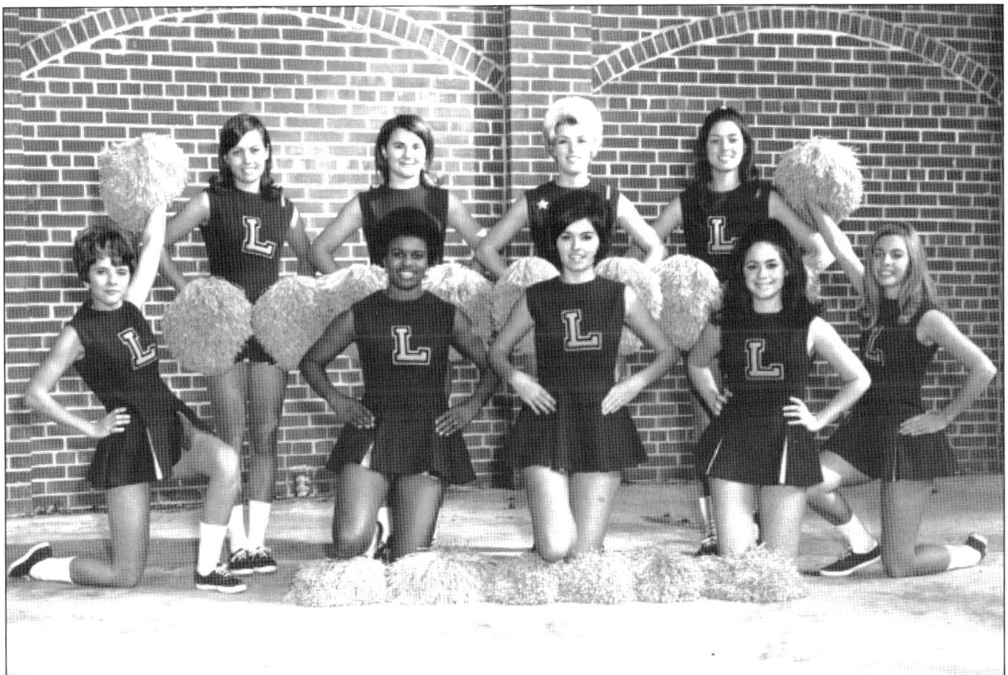

These Lander cheerleaders, shown in 1970, wear more contemporary blue and gold uniforms than their 1930s counterparts. Pictured from left to right are (first row) Pat Butler, Emma Babb, Penny Wood, Betsy Goldstine, and Dale Driggers; (second row) Nancy Jones, Sue Sudlow, Margaret Igleheart, and Julie Rogers.

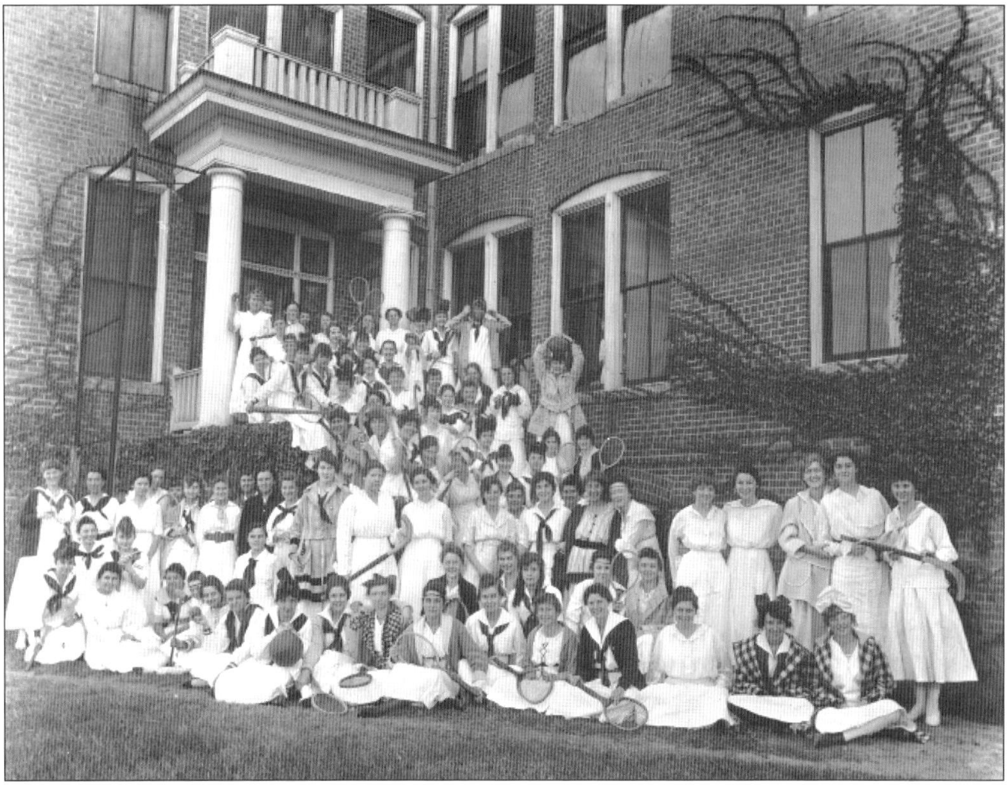

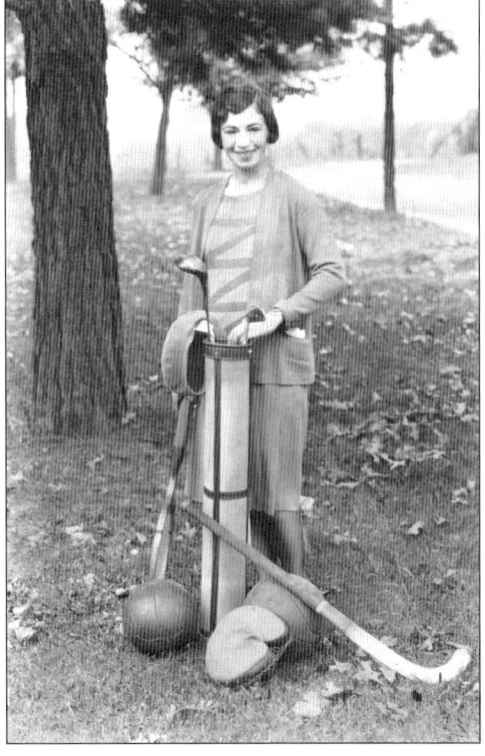

Students in athletic attire stream out of Willson Hall while posing with sports equipment in this early-20th-century photograph. Sports at Lander during this time were intramural. The 1933 *Naiad* describes "a keen spirit of rivalry between class teams, but a spirit of true sportsmanship and loyal enthusiasm characterize the college athletics."

This portrait of Louise Hodges, athletic director, was taken in 1930. She poses with a variety of athletic gear because she oversaw and coached all sports as well as any athletic demonstrations—no small feat. She attended Mary Baldwin Seminary in Stanton, Virginia, and graduated from the Central School of Hygiene and Physical Education in New York City in 1924 with a degree in physical education. At age 91, she was awarded the prestigious Order of the Palmetto from the State of South Carolina for her selfless service to the Greenwood community. She lived to be 100 years old and is buried in Greenwood's historic Magnolia Cemetery.

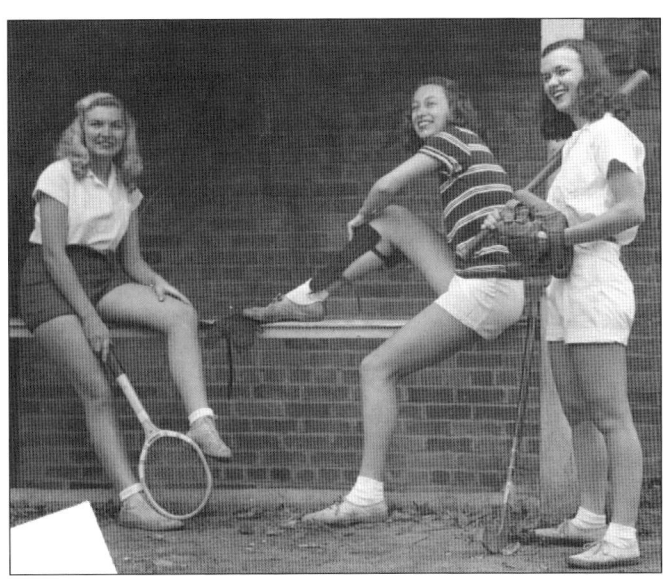

Student-athletes pose with their gear in this photograph that appeared in the 1949 *Naiad* with the caption "Chris, Duck and Grem." All three students were members of the Order of the L, an honor bestowed upon students whose participation in various sports was exceptional. From left to right are Christine Hatcher, Wilma Duckett, and Betty Turner. Duckett served as senior class representative for the Athletic Council that year, and Betty Turner was president of the council.

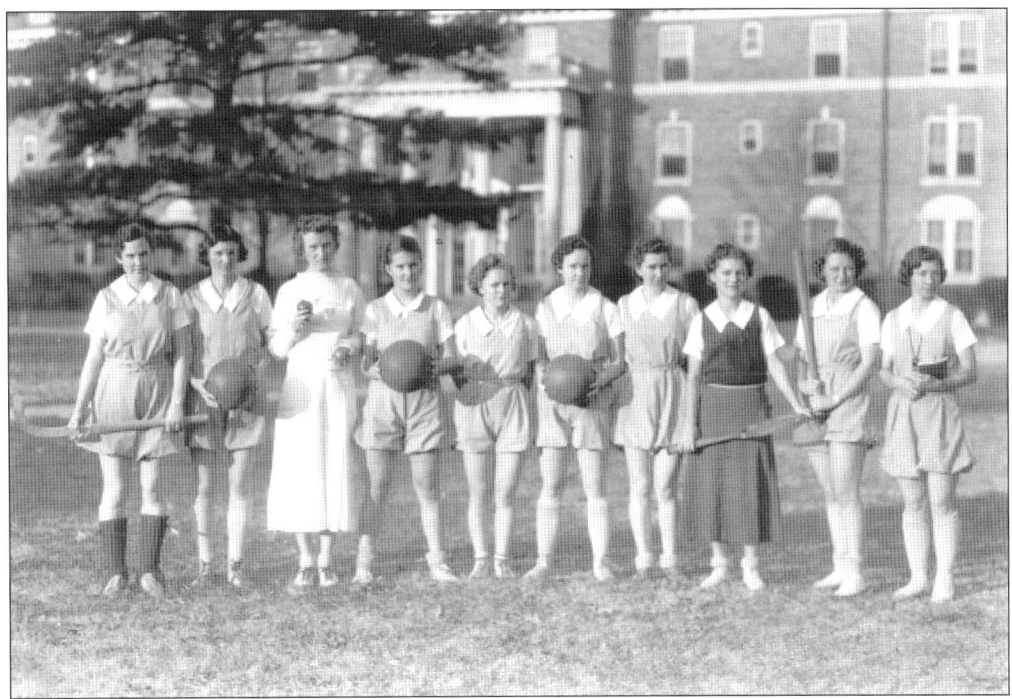

These are the Athletic Council members for 1934. The officers of this association, the athletic director, and the four class representatives formed the Athletic Council. It was the work of the council to provide athletic programs and parties and to look after the welfare of the association. Pictured from left to right are Clara Parkman (hockey), Miriam Jones (speedball), Mary Anderson (hiking and skating), Alice Griffin (basketball), Esther Messick (stunts), Ruth Jeffcoat (volleyball), Evelyn Chambers (track), Louise Cope (tennis), Lillian Cannon (baseball), and Louise Hodges (athletic director).

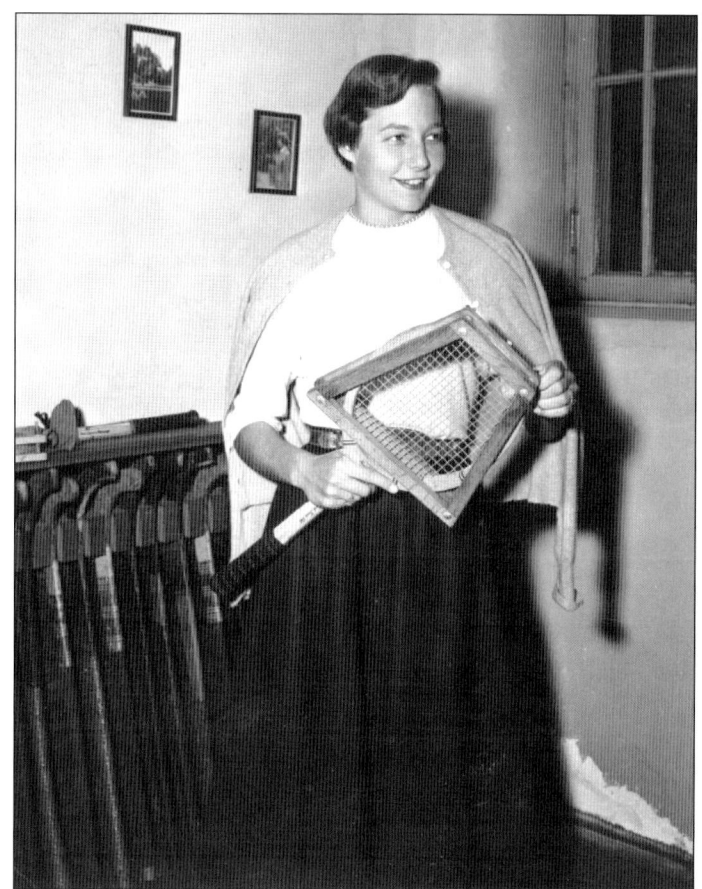

Physical education department faculty member Ella Claire Lee Mays poses with a tennis racket and other athletic equipment in 1954. Mays, a former Lander student herself, was an advisor to student swimmers in the Dolphin Club as well as the student council. The photographs on the wall behind Mays are of equestrian activities.

For many decades, Lander had a point system for participation in sports. In the 1950s, the proud possessors of Block Ls are those who had earned 25 points for participation in athletic activities; a star was awarded for an additional 10; and a crescent for 10 more points. Showing off their Block L in this 1951 photograph are, from left to right clockwise, Jean Smith, Gloria Glymph, Ruby Johnson, Rachel Johnson, Betty Coleman, and Hazel Perritt.

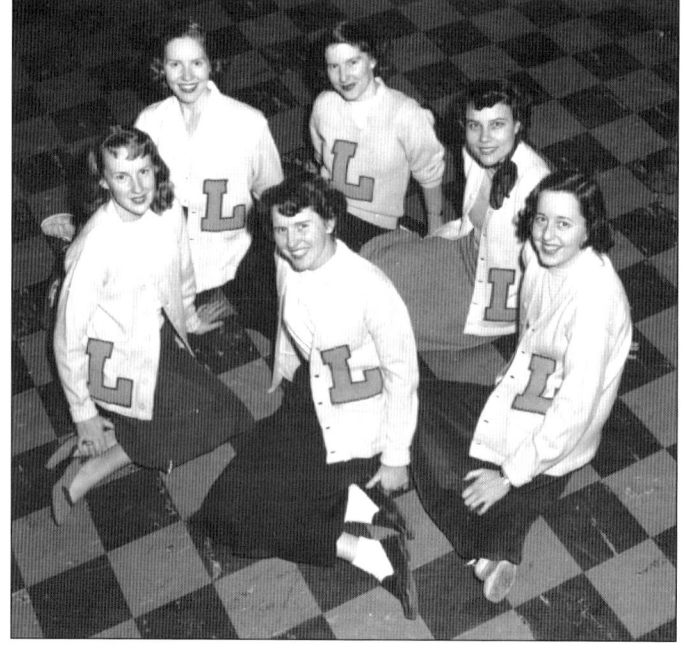

In this 1931 photograph, Margaret Lander (left) and Dorothy Booth (right) pose with their tennis rackets. The hexagon-shaped leather patch on Margaret Lander's sweater is an Order of the L emblem, an early version of the varsity, or Block L. In the 1930s, the criteria for obtaining a letter was based on winning 1,500 points for successful participation in athletics. A student must be outstanding in athletics for at least three years. For each team made, she won 100 points, and additional points could be gained through various other activities such as hiking, skating, stunts, and clogging. If one wins as many as 2,000 points, she was entitled to a sweater. The letter was usually earned during junior year and awarded on Field Day.

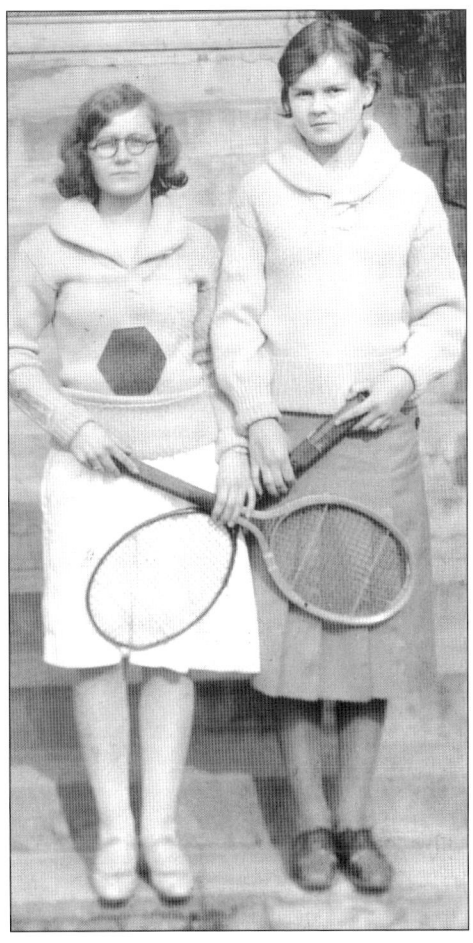

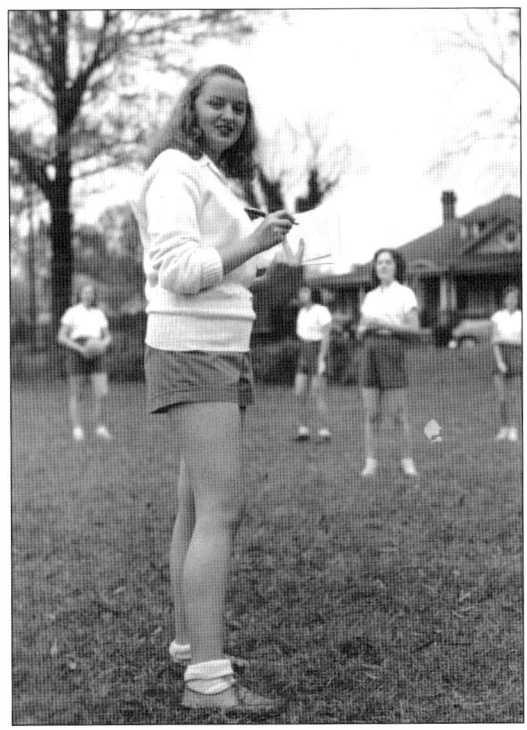

Lucille Edwards keeps score during a speedball game in 1949. The game is a combination of basketball and soccer. Further detail about speedball is given in the 1953 *Naiad*: "Every player must always remember to execute the correct techniques of the game and to play her position on the field. Although the players may get very exhausted and get a few bruises and bumps, they have a wonderful time playing the game."

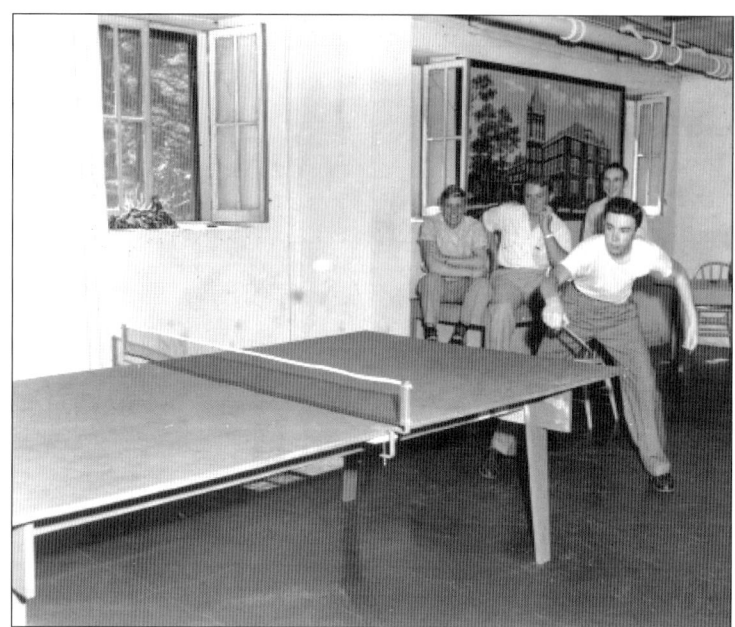

Ping-pong competitions at Lander are mentioned in the local newspaper, the *Index-Journal,* as early as 1936. Male students were first admitted in 1944, and ping-pong became a very popular option, perhaps due in part to insufficient enrollment in the early years to form full intramural teams in other sports.

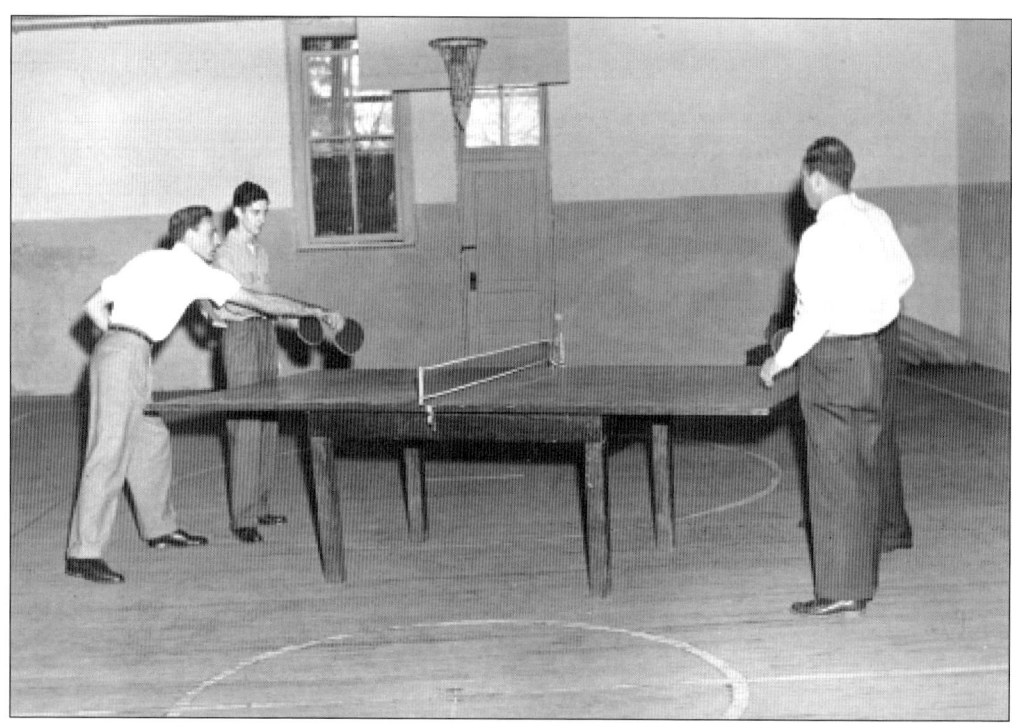

Photographs of students playing ping-pong often appeared in the *Naiad*: "Every day is ping-pong day at Lander. The boys have a special 'nack' for this game and keep the ping-pong table busy in the canteen." Charles Henderson, second from left, plays a game of doubles around 1952. The other players' names are not known.

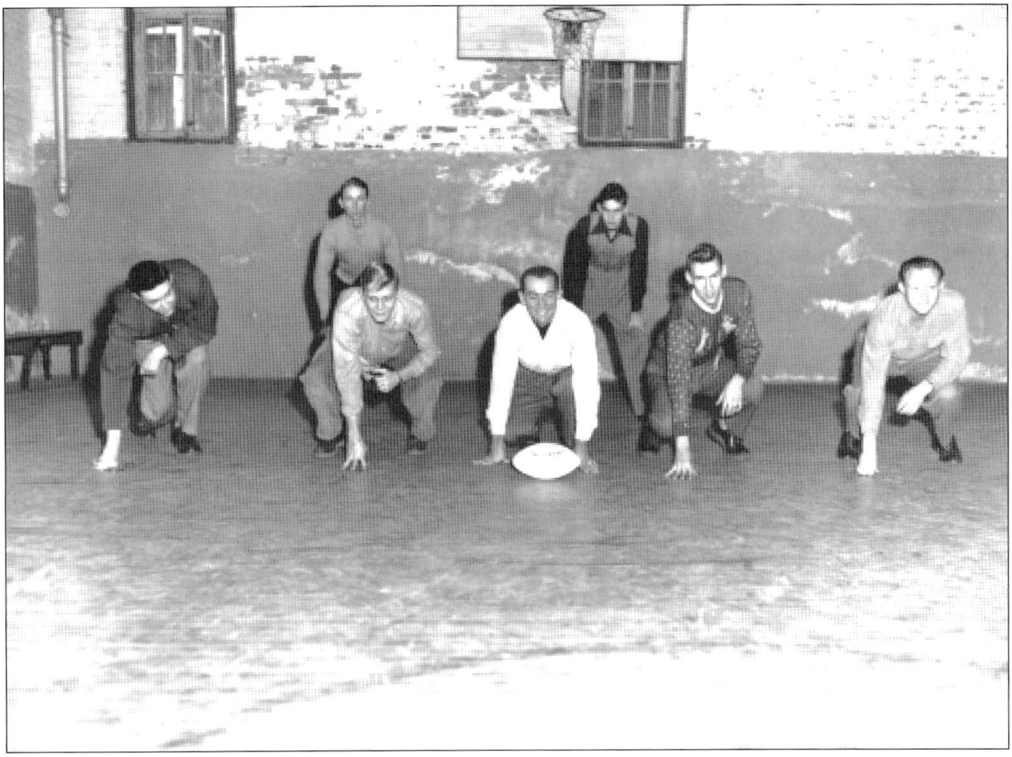

A section featuring men's football appeared in the 1952 *Naiad*: "The Lander 'Willies' got under way this year the first Lander football team with the venerable Charles Henderson as their coach. With Ray Chronic and Hugh Pratt as stars, who could stop them? Anyway, this touch football team played several games with men's clubs in the town. Keep working, boys! Some day . . . " Pictured here in 1952 are, from left to right, (first row) Hugh Pratt, Ray Cronic, Charles McNeil, Mack Jones, and George Teasley; (second row) Hulon Brown and Charles Henderson.

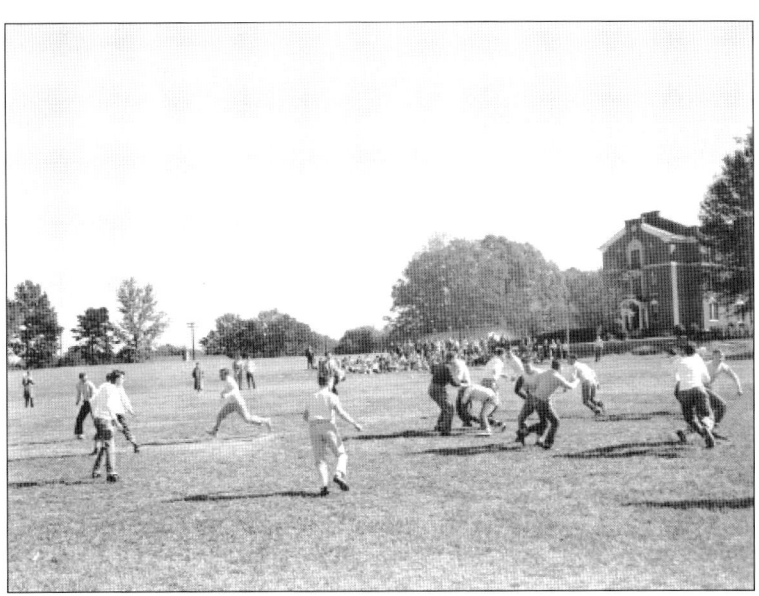

In this 1956 game of touch football, Chipley Hall can be seen to the right. The roof of the equestrian stables is directly behind the spectator crowd. Upon enlargement, Dr. Boyce Grier— Lander's seventh president—can be seen on the left edge of the spectator crowd in a black suit.

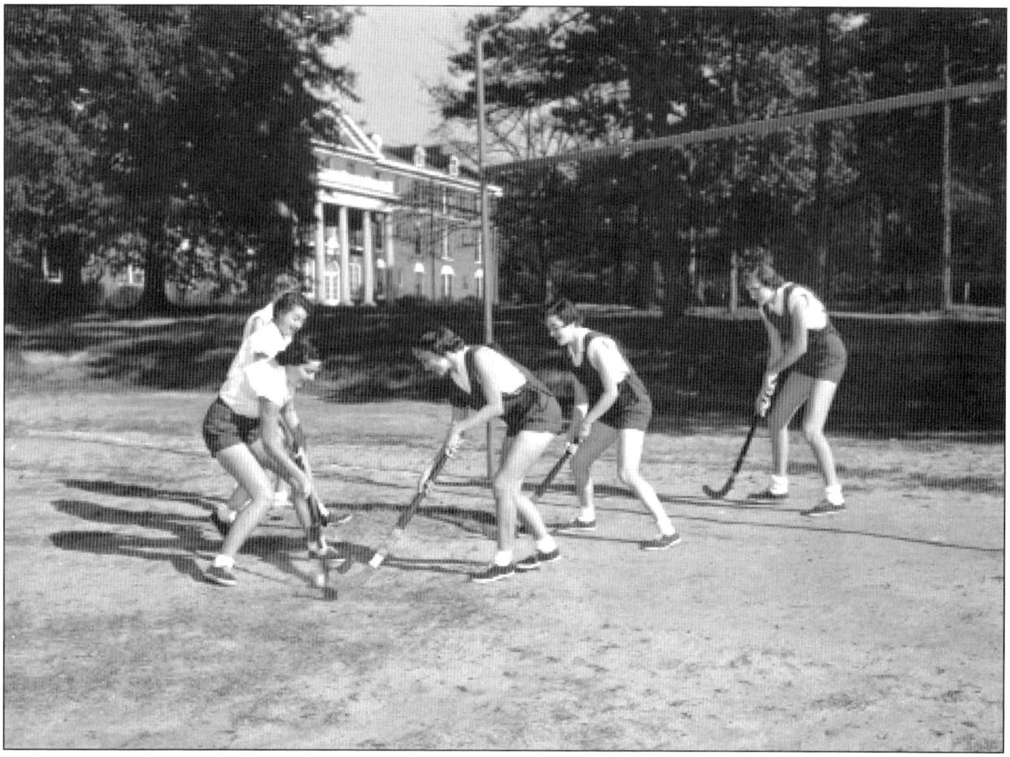

According to the *Naiad* annual, field hockey season opened in the fall when "students buckled on shin guards and picked up sticks in order to perfect left-hand lunges or dribbles down the field." Pictured in 1955 from left to right are Janice Curran, Delores Johnson, Ouida Miller, Norma Owens, Jean Fowler, and Frances Moore.

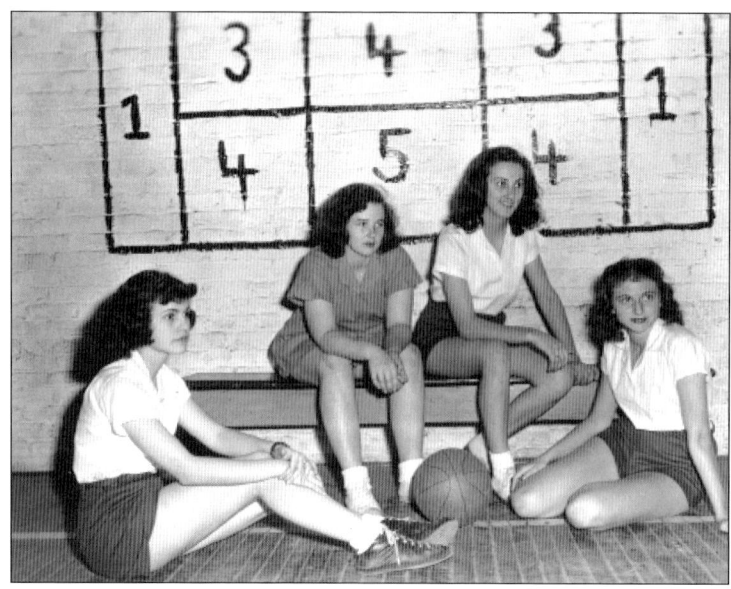

"When do we play basketball?" was reportedly the most often heard question on campus. The season for basketball began with a practice tournament in December, and then the main tournament was held after Christmas. The varsity basketball players in 1949, pictured from left to right, are Juanita Cerda, Ethel Watson, Marjorie Hipp, and Jimmie Rhode.

A column in the 1935 *Naiad* called "Writin' 'Em Up" recalls the final game of Lander's speed ball season: "At 5:15 on Thursday afternoon these astounding messages click-clacked from electric sparks through the Associated Press automatic printers in the *Lander News* editorial room. The juniors had just scored a big success in that championship-determining speed ball game over the seniors. Already the juniors had scored against the sophomores and freshman, although both classes put up a good fight."

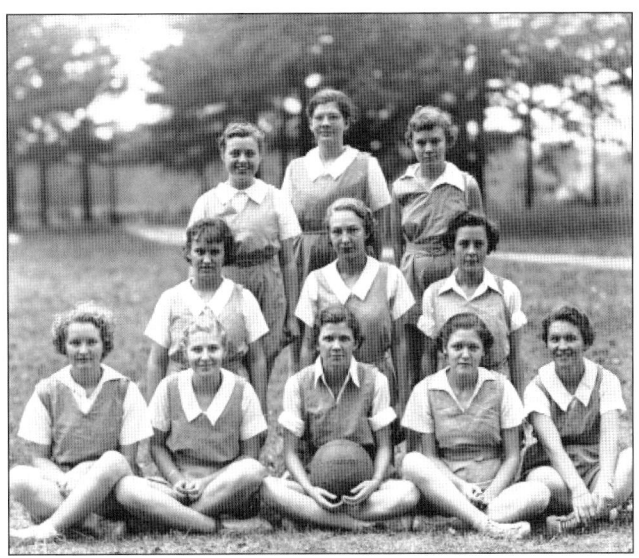

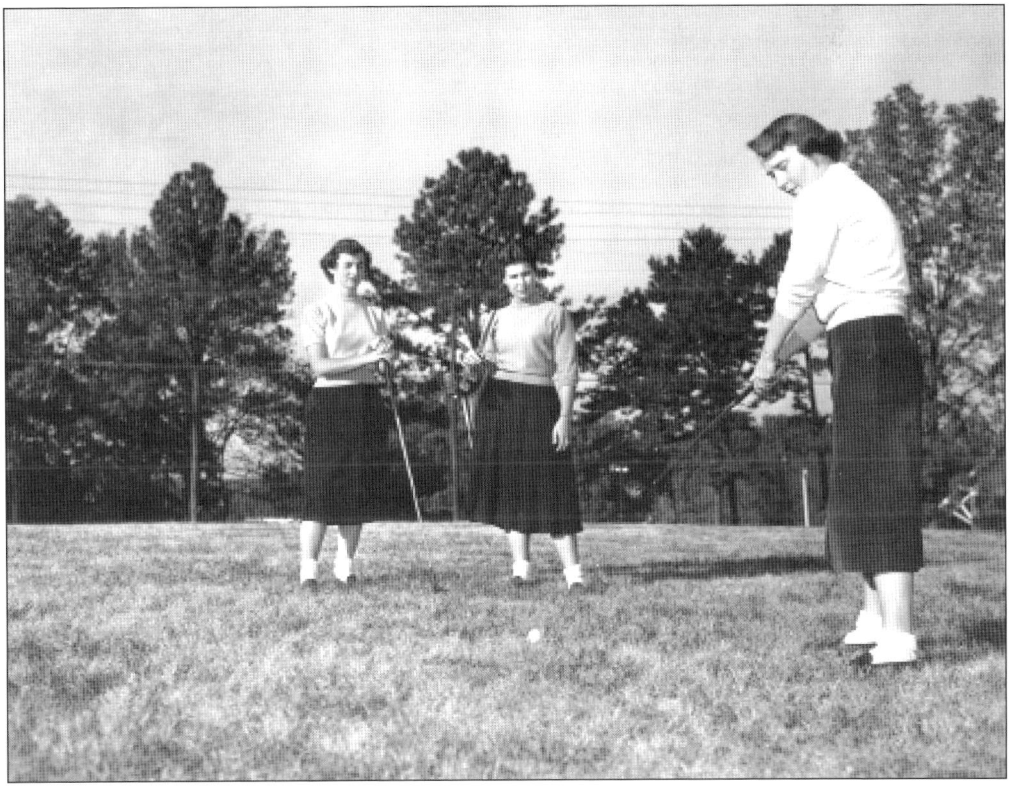

The 1951 *Naiad* provides insight into golf in the early days of interest in the sport at Lander: "Sandtraps and roughs are a part of the fun of golf, a sport in which more and more students at Lander are taking part. Though not one of the major features of the curriculum, students can often practice chip shots or putts on the athletic field in preparation for the days when they got to the Greenwood Municipal Golf Course. Golf battles between faculty members and also the students themselves help to keep interest alive." Pictured in 1955 are, from left to right, Mary Frank Gantt, Vera McMillan, and Betty Saunders.

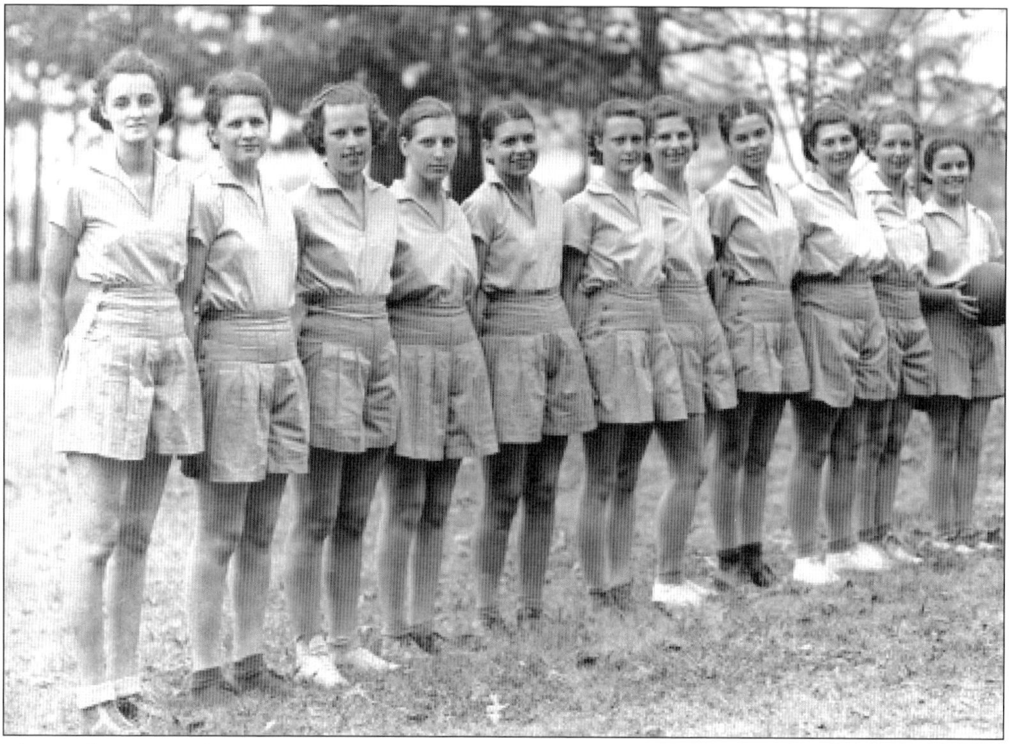

The *Index-Journal* describes an event held in November 1934 at the fairgrounds called "Greenwood Monday," where alumni from different sports teams competed against current students. While the major headline was about Greenwood High's football team, there was mention of Lander's speedball team: "Color and flavor will be added to the gridiron battle when Lander college's two all-star speedball teams clash between halves. Louise Hodges (athletic director) promises plenty of action and thrills in the clash and if you haven't seen a speedball game you had better see this one." The freshman speedball team of 1934 is pictured.

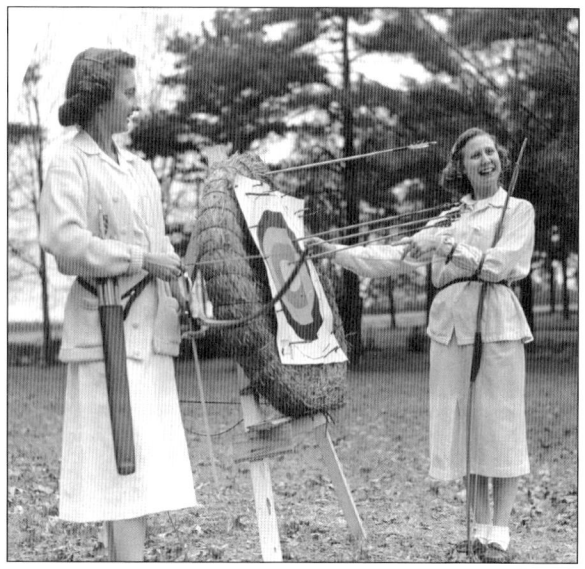

The 1955 *Naiad* describes archery at Lander, "Stand tall . . . sight the target, raise the bow arm… draw . . . aim . . . release. This is the secret of the perfect form and accuracy of the girls who enjoy archery. Archery is liked by many whether in class or just shooting for enjoyment and relaxation." This photograph appears in the 1949 yearbook with the caption "I Hit It!" Pictured are Callie Self Coker (left) and Tweedie Ann Durst.

This is an early photograph of baseball players (some posing with equipment) taken around 1919 and found in the Lander memory book of Dorothy Rayson Stokes. From left to right, as identified by Stokes, are (first row, seated) Lila Peden and Mary Louise Heustess; (second row, standing) Effie Graham, Lizzie Peden, Martha Shuler, Elizabeth Coskrey, and Roy Garrison.

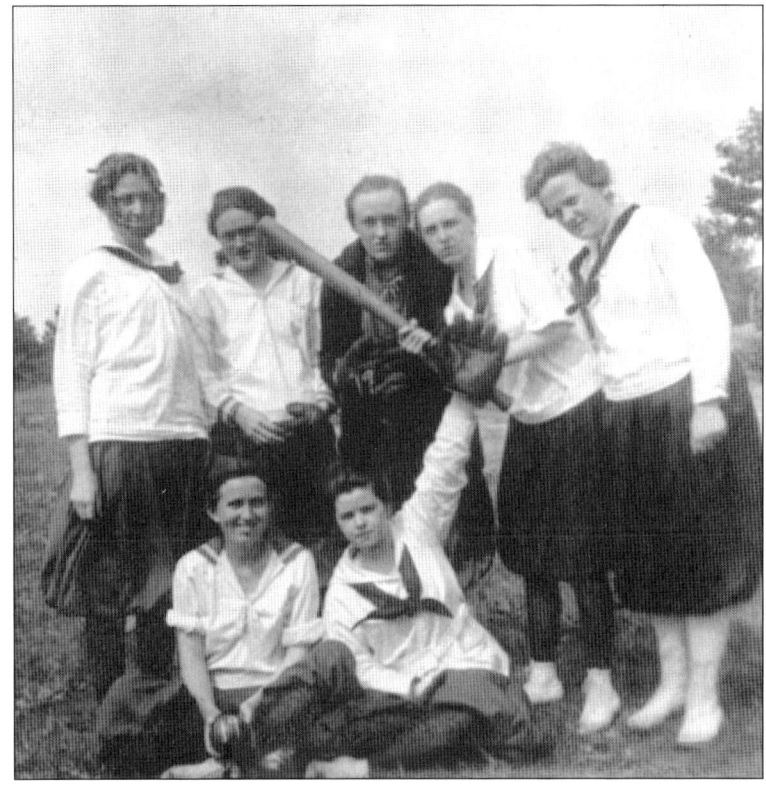

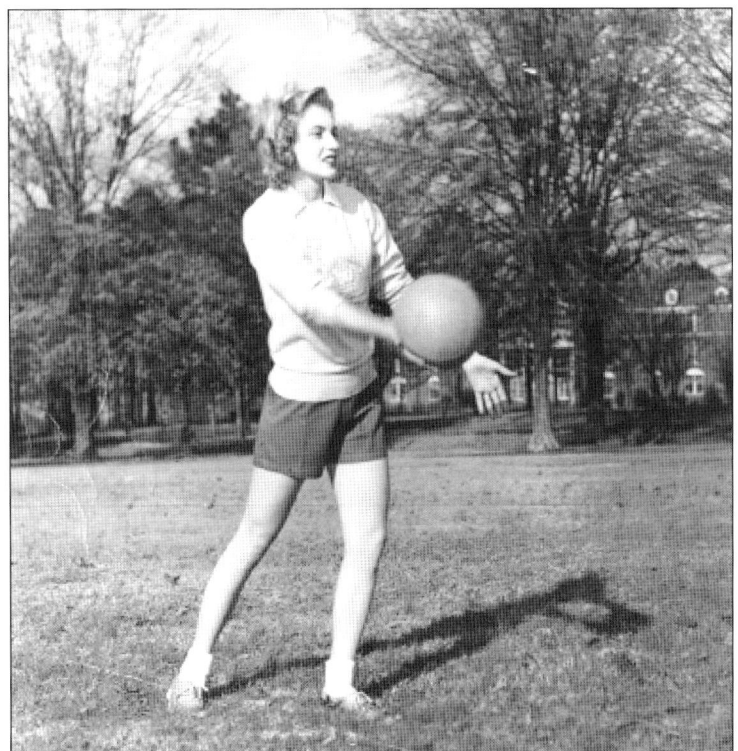

Jean Redden, pictured wearing a Lander athletics sweatshirt and serving a ball in this 1951 photograph, was a member of the Athletic Council. The council had eight members who planned Pep Night, Field Day, and May Day. In addition, per the 1951 *Naiad*, they were responsible for "stimulating interest in all sports and tournaments."

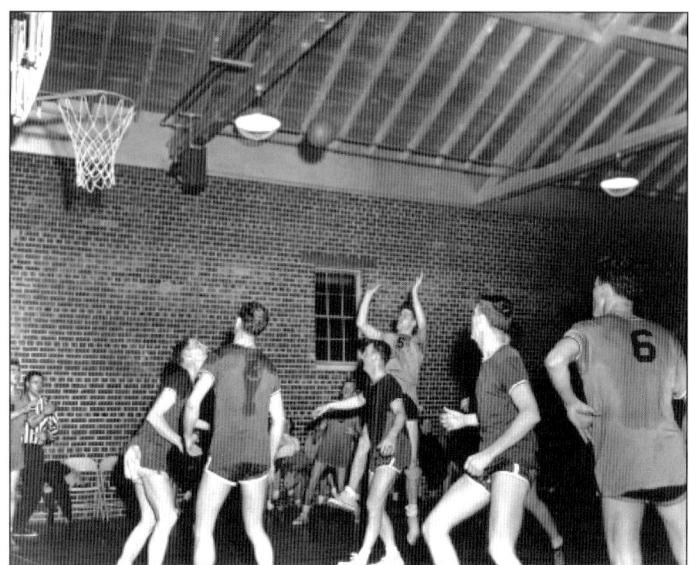

The Lander men's basketball team played in the Greenwood Recreation Center League. Although the name does not appear in any of the Naiad annuals, reports in the *Index-Journal* refer to the team as the Lander Bullfrogs. This could have been the official team name or just a way to refer to male Lander students since the female students were often referred to as Lilies. In this photograph from 1958, James Nixon takes a shot during a game in the recreation center.

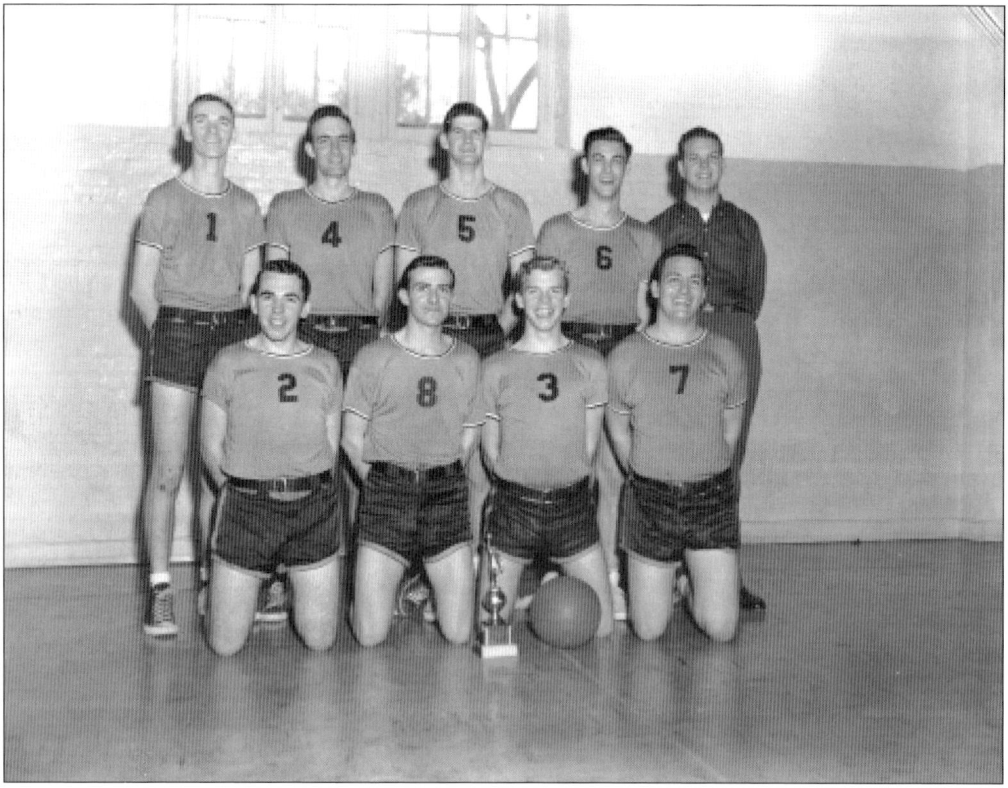

Lander Bullfrogs pose with a trophy in this team portrait from 1958; from left to right are (first row, kneeling) Joe Langley, Willie Falls, Doug Jones, and Claude Simmons; (standing) Jerry Clegg, Bob Miller, James Nixon, Bill Scurry, and Harold King (second row, manager).

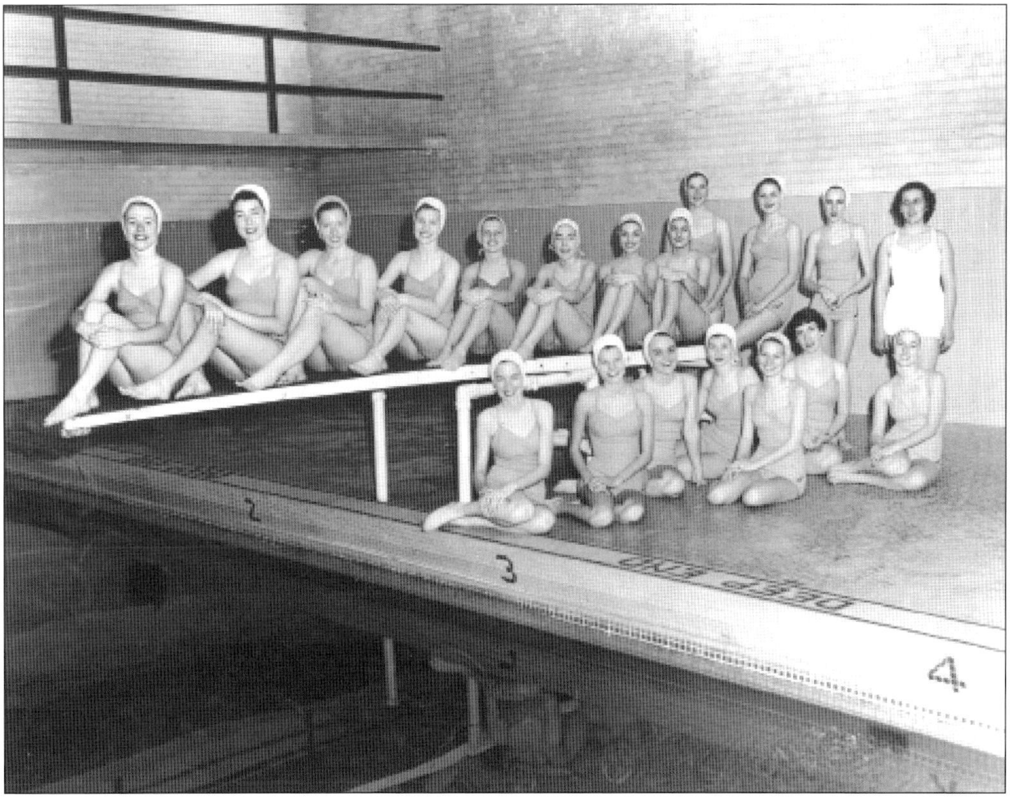

The Dolphin Club was formed in 1951. Swimmers met at the new pool at the Greenwood YMCA. The 1952 *Naiad* reported that "activities for the year included a swimming exhibition in January, an aquacade in March, and relays and games which took place in the spring. The proceeds of these functions were used to send some deserving Sophomore or Junior girl to the Aquatic School held in the summer." Pictured in this 1952 photograph, from left to right (first row) Ray Crowder, Ruth Burnett, Beth Sheridan, Mary Frank Gantt, Dian Belk, Dot Burgess, and Shirley Arant; (second row) Evelynne Norris, Marian Hagan, Dot Breazeale, Deebie Bessinger, Carolyn Summer, Carolyn Miller, Charles Andrews, Frances Cuttino, and Mrs. R.W. Anderson (advisor).

Members of the Dolphin Club are shown in this photograph from 1953. The *Naiad* yearbook describes swimming at Lander, "Stringy hair and wet bathing suits are part of swimming . . . students eager to become champion swimmers practiced breaststrokes, crawls and frog-kicks." From left to right are (first row) Betty Stone; (second row) Joan Bonnett and Charlie Andrews; (third row) Dot Burgess, Marian Hagan, and Betsy Boyer; (fourth row) Winnie Newman, Sally Bald, Dorothy Clyburn, and Barbara Theophanis.

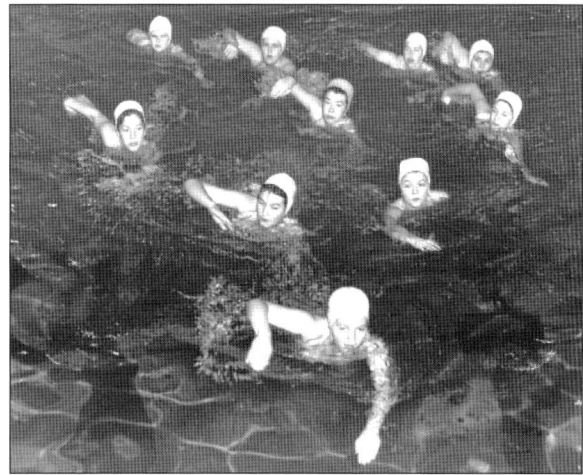

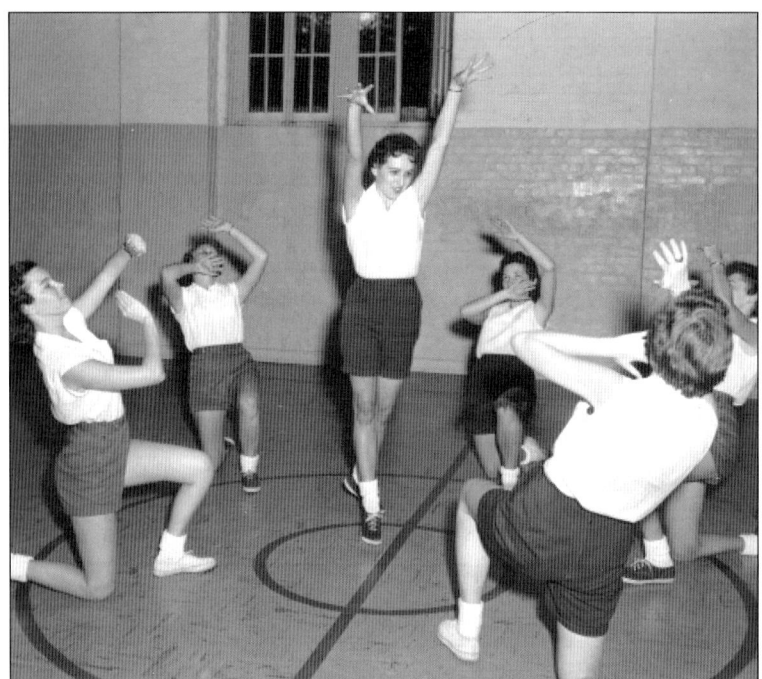

Modern dance class at Lander in the late 1950s was described in the *Naiad* annual as, "filled with potential dancers practicing mazurkas and leaps or learning steps for dances performed at the Harvest Festival and at the Christmas Dance." From left to right are Charlise Hughes, Maggie Garrison, Eleanor Seel, Mary Jo Harrison, Dot Terry, and Anne Heyward.

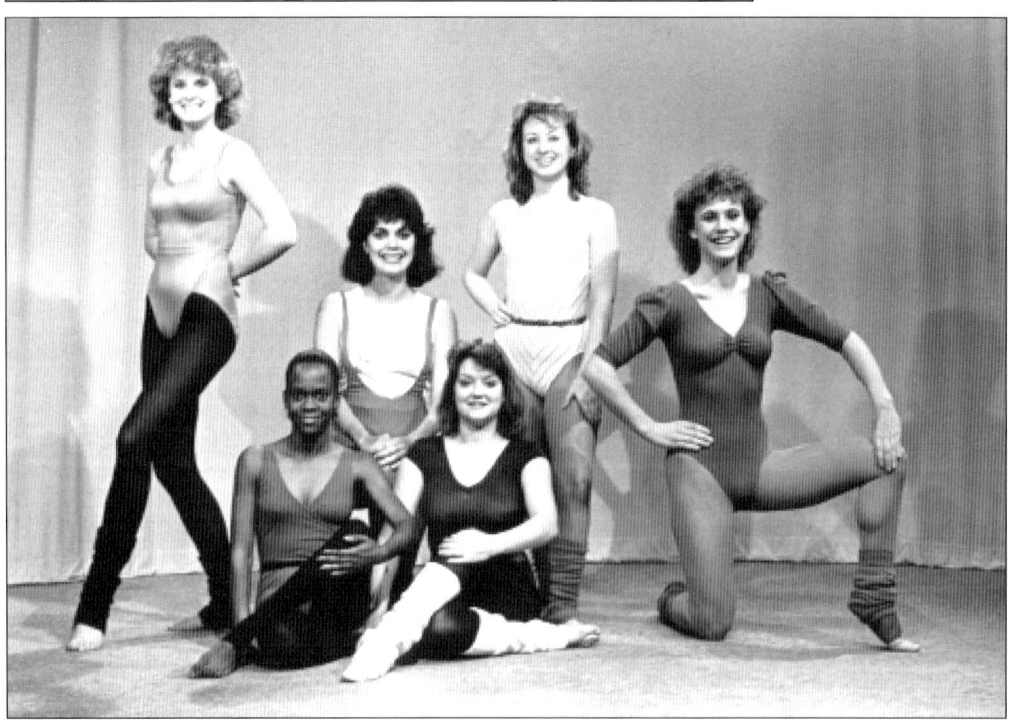

In 1986, under the direction of Carole Neubner, assistant professor of dance, this subset of the Lander Dancers dance troupe suited up in leotards and leg warmers to continue the tradition of movement and dance as a means of expression and a way to stay physically active. Pictured from left to right are Sheree Johnson, Sonja Williams, Leitreanna Terry, Caroline McCall, Robin Lee, and Tina Haskins.

Lander College cheerleaders work together to create this tower formation in the early 1980s. In this photograph, the addition of male students to the squad bolstered the foundation of the pyramid.

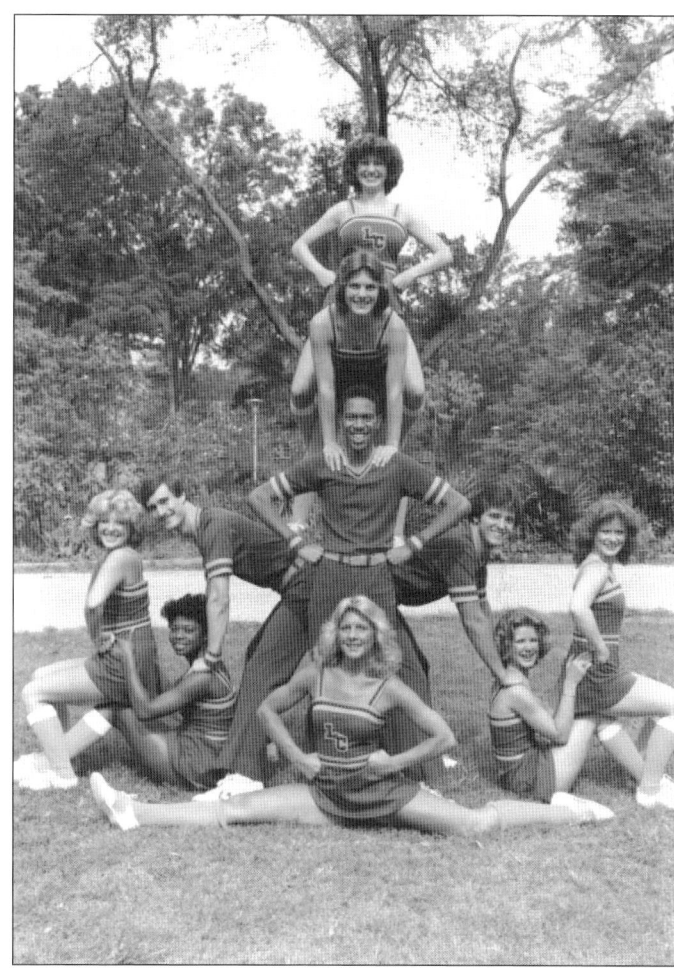

Members of this 1953 tumbling class learned formations for a variety show act where they rolled and tumbled to the music of the Virginia Reel. Doing headstands are Mot O'Shields Patterson (left) and Ann Byrd. From left to right on the pyramid are (bottom row) Marian Hagan, Betty Jean Dean, and Catherine Corley Wilson; (middle row) Jo Lusk and Beth Sheridan; (top) Dot Shirley.

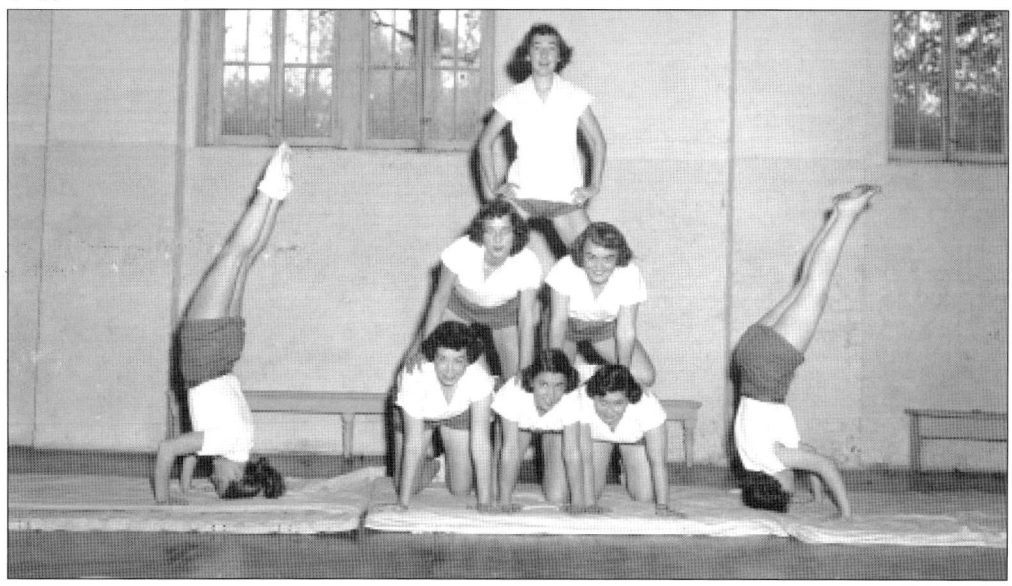

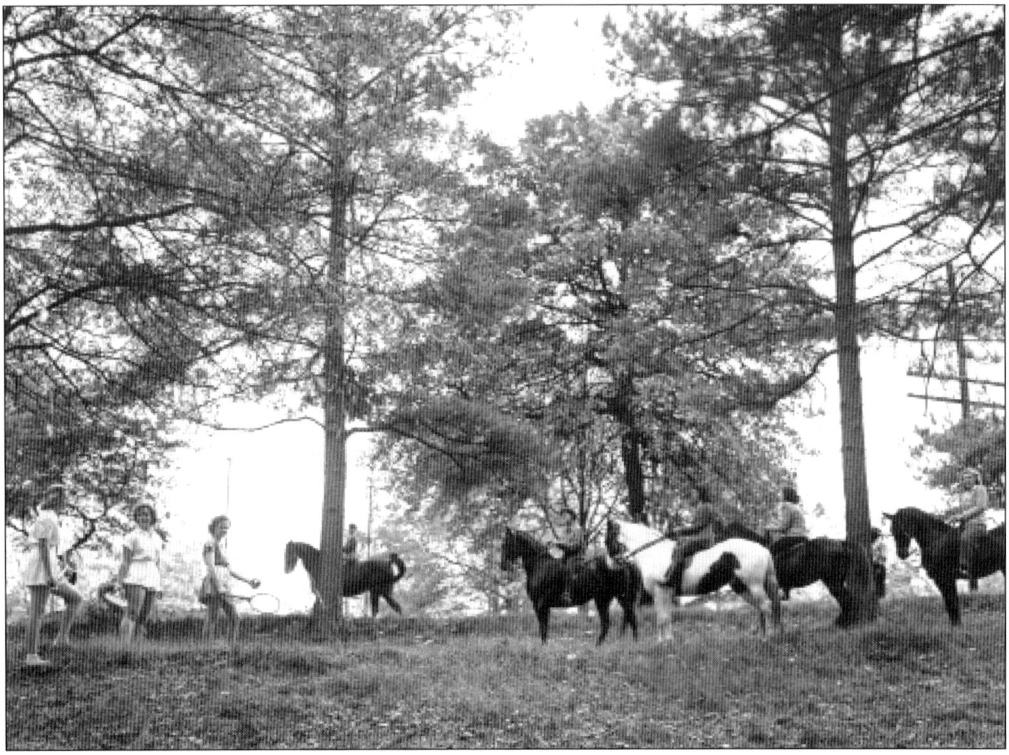

In the 1940s, equestrians could exercise their horses on the campus bridle path. This path also led to the tennis courts. In this image taken in 1943, tennis players and equestrians meet up on the path in the woods. It is uncertain how the right-of-way was determined.

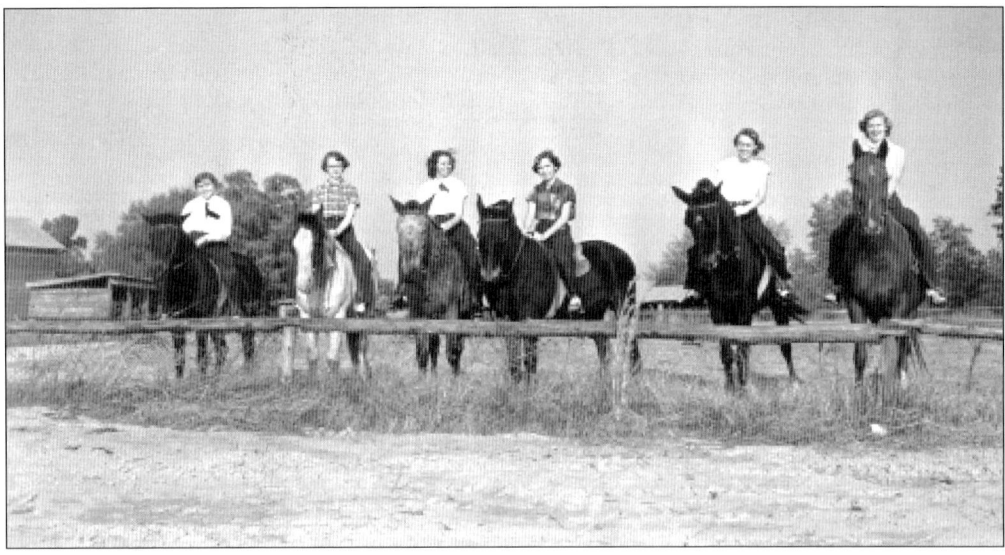

Equestrian sports were introduced at Lander in 1939 under the leadership of Lander faculty member Alice Spencer. The stables were directly behind Chipley Hall, and the riding ring was on the east side of Chipley. This photograph shows the equestrian team in 1953. From left to right are June Kelley, Esther Waters, Margaret Ward, Nancy Saxon, Carolyn Spelts, and Ann Simmons.

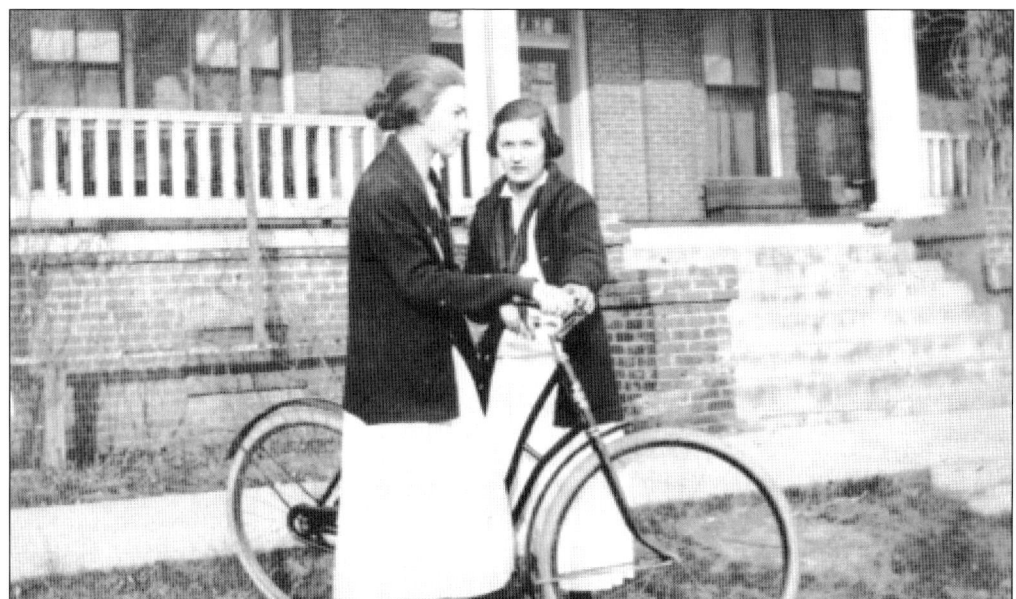

When Rev. Samuel Lander chose the site for the college in Greenwood, he told the selection committee, "Gentleman, we must find a lot within easy walking distance of the churches and the shopping district." This photograph was taken around 1919 and was found in the memory book of Dorothy Rayson Stokes. Frances Bolton is the student who stopped for a moment to have her photograph taken with a friend before heading out on a bike ride, possibly into town.

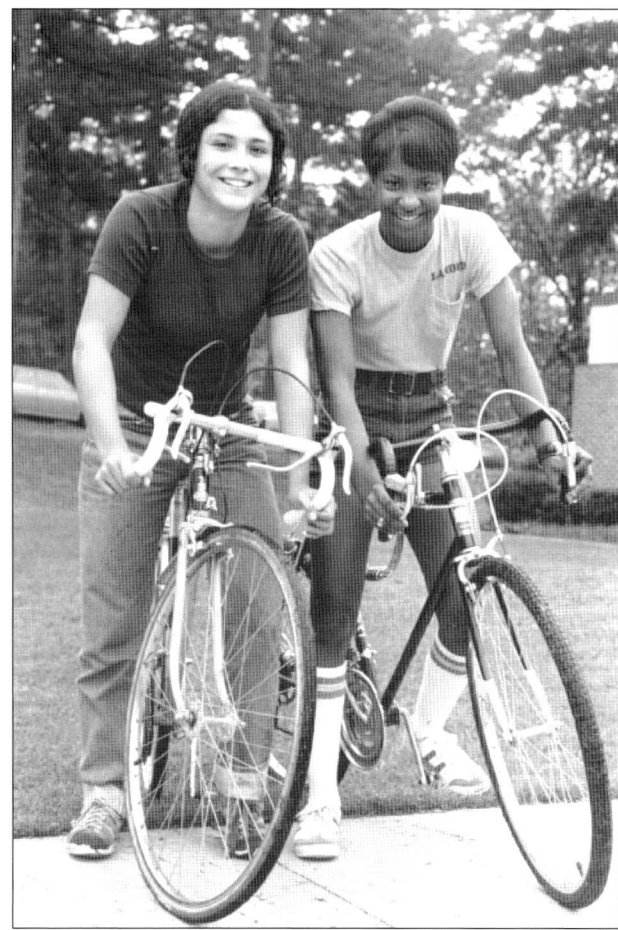

Students pose in this undated photograph on their 10-speed bicycles before setting out for a ride. Even today, interest in bicycle riding is supported and encouraged with a bike path leading from Montague Avenue through the main campus entrance. Bicycles can also be borrowed from the campus recreation department.

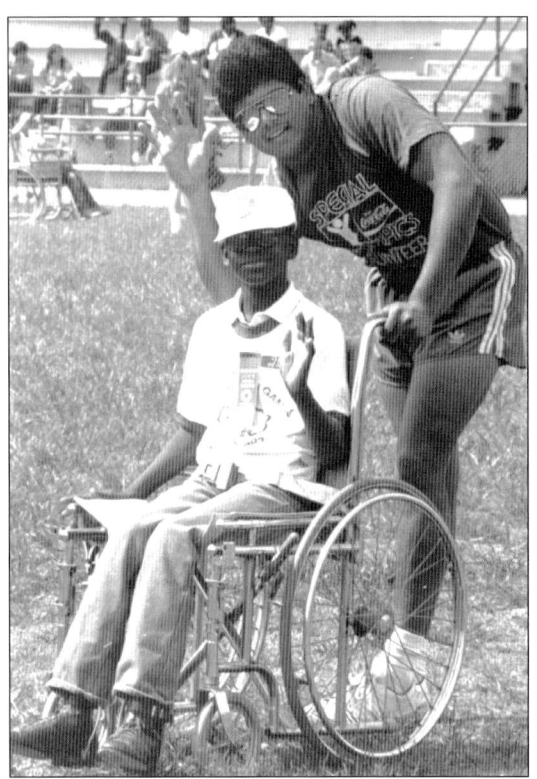

The annual Lander-Civitan games (Special Olympics) was a day of fun and games for the physically and mentally disabled, co-sponsored by Lander and the Greenwood Civitan Club. In 1983, Lander student Ravi Sastry, a chemistry major from Simpsonville, was a volunteer at the event held at Greenwood High School. There were numerous games for entrants to participate in, including a wheelchair race.

Athletes in the 1983 Lander-Civitan games take time to get hydrated with a volunteer. The Greenwood community was very committed to supporting this event, with over 200 volunteers from the high school and Lander. The Greenwood Civitan Club who co-sponsored the games with Lander raised funds for disabled children in the county. In 1975, Mayor Thomas Wingard proclaimed November 8 as Greenwood Civitan Day in honor of the efforts of the club.

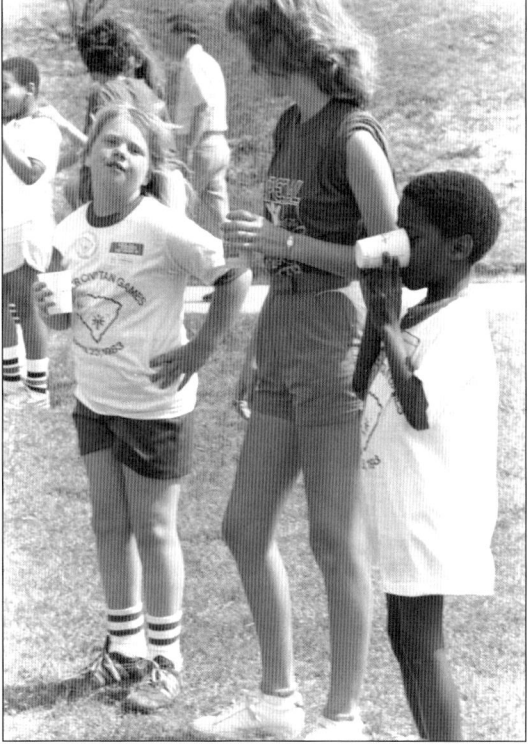

Volunteers give directions to athletes at the start of a race at the Lander-Civitan games in 1983. The track is at Greenwood High School. Games included basketball events, a football throw, a wheelchair race, a frisbee toss, sack races, and parachute games. More than 450 people participated.

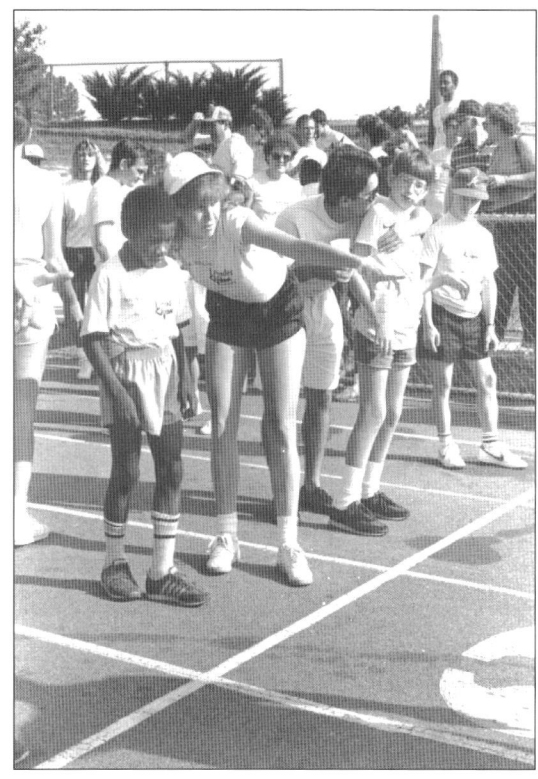

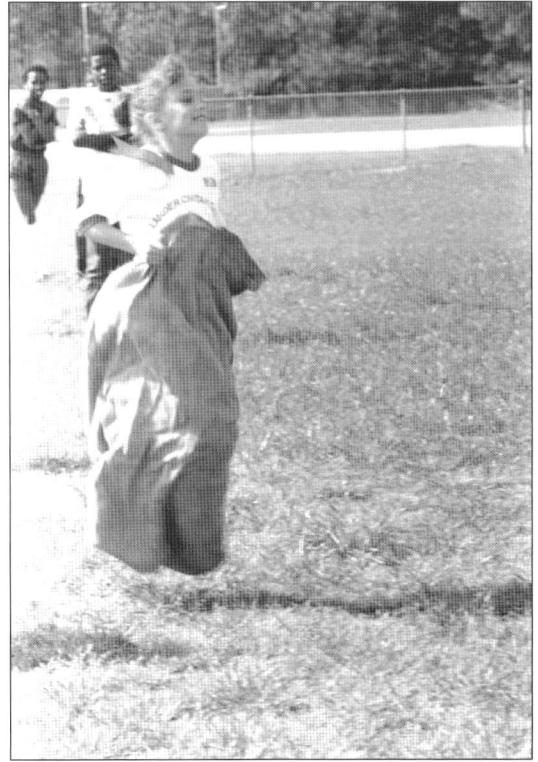

A young entrant at the Lander-Civitan games leaps into the air during the sack hop race in 1983. This participant appears to have already won a ribbon in another competition. According to the *Index-Journal*, "The event was believed to be one of the best days in South Carolina for the mentally and physically handicapped."

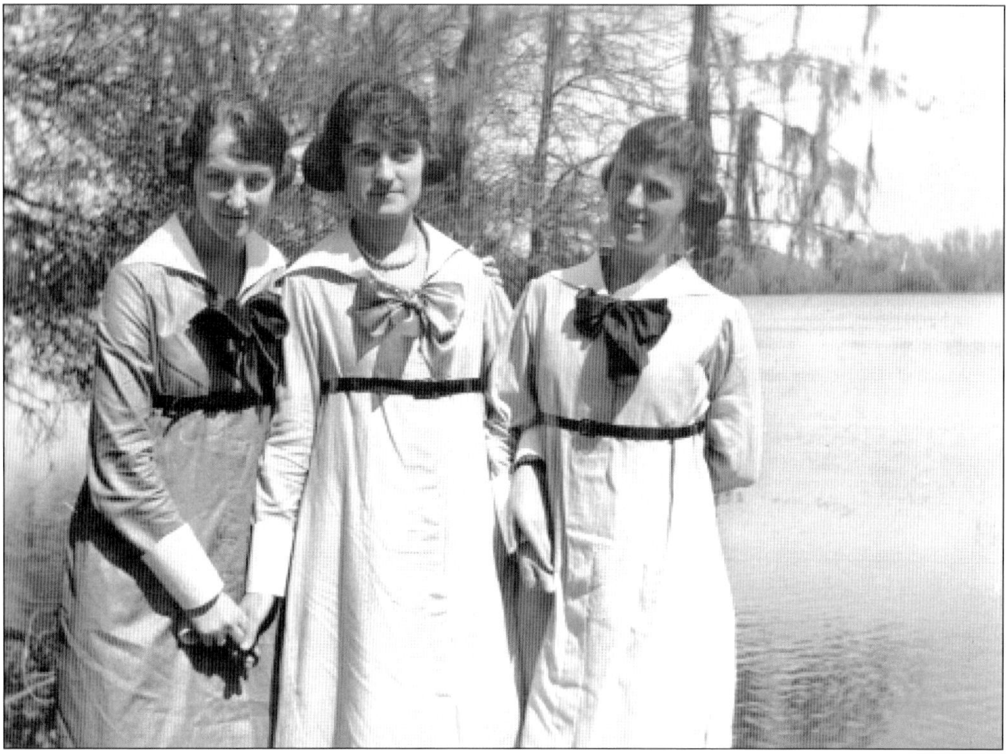

Perhaps the greatest lesson in physical culture learned at Lander was the appreciation and enjoyment of active time outdoors with friends, whether on campus engaged in physical education classes and organized sports or on their own while on holiday. This photograph is from the 1918 memory book of Marian Sheridan.

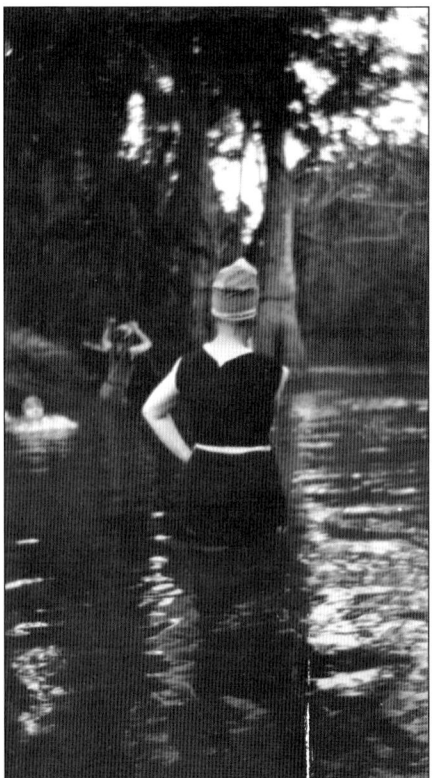

The final photograph, in the physical stream of learning, evokes the spirit of Lander's *Naiad* as students on summer break enjoy a freshwater swim. This tranquil image, from the 1918 memory book of Marian Sheridan, pairs well with Rev. Samuel Lander's sermon notes on the desirableness of peace and the human ability to produce it: "As a river. (1) Copious (2) Increasing (3) Overcoming Obstacles (4) Tending to the ocean of Heavenly Peace."

Five

THE AESTHETIC STREAM OF LEARNING

Music and the arts were important from the first day at Williamston. Of the tiny faculty of eight in 1872, three are listed as instructors in music and art. Students could take courses in vocal music, piano, guitar, and reed organ. By way of art, the 1872 catalog describes an "Ornamental Department" that provided instruction in how to make wax flowers, wax fruit, jewelry, "and other fancy work." Though rudimentary at the time, including these skills from the very beginning instilled in the college a culture dedicated to aesthetic beauty. Over the years, this culture matured and expanded. By the time of its last year in Williamston, Lander students were participating in art exhibits in Charleston.

In 1884, the Mendelssohn Club was formed. For the first meeting after the club elected officers, the *Naiad* newsletter notes, "It was decided to discuss the history of music before the Christian era. Miss Bonnette was appointed to prepare an essay on Hindu and Egyptian music; Miss Leard, one on Chinese and Japanese; and Miss Lander, one on Grecian, upon which our present system is grounded."

In 1904—the first year in Greenwood—the college had a fine arts department. The academic catalog for that year lists a student organization called the Bonheur Club, "so called from the pupils' admiration of the famous artist Rosa Bonheur." The club met "once a month to study artists and their pictures, history of art, and the different schools—Italian, Dutch, French, etc."

The 1910 academic catalog highlights the art department: "Our Art Department is one of the best features of the College. . . . We have two well-lighted studios, equipped with all necessary appliances, including a gilding wheel and a 'New Revelation Kiln' in which all china is fired. The branches taught in this department are Drawing (charcoal, ink, pencil, pastel, and crayon), Painting in oil and water colors, China Painting, Tapestry, Stenciling, Tooled Leather, Blockwork, Pyrography, Pierced Brass and History of Art. The text-books used are Van Dyke's History of Painting and Goodyear's History of Art."

Beautiful pageants and plays were also a prominent feature of celebrating aesthetic expression.

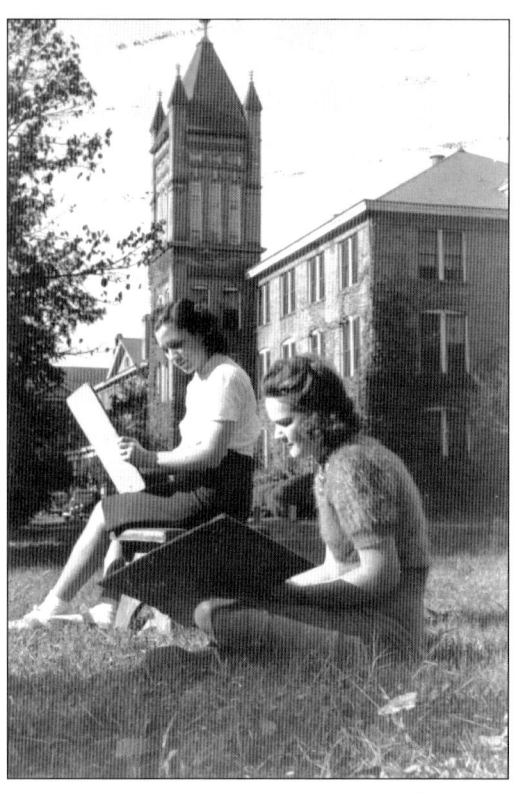

Laura Lander Hall provides the perfect inspirational backdrop as these students work on their artist's sketches in 1941. Pictured are Mable Edwards (left) and Harriet Minus. Both students were officers in the Art Club. Minus won a blue ribbon that year at the Greenwood County Fair for her "Landscape from Nature" piece, and Edwards won a blue ribbon for her "Flower Study."

A new building was added to the Williamston campus shortly after 1872. In 1876, a single large bell was placed on the peak of its roof. It was forged by one of America's most famous bell casting foundries, Meneely and Kimberly of Troy, New York, the same foundry that made the bell that currently hangs in the bell tower of Independence Hall, Philadelphia. When the school moved to Greenwood, the bell was relocated to the current bell tower. Pictured here is a demonstration carillon that was installed overlooking the Dingle on campus in 1951 by the Van Bergen Bell Foundry. This carillon remained on campus until 1957. In 1978, Lander purchased a new carillon with 35 bells, created by the same foundry. The original bell, now housed in the Lander Archives, was replaced with the new carillon which remains in use today.

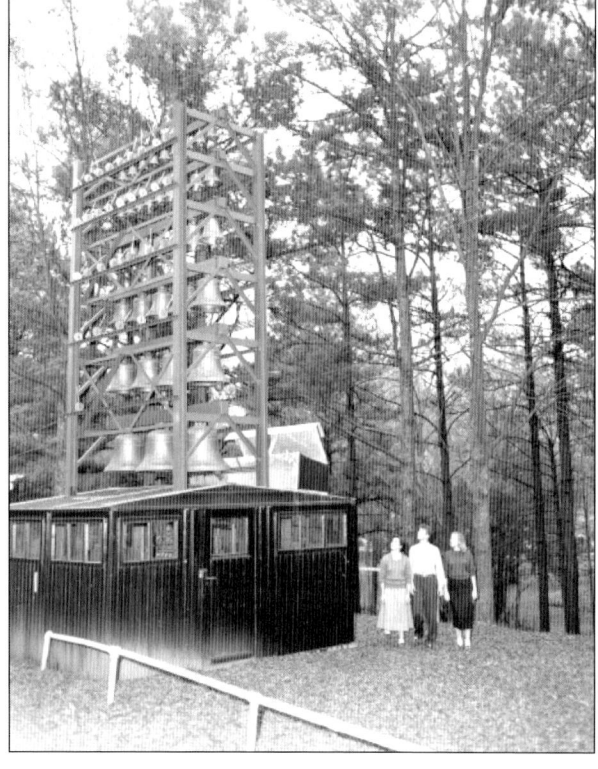

This recital program was found in the memory book of music faculty member Annie Elizabeth Aunspaugh. Janet Bailey, the accompanist for this recital, composed the Lander Alma Mater. Bailey also served as president of the B-Sharp Club, to which all students of music belonged. The club studied all things musical, the biographies of the great masters, their compositions, and current events in the musical world. Music was rendered by the students and the faculty. Their meetings were held monthly.

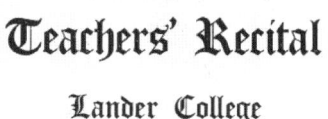

Teachers' Recital
Lander College

March 16, 1916

Mr. O. M. Tully	Organ
Miss Mary W. Newton	Piano
Miss Annie E. Aunspaugh	Violin
Miss Ethel M. Crockett	Soprano
Miss Janet M. Bailey	Accompanist

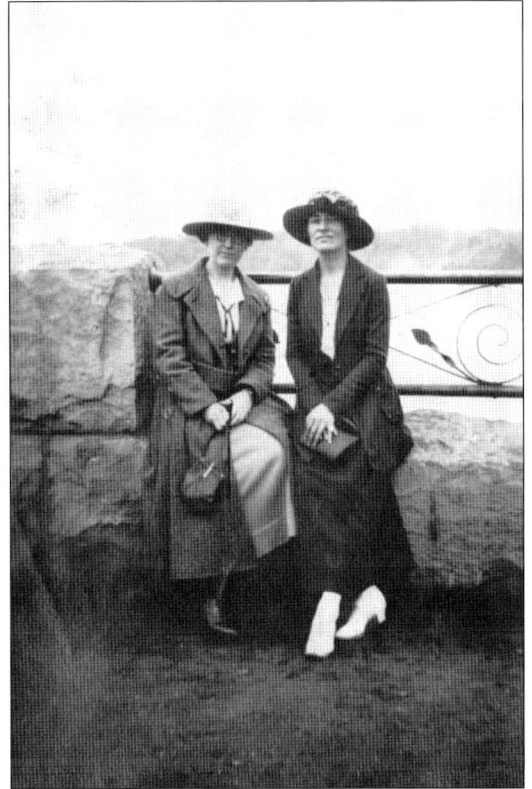

In addition to a "high-class Lyceum Course," where the college arranged for speakers and musicians to be brought to the area for both the students and the Greenwood community, a Thursday lecture series (mostly given by Lander faculty) was also organized for the entire school year. Annie Elizabeth Aunspaugh, a violin teacher (pictured on the right), gave a talk in 1912 called "The Violin and its Possibilities."

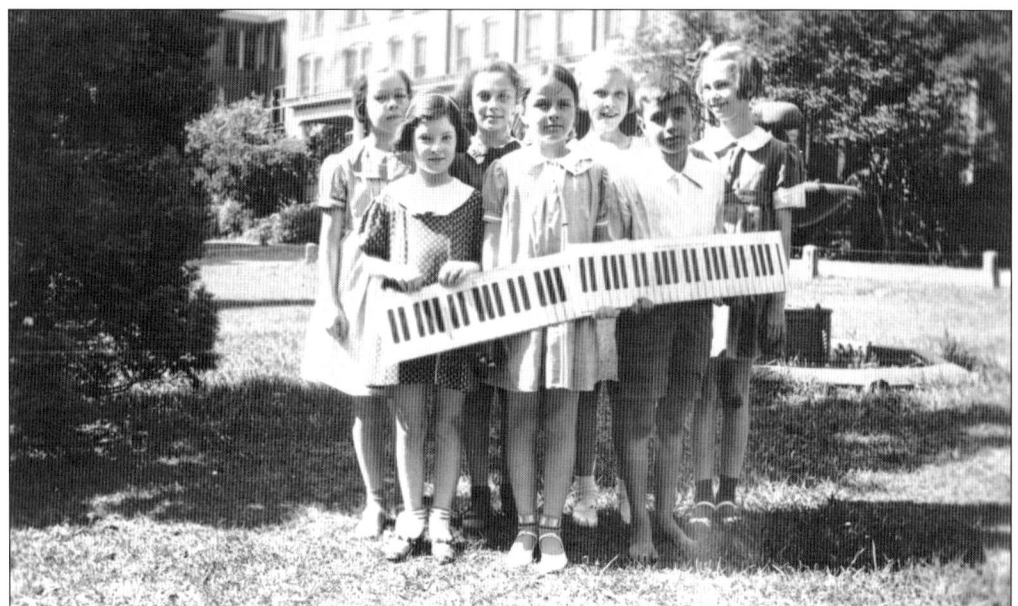

This is a group portrait of Kinscella program children in 1930. Estill Blocker of the Lander music faculty studied at the University of North Carolina and Furman University to learn the Kinscella method of teaching piano to children. Lander College sponsored the establishment of a Kinscella piano program for local children led by Blocker. Students in the program, which lasted into the 1950s, presented public recitals on campus, participated in state and national competitions, attended conventions, and even traveled to be broadcast on radio stations in Greenville (WSPA), Columbia (WIS), and Anderson (WAIM). Music majors in the college could take courses in the Kinscella method as part of their professional preparation.

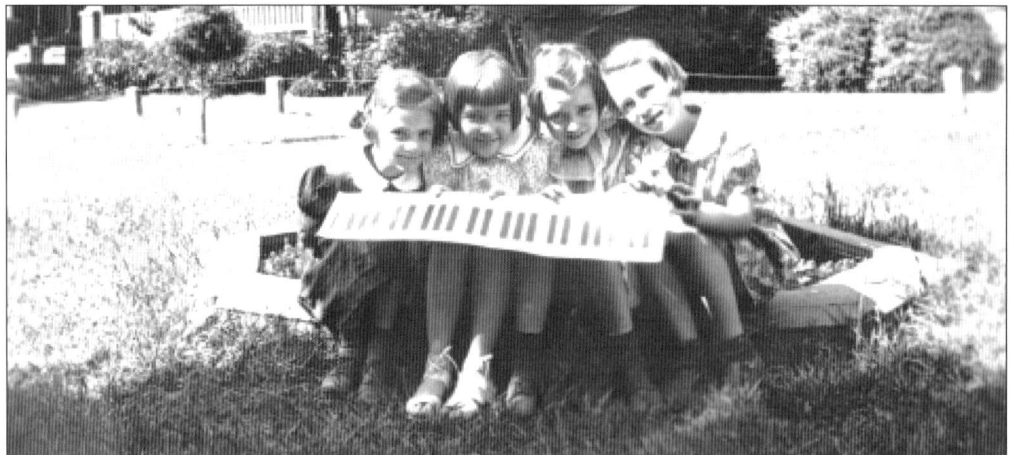

Group portrait of Kinscella program children in 1932. Dozens of local newspaper articles and recital notices about the program reveal how the local community treasured its benefits. This quote from an article in the *Index-Journal* on May 3, 1929, is typical: "At eight o'clock Thursday evening in the Lander College auditorium a recital was given by the first year Kinscella Piano class under the direction of Miss Estill Blocker. . . . The children showed a keen accurate sense of rhythm and accent both in their marking of time and their playing; their knowledge of the scales put the adult audience to shame, their bodily response to musical selections demonstrated a true appreciation of the composers mood."

Lander also sponsored a music club for child vocalists from the community under the direction of Estill Blocker. The girls in the back row formed a quartette that won first place at a competition in Columbia in 1934. Though uncertain, they may be Jean Campbell, Dorothy Holloway, Mary Jean McCleskey, and Elise Nicholson. The two girls in the first row formed a duet that won second place at a competition the same year; however, their names are not in Lander's archive records.

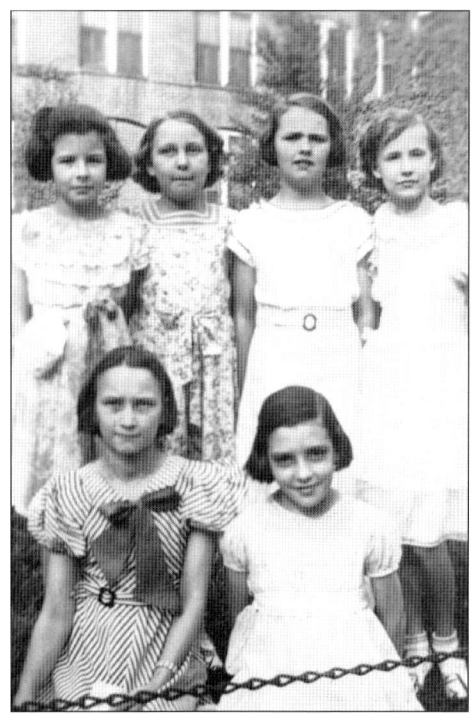

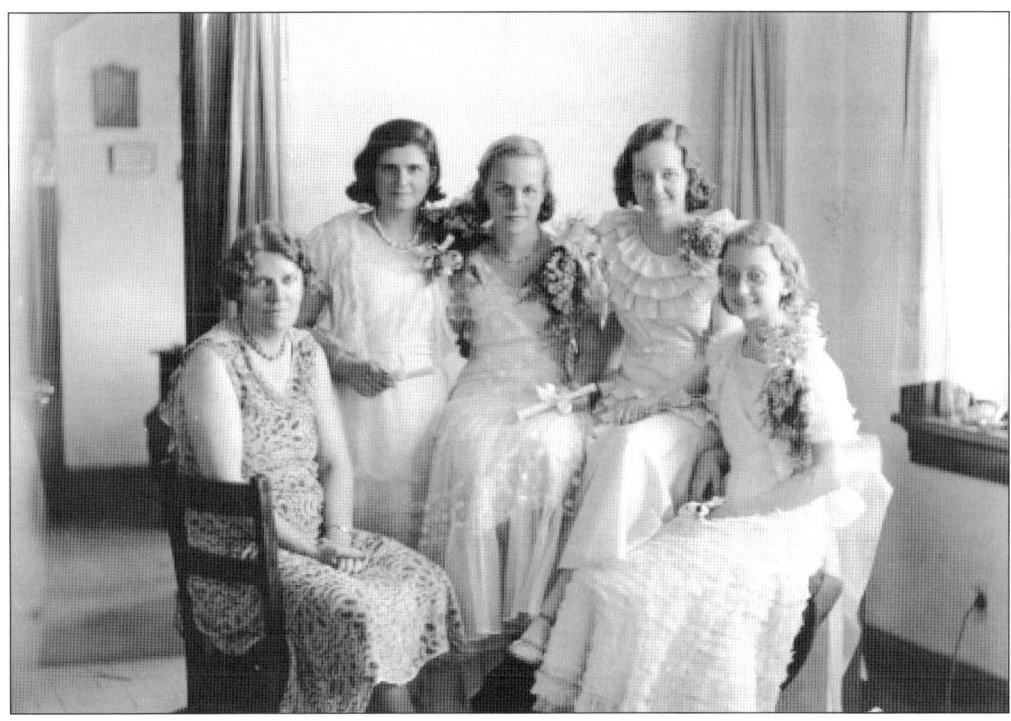

Estill Blocker (left) is pictured with Kinscella program graduates in pretty graduation dresses and holding certificate scrolls in 1929. Lander students were able to earn certificates in the Kinscella technique as part of training for professional music instruction, and they would share a graduation ceremony with the young students in the program.

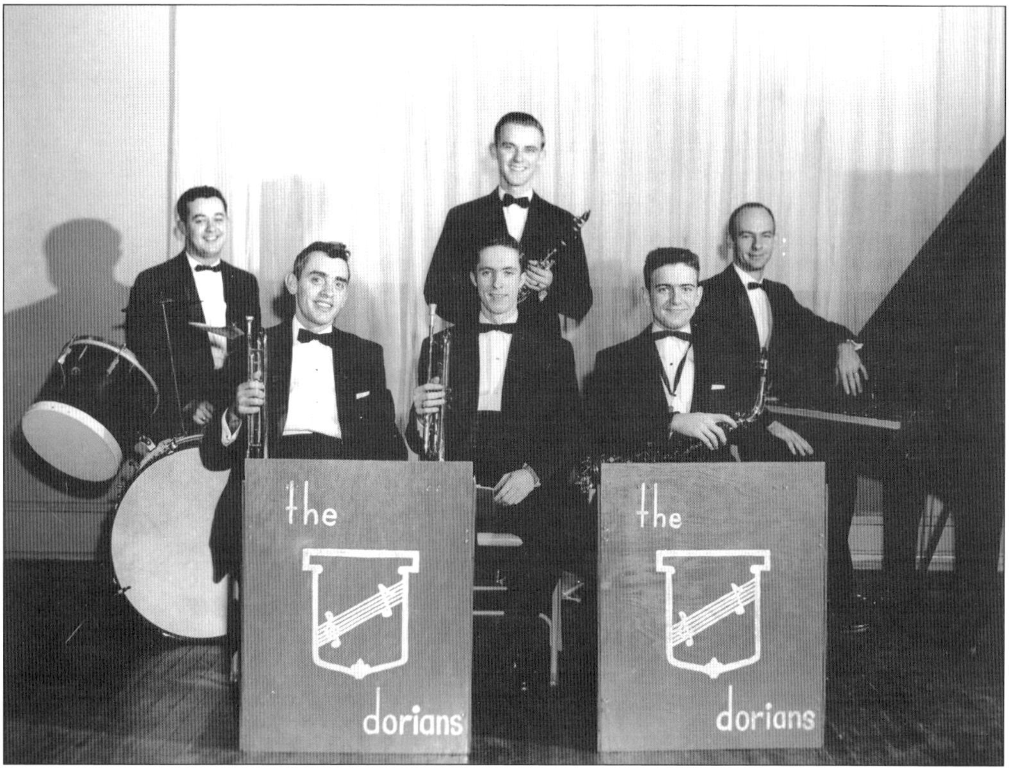

The Lander College Dorians, a six-man combo who made public appearances throughout the state winning first place in multiple talent competitions. The group appeared twice on WFBC Greenville television's *Talent Parade* and won a trip to New York City to audition for Ted Mack's *The Original Amateur Hour*. Members of the band in 1957, from left to right, are (first row) Preston Lollis, Ray Berry, and Malcolm Stribling; (second row) Henry Hodges, Louis Polatty, leader, and Bill Wilson.

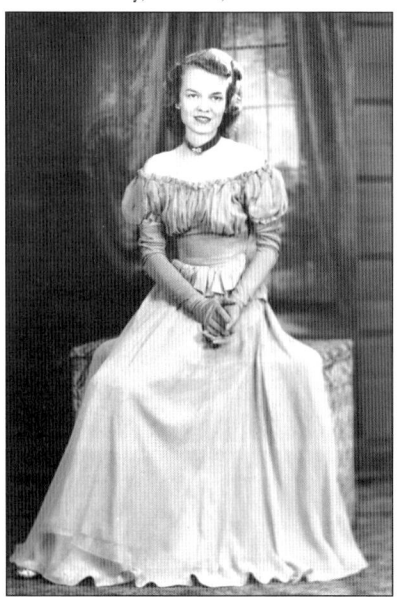

This photograph of student Mildred Bailey Mullikan of Greenville, South Carolina, was taken in the late 1940s at her voice recital. Mullikan graduated with a degree in English and had a variety of interests. She was a member of the Poetry Club, Biology, Glee Club, Lander Lyrikers, Lander College Christian Association, Thespia, business manager to the *Erothesian,* Methodist Council, and French Club.

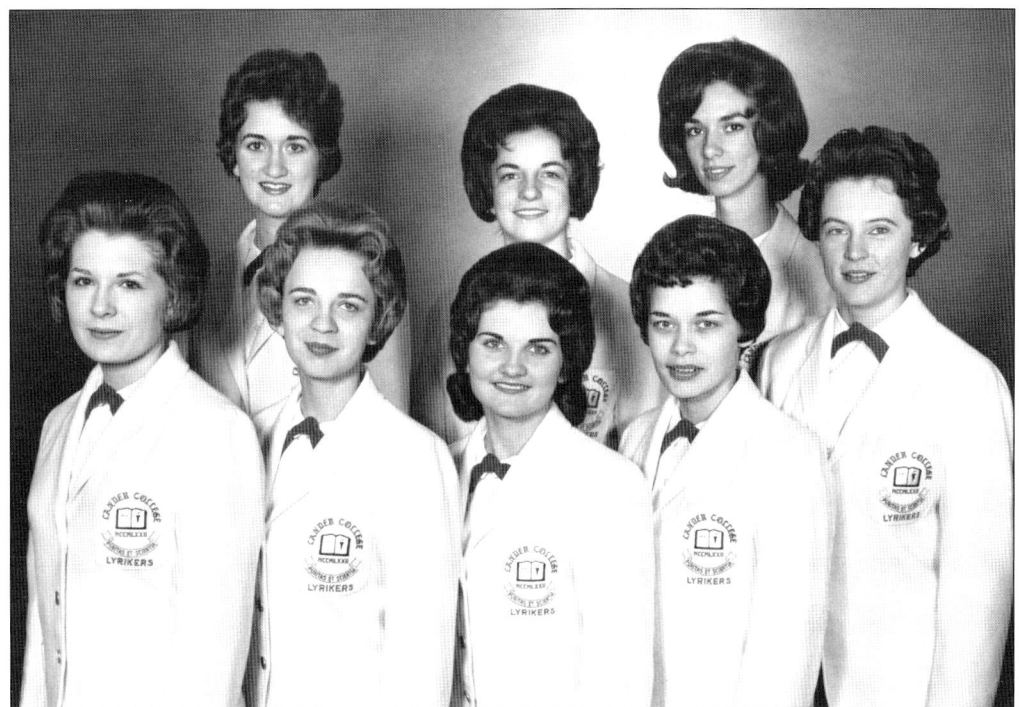

This is the Lander Lyrikers' spring 1963 tour photograph. The Lyrikers visited numerous South Carolina venues on their tour and made a stop for a TV appearance on WSPA-TV (Channel 7) for a special Christmas music program. The group was directed by music faculty member Roberta Major. From left to right are (first row) Susan Lander, Jo Shirley, Norma Ford, Kitty Young, and Linda Dobson; (second row) Henrietta Bowers, Linda DeLoach, and Penelope Galloway.

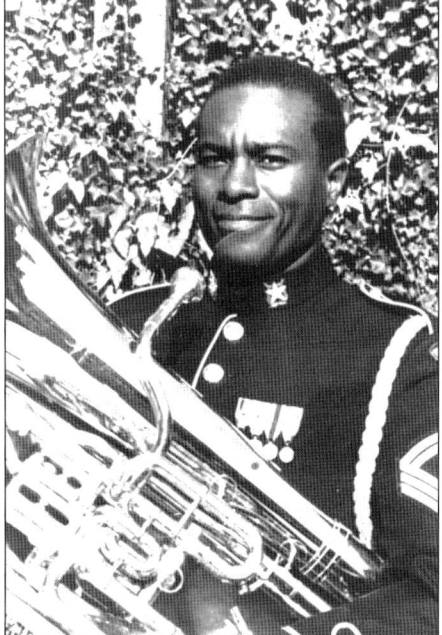

This is a portrait of Richard L. Wilkins, a 1982 music education graduate. Wilkins was a member of Pershing's Own, the US Army's premier band. He performed during presidential inaugural parades and balls, an economic summit, and at arrival and departure ceremonies for visiting international dignitaries. He returned as an alumnus to perform at the 1993 inauguration of Dr. William C. Moran, 10th president of Lander. He also established an instrumental music scholarship at the university.

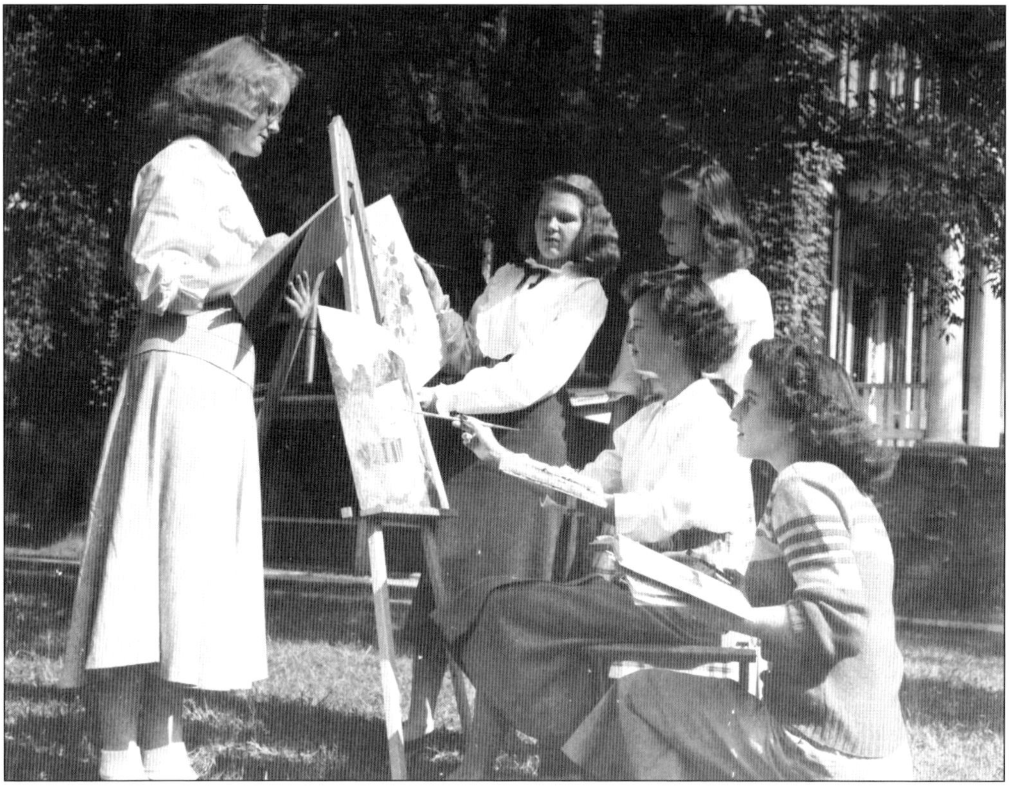

In this 1940s photograph, students paint outdoors in natural sunlight. The image pairs well with Rev. Samuel Lander's notes from his sermon No. 33, in which he discusses the importance of light: "1. Light is mysterious a. In its origin b. In its mode of propagation. 2. Yet we may know some of its laws, properties, and effects. a. It radiates constantly, abundantly, and in all directions. b. So that the reception of its influences depends upon the attitude of the object (1. Angular relation 2. Relative proximity). c. It is necessary for the manifestation of beauty (1. Objectively 2. Subjectively). d. Also for the development of beauty and vigorous life. e. For the attainment of accuracy. f. For the enjoyment of safety. g. In a word, for perfect happiness."

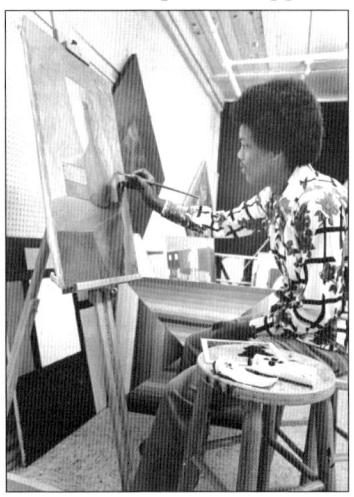

Art major Ronald Sullivan works on an abstract oil painting. Sullivan's sketch of the Rock Church Graveyard, believed to be the oldest church in Greenwood County, was published in the book *Greenwood County—the Artist's View*. The sketch was made during his time as a Lander student in the mid-1970s.

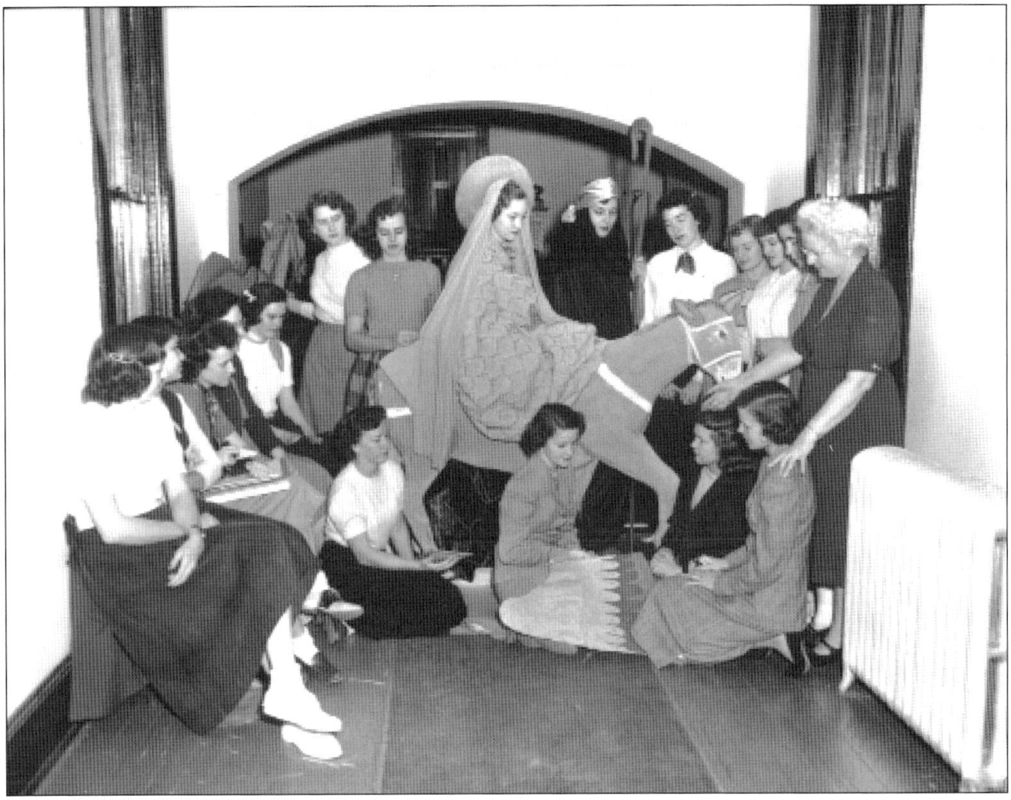

In 1951, the Art Club presented this Christmas scene. Pictured from left to right are (seated on floor) Reba Riddle, Martha Jean O'Shields, Gwen Laramore, and Ruth Burnett; (clockwise from the person seated first on the bench) Betty Coleman, Nandy Miller, Carolyn Hendrix, Eloise Coleman, Orpah DuBose, Farris Bush, Doris Dorn, Joye Angel, Lynn Sweatte, Marian Hagan, Helen Howell, Joyce Land, Betty Jean Dean, and Marie Chisholm (advisor).

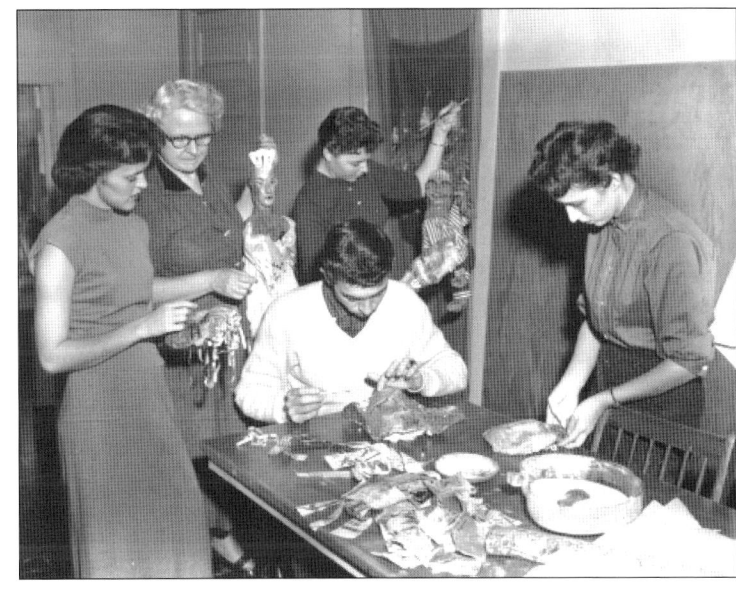

Faculty member and advisor to the Art Club, Marie Chisholm instructs students as they create papier-mâché puppets. This may have been the arts and crafts class described in the college catalog: "A course primarily planned to meet the requirements of elementary teachers. Toy making, poster making, murals, lettering, braiding, and knotting, etc. at different grade levels."

99

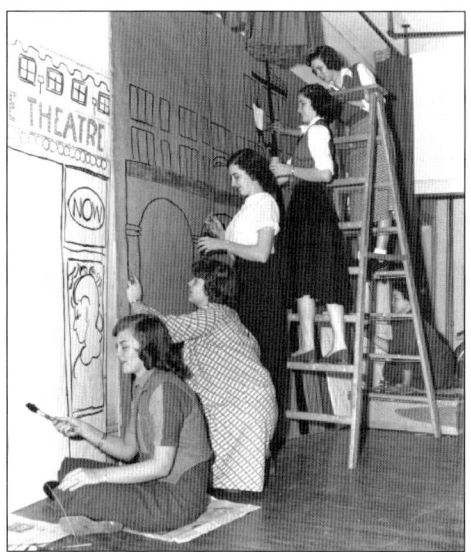

Members of the Lander Art Club prepare scenery for a variety show in 1953. Pictured from left to right are Mary Bowen, Sara Carolyn Bald, Josephine Leaman, Agnes Cooner, Claire Lyon, and Helen Hollingsworth (behind ladder).

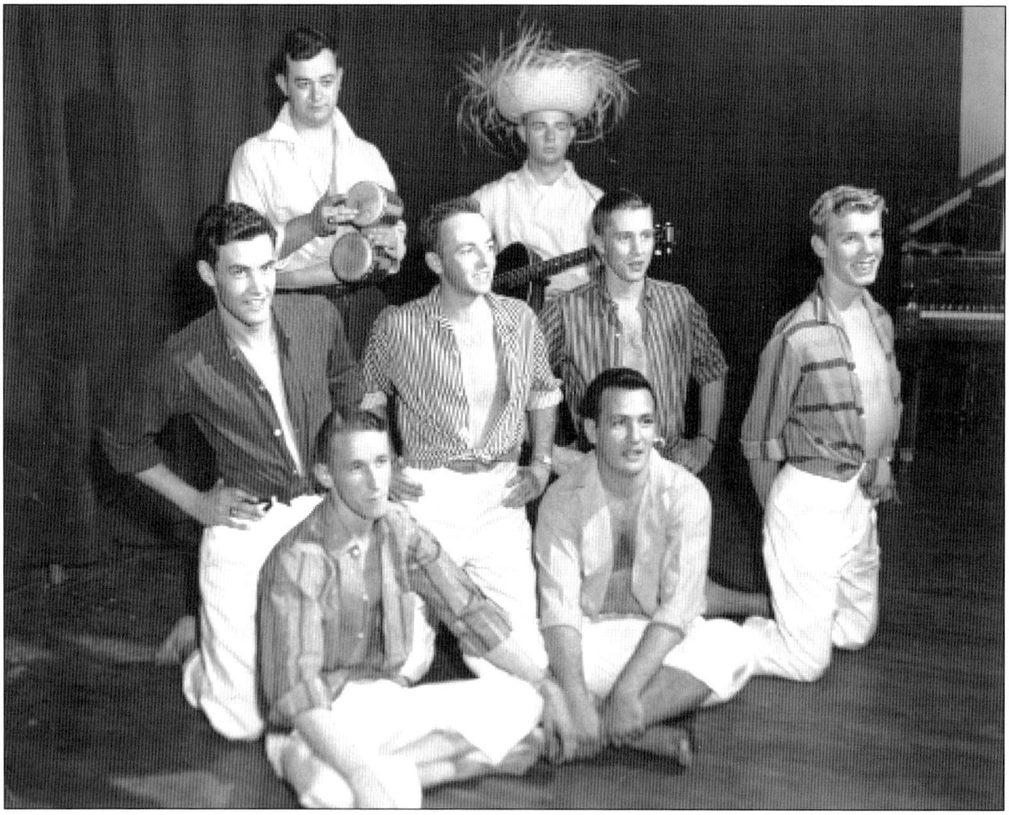

This group, called the Calypso Bullfrogs, performed in the Lander Men's Club presentation of "Bullfrog Follies" on March 30, 1957. In the early years of male attendance at Lander, the men were referred to as "Bullfrogs," a water creature, perhaps as a tribute to the water naiad and the female students' nickname: "Lilies." Pictured from left to right are (seated) Wes Brown, Claude Simmons; kneeling: Bill Scurry, Tim Etheridge, George Beaver, and Doug Jones; (standing) Henry Hodges and Johnny Bailey.

This image is from Lander's 1989 production of Lorraine Hansberry's play *A Raisin in the Sun,* directed by Prof. Frank Jackson. From left to right are Willie McBride as Walter Lee and Troxy Minyard as Ruth Younger.

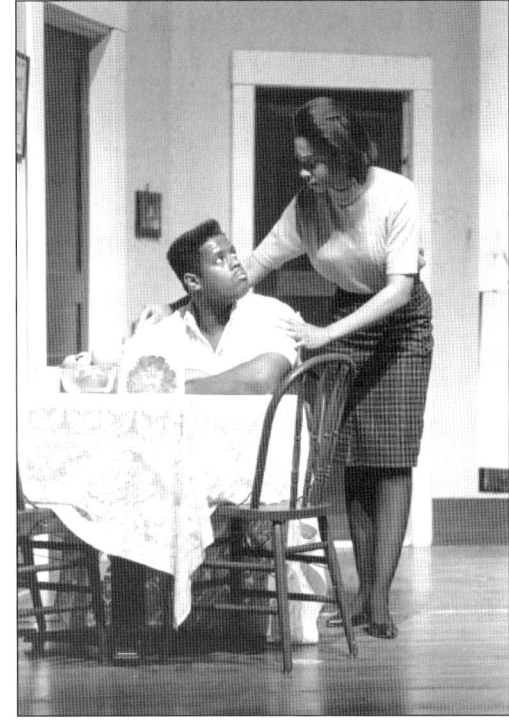

This is the 1957 cast of *The Day After Tomorrow*, a play about a woman who shows up on her estranged daughter's wedding day after she had spent time in prison. Pictured from left to right are Elizabeth Goldwire, Delores Smith, Gail Rice, Phillip Robuck, and Mary Alice White.

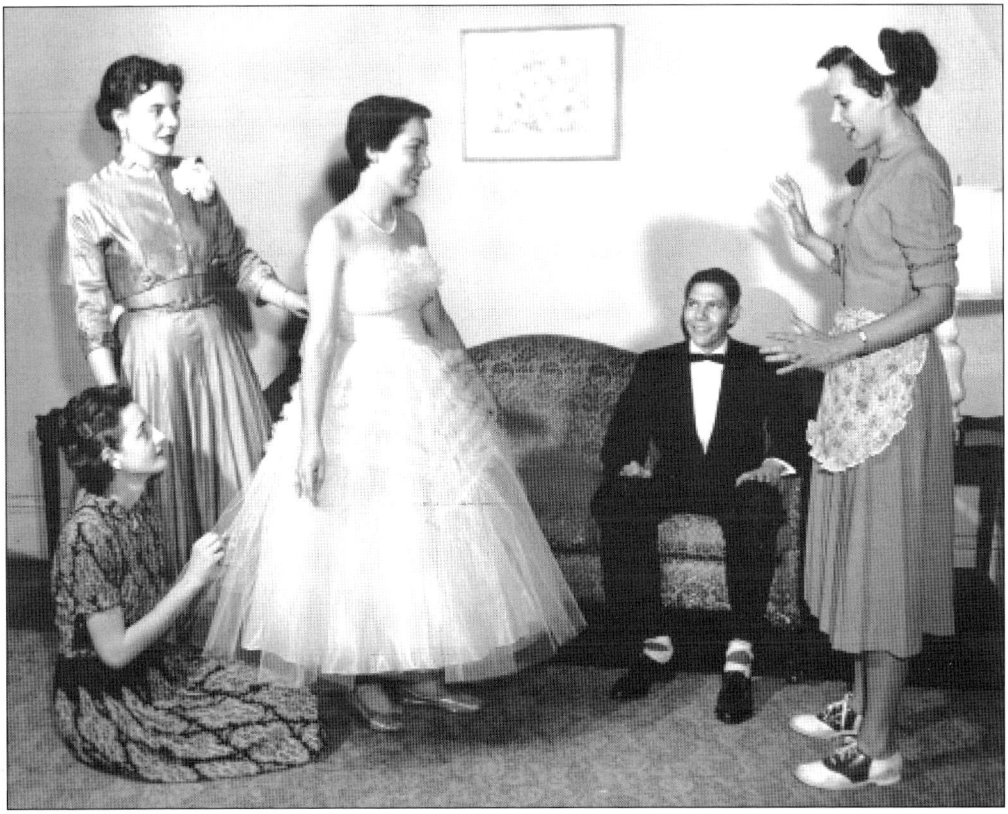

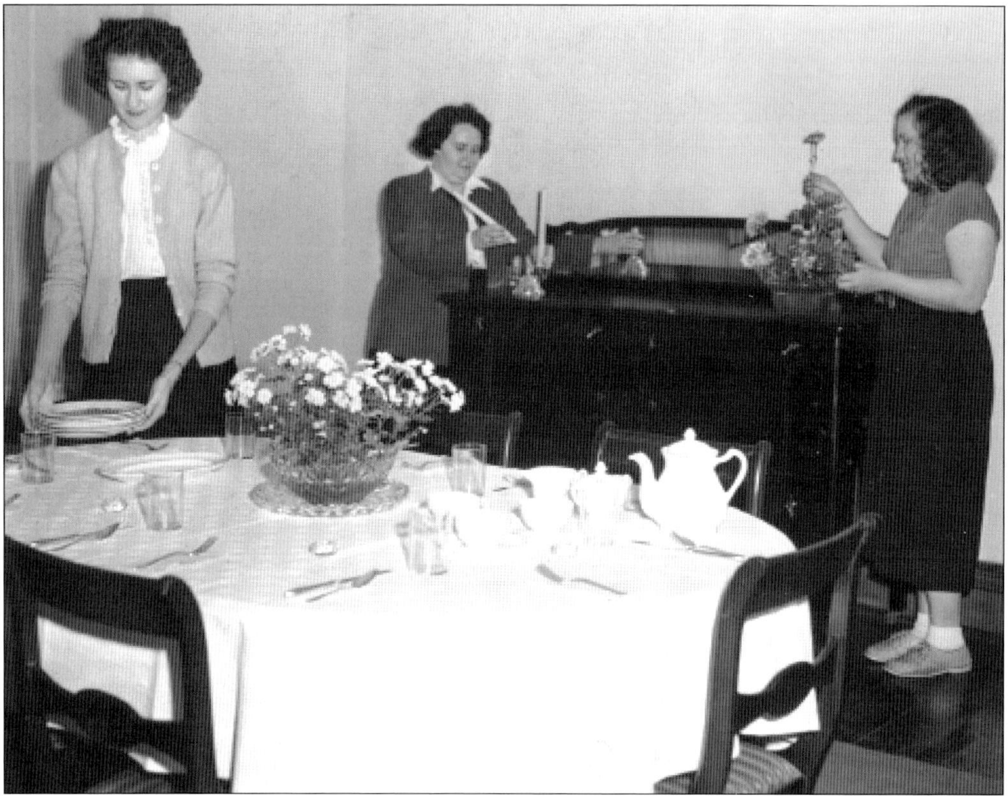

Part of the aesthetic stream of learning included the art of arranging, embellishing, and setting up formal dinner parties and other events. Home economics students in this image are setting the table and working on floral arrangements in the practice house dining room. From left to right are Mary Miller, Jeanette Saunders, and Lucy Rowland in 1950.

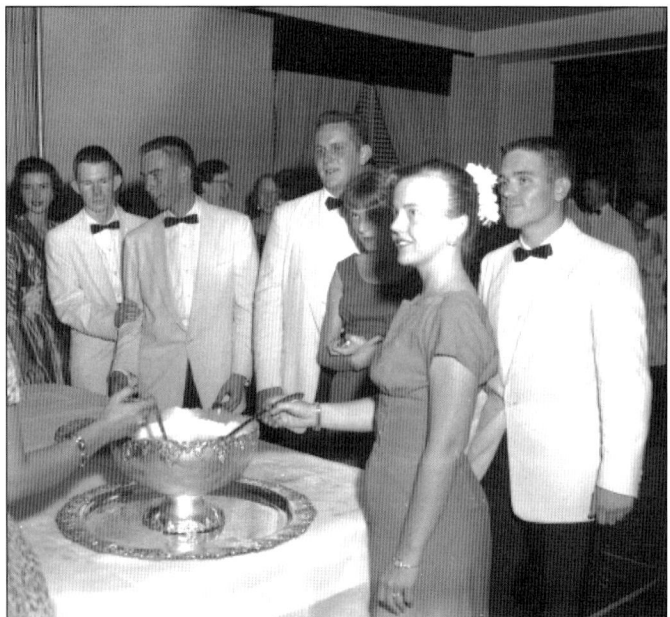

The class of 1958 left as its gift to the college a strikingly beautiful silver punch bowl and a silver serving ladle, which enhanced many college functions. Formal dances, dinners, banquets, teas, and receptions allowed students to cultivate and develop poise as future hosts and hostesses.

A bygone tradition at Lander is the freshman-junior wedding. The freshman class would elect the "bride," and the "groom" was chosen by the junior class. A "wedding" with authentic detail was held to express the bond of friendship and acceptance of the freshmen. This tradition was also a part of school life at other women's colleges, such as Columbia College in Columbia, South Carolina, and Simmons College in Boston, Massachusetts.

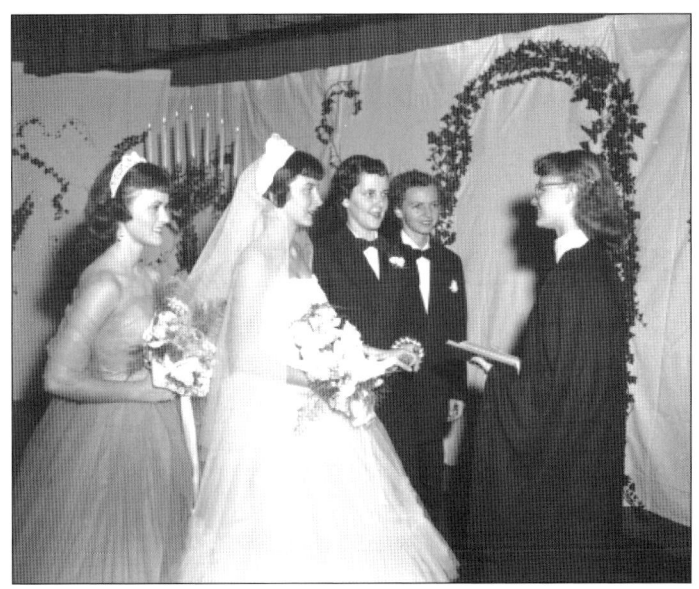

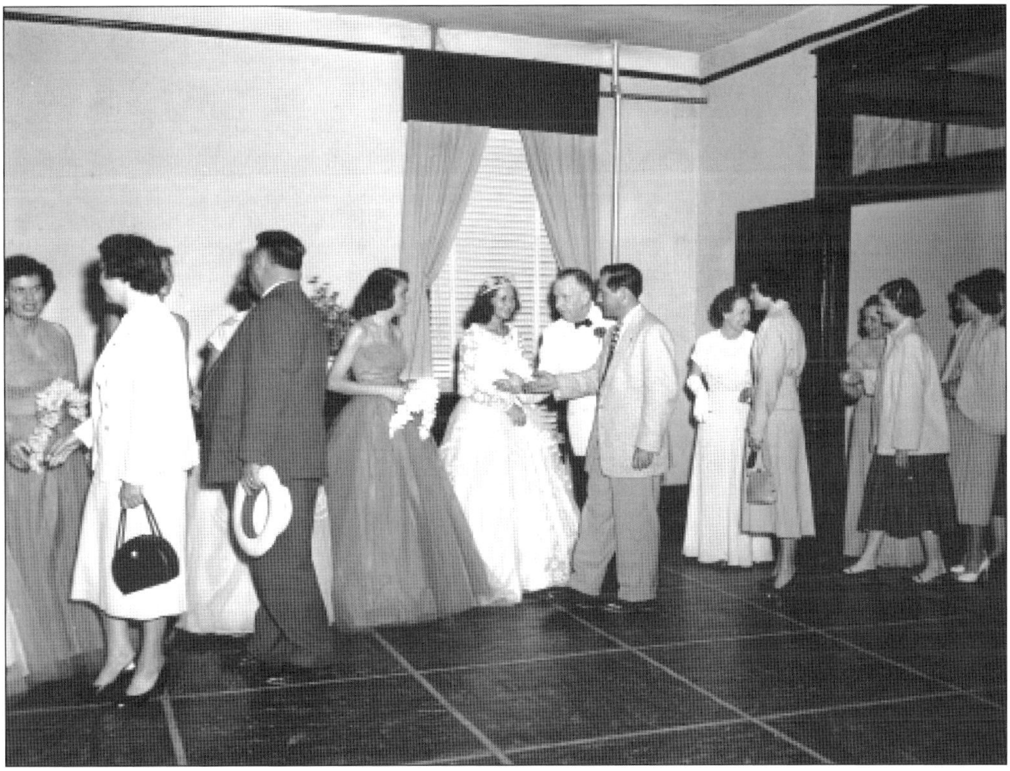

Receiving lines were typically held after the Annual Beauty Review, the May Day pageant, and the freshman-junior wedding. This helped students to learn how to set up, organize, and take part in more formal social events. The president of Lander and his wife were part of the receiving line. Dr. Boyce Grier is pictured in a bowtie paired with a white suit coat (center).

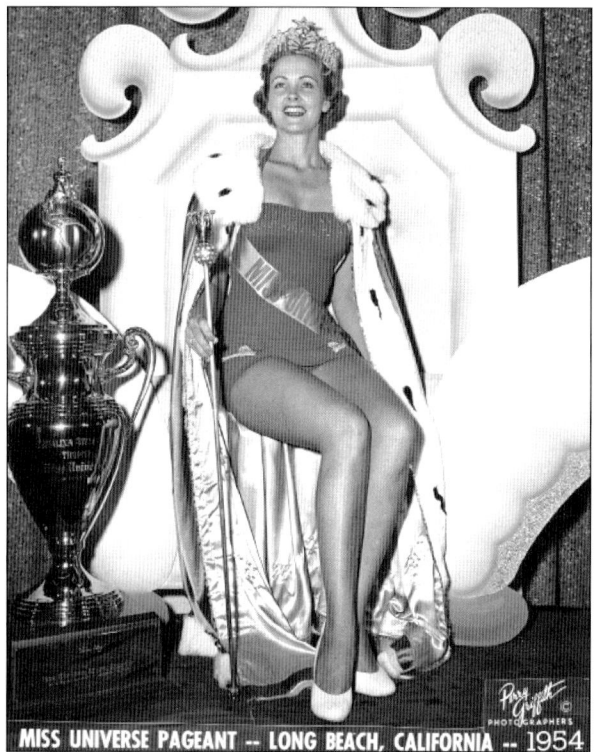

MISS UNIVERSE PAGEANT -- LONG BEACH, CALIFORNIA -- 1954

Lander student Miriam Stevenson of Winnsboro, South Carolina, poses with her trophies after winning the titles of Miss USA and Miss Universe in 1954. She was the first woman in the history of the contest to win both titles.

A large celebration and parade were held in Miriam Stevenson's honor upon her return from winning the Miss Universe pageant in 1954. According to the *Index-Journal*, "The widest street in the world was adorned with flags and bunting more lavish than the Fourth of July ever saw. Approximately 20,000 admirers welcomed her home."

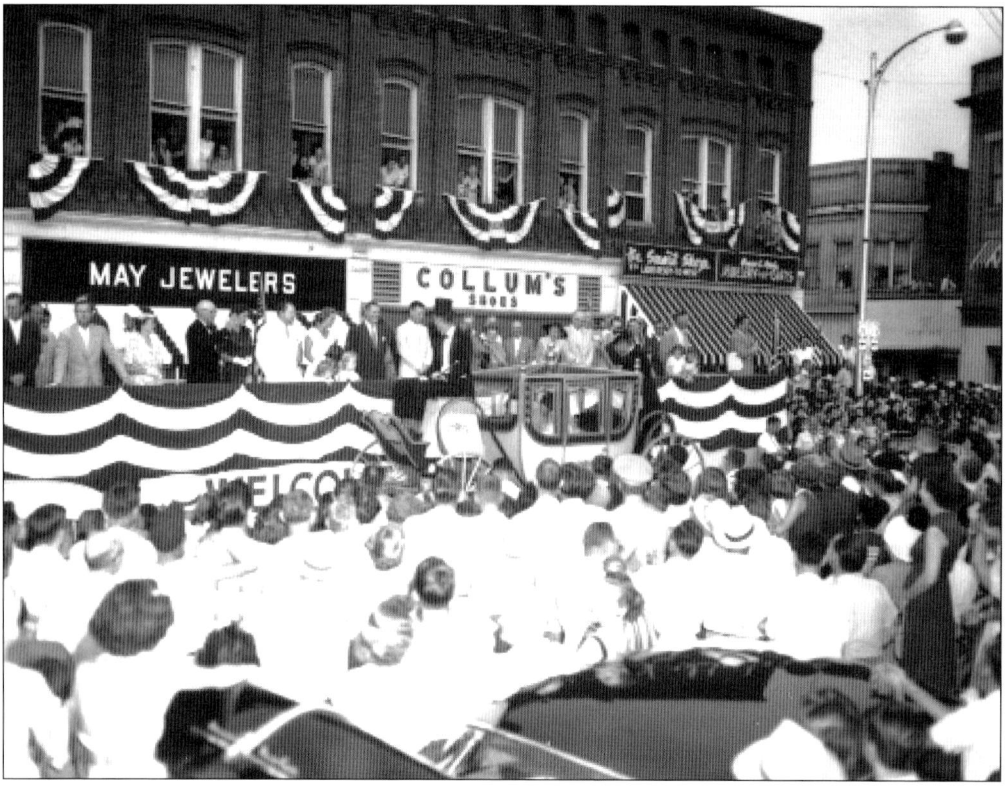

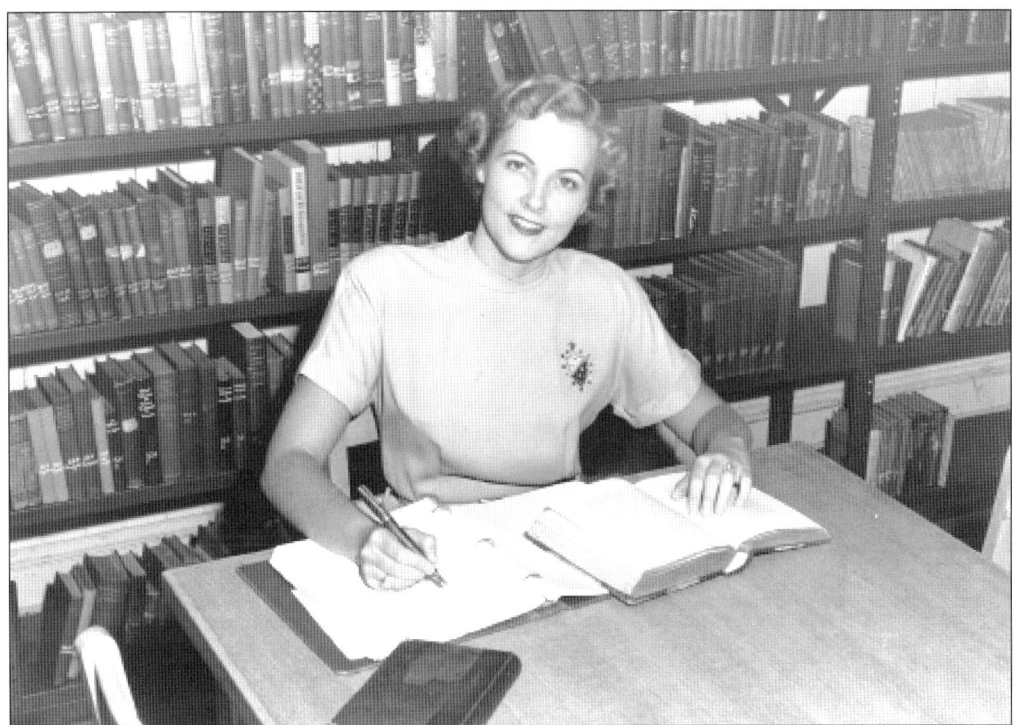

After returning from winning the Miss Universe pageant, Miriam Stevenson resumes her studies in the college library. Stevenson graduated in 1955 with a degree in home economics. She enjoyed interior and fashion design. Stevenson was involved in numerous activities while she was a Lander student, including serving as president of the freshman class, vice president of the Home Economics Club, vice president of the State Home Economics Club, student council representative, vice president of the Art Club, and vice president and president of the Westminster Club Fellowship. She was part of the Lander College Christian Association cabinet, on the Rednal staff, and was on the honor roll. Additionally, she was in the "Who's Who" in American colleges and universities and was chosen as "Senior Class Beauty," May queen, and as a bride in the freshman-junior wedding. Stevenson also served as Miss Lander, Miss South Carolina, Miss USA, and Miss Universe.

During her time as a student, Miriam Stevenson was selected as the bride in the freshman-junior wedding in 1951. The classes had many rivalries, especially when it came to athletics, so this tradition was a nice reminder of the importance of forming bonds of friendship between classes. Pictured in this photograph are, from left to right, (first row, kneeling) Opal Ruth and Miriam Stevenson; (second row, standing) Jean Redden and Mary Frances Bailey. The officiant is unidentified.

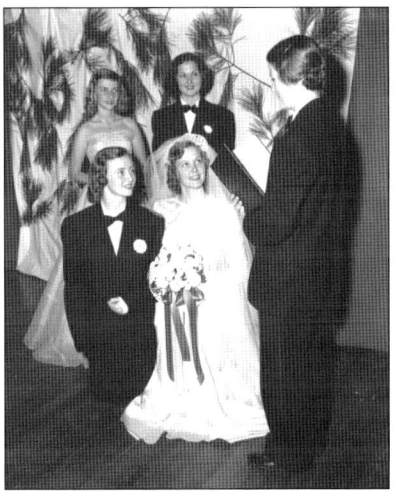

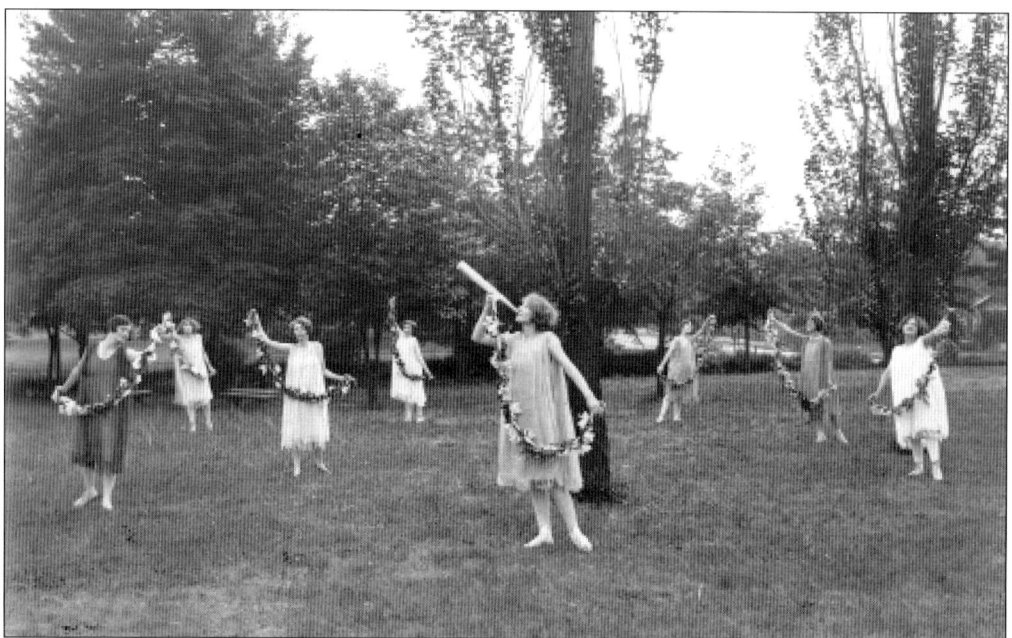
Lander students celebrate May Day, an ancient festival marking the first day of summer, appearing in Lander student memory books as early as 1914. The photograph from the May Day pageant of 1927 appears in the *Naiad* with the caption "The Herald of May." The herald, played by Rachel Edwards (center) with her silver trumpet, sounds the approach of the queen.

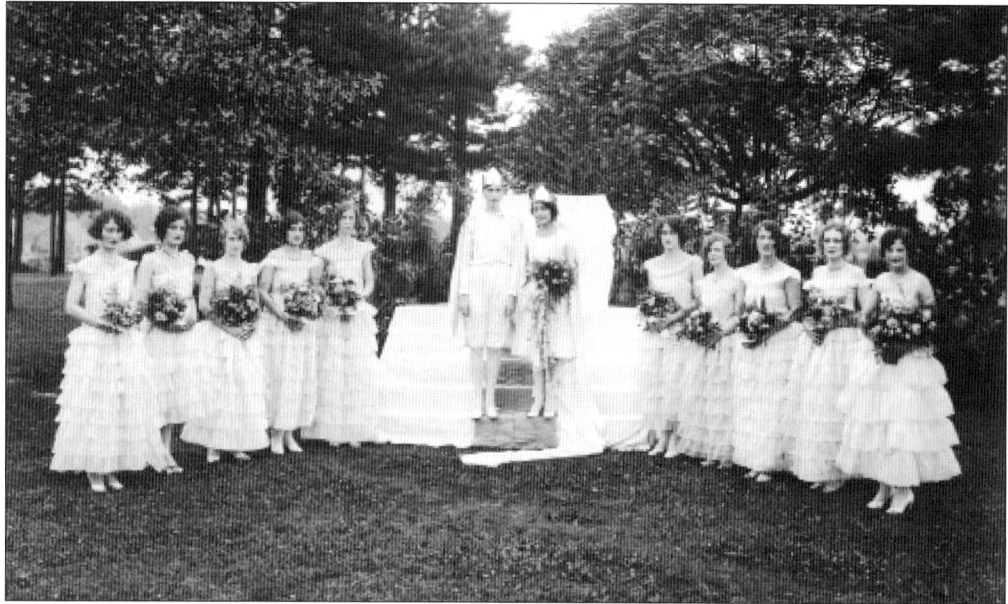
This photograph of the May Day court in 1930 shows a smaller subset of the May court, which would usually also include child attendants. Some years, the person in the May court who is also wearing a crown and standing directly next to the queen would be referred to as a page; other years, a prince and others a king. Female students would play the role of the page, prince, or king prior to Lander becoming co-educational.

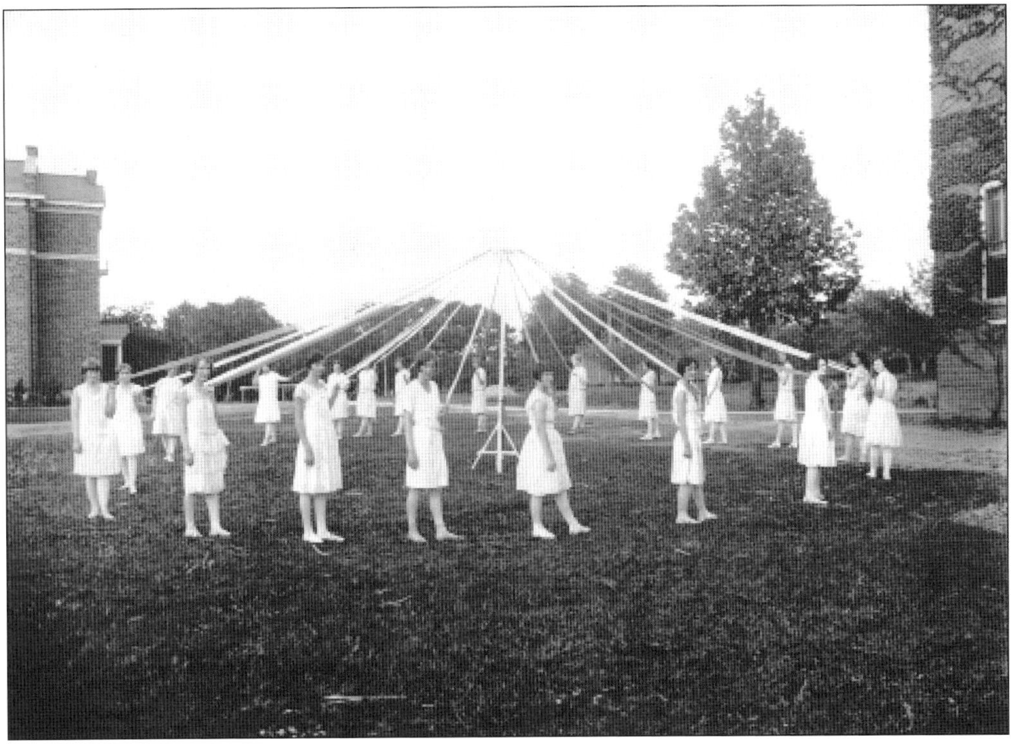

In this c. 1927 photograph, Lander students practice for the upcoming Maypole dance. The Maypole dance is a "ceremonial folk dance performed around a tall pole garlanded with greenery or flowers and often hung with ribbons that are woven into complex patterns by the dancers. Such dances are survivals of ancient dances around a living tree as part of spring rites to ensure fertility," according to the *Encyclopedia Britannica*. During the celebrations on May Day, a May king and queen would be crowned.

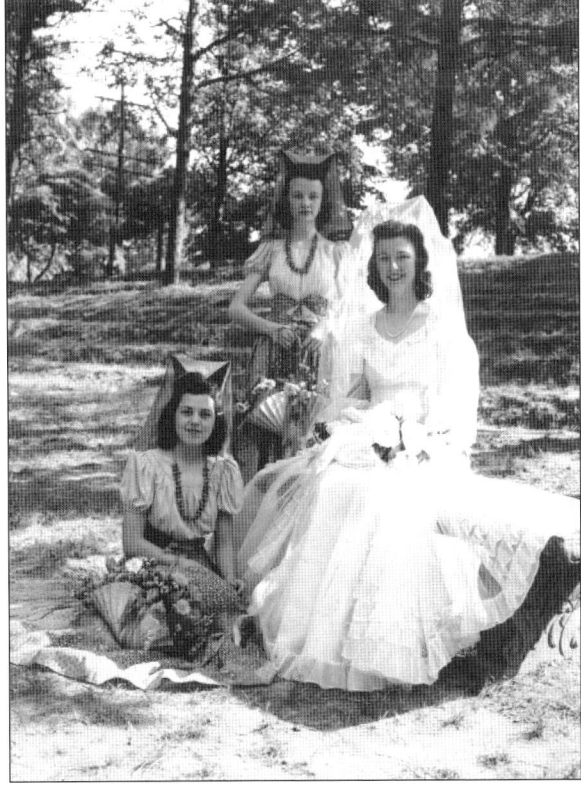

Sarah Watkins (right) was the May queen in 1942. She performed in the musical comedy *The Belle of Barcelona* with her maids of honor, Pauline Graham (center) and Ruby Thomas (left). This photograph is from the memory book of Alice Spencer, Lander faculty member. (Courtesy of Allie and Glenn Williams.)

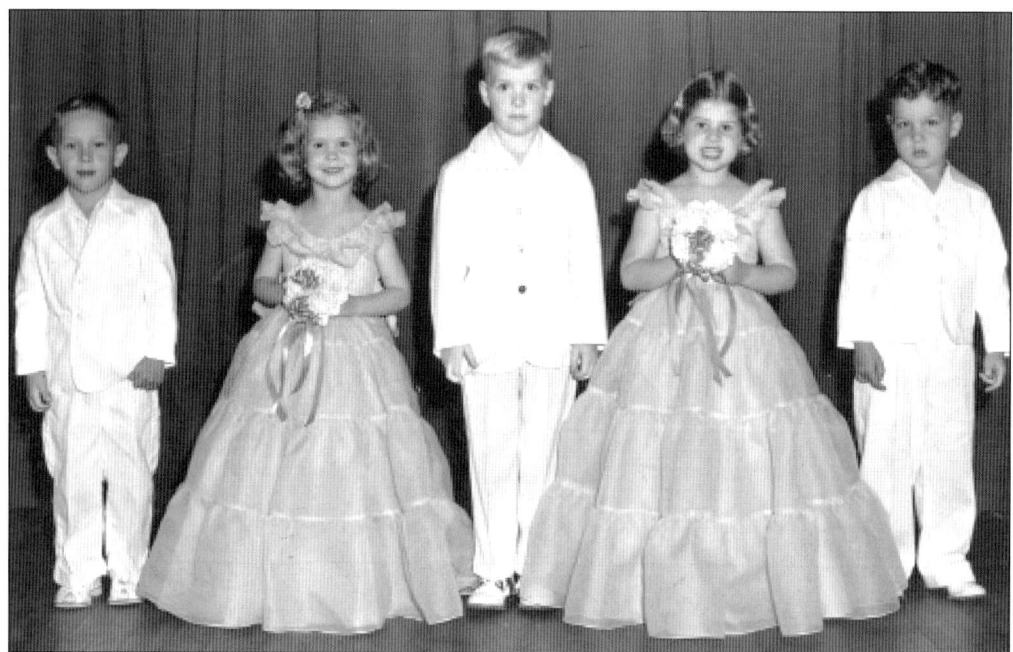

In 1954, a cast of 125 students was part of the May Day pageant directed by Leotus Morrison, head of physical education. Additionally, local Greenwood children were included as attendants (flower girls and train bearers) in the May court. From left to right are Steve Fisher, Pamela Scurry, E.B. Grier, Karen Park, and Marshall A. Leaman Jr.

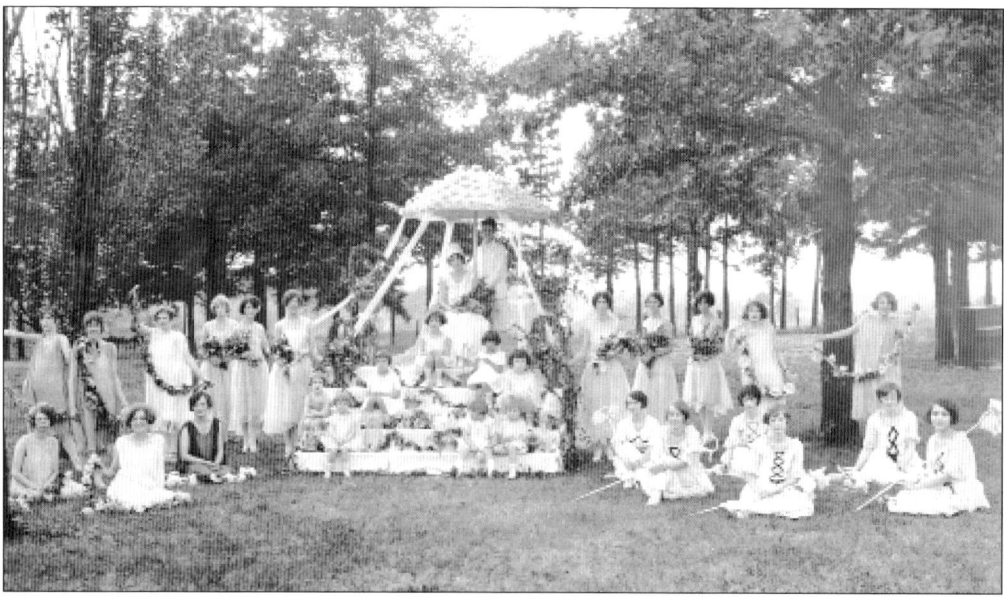

May Day queen Willard Webb and her page Margaret Cope pose with the court in 1927. The six attendants holding bouquets and standing on either side of the platform were listed (order of appearance unknown) in the 1927 yearbook as Evelyn Miller, Louise McMeekin, Nora Grant, Betty Gambrell, Clara Sapp, and Murrell Jones. The eight flower girls are listed as Nancy Gilmer Coleman, Mary Sue Gambrell, Ann Lomax, Dora Sterghos, Neva Jackson, and Eileen Runge.

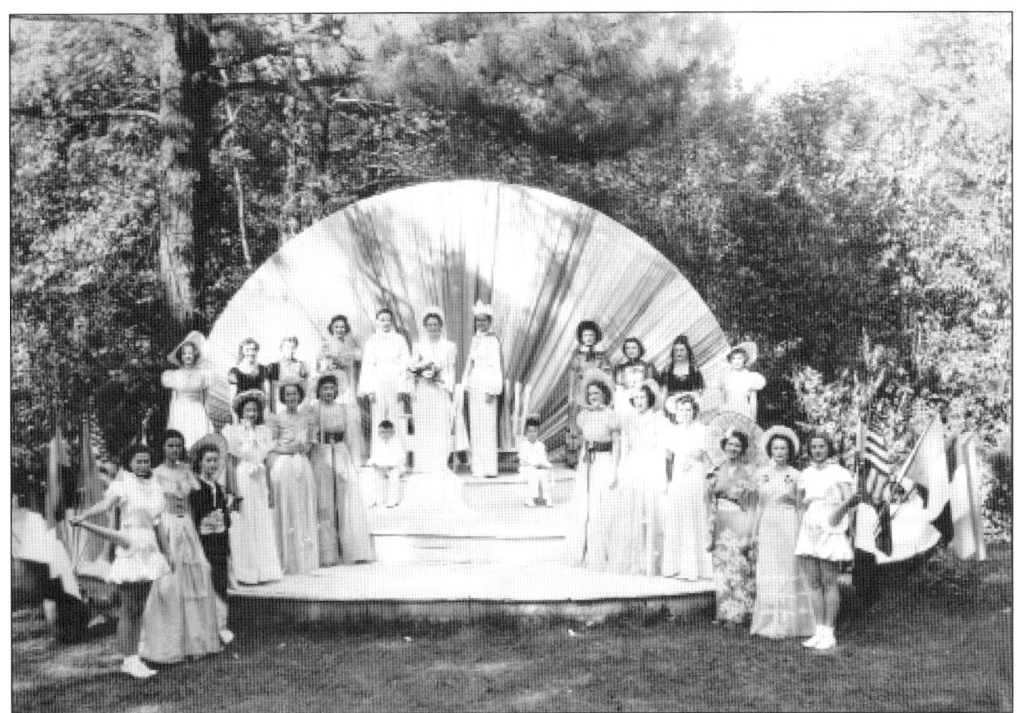

The theme of the 1938 May Day program was "The Melting Pot." May queen was Catherine Rogers, May king was Sara Blackman, maid of honor was Emily Page, the crown bearers Thomas Keller and Bruce Barksdale (who also served as a senior class mascot in 1935), and the flower girls Danny Reynolds, and Mary Dudley Steer. The junior attendant, who was also the senior class mascot, for that year was Viola Keeter Pierce. The program was arranged and directed by the head of the department of physical education, Alice Spencer, and this photograph was found in her memory book.

This is a portrait of sophomore class May Day court attendants in 1957. Representatives from each class were selected to be members of the May Day court. From left to right are (seated) Eleanor Green and Gwen Herring; (standing) Ann Long and Betty Ann McFadden.

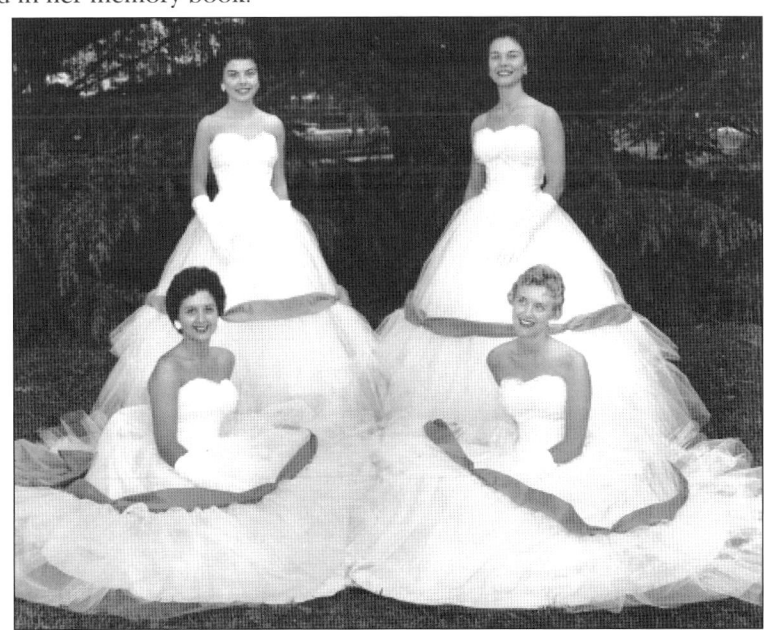

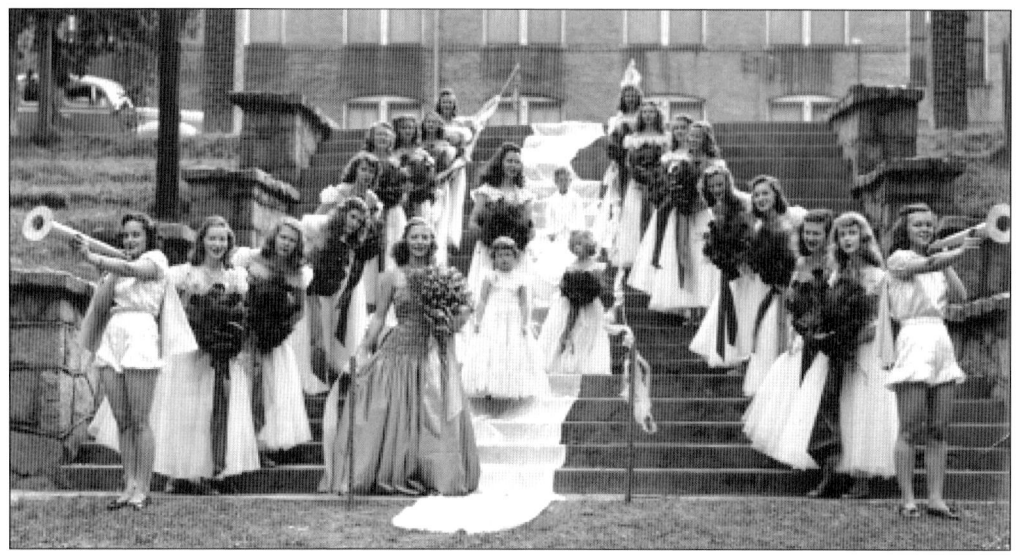
Betty Brown, the "queen of the May," makes her entrance with her maid of honor Ella Claire Lee and the royal court in 1948.

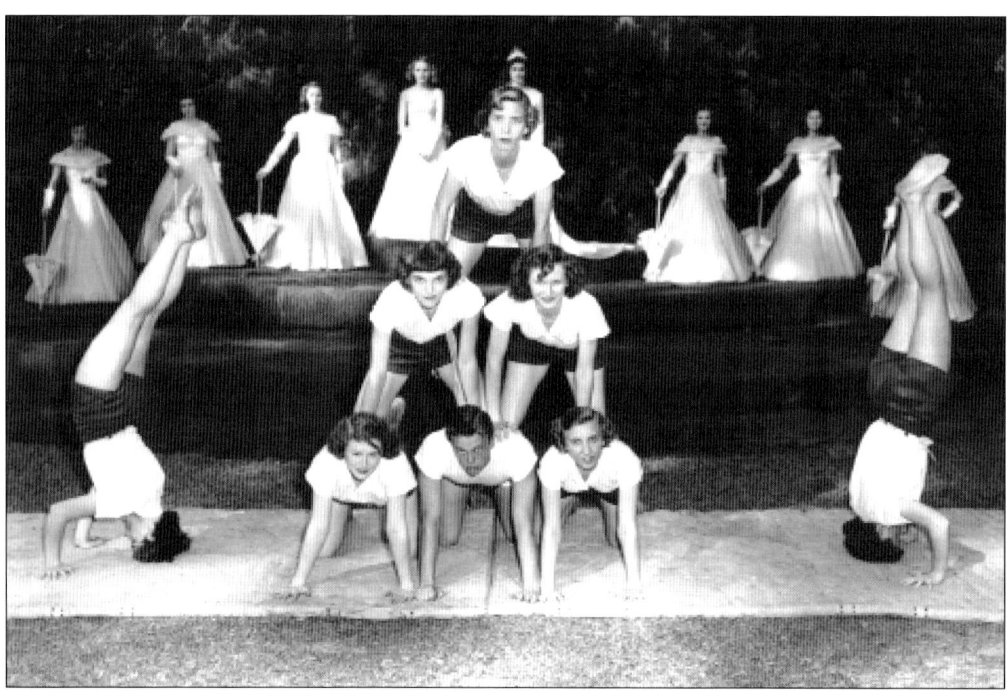
Students demonstrate the hard work they did all year in tumbling class at the May Day pageant in 1951.

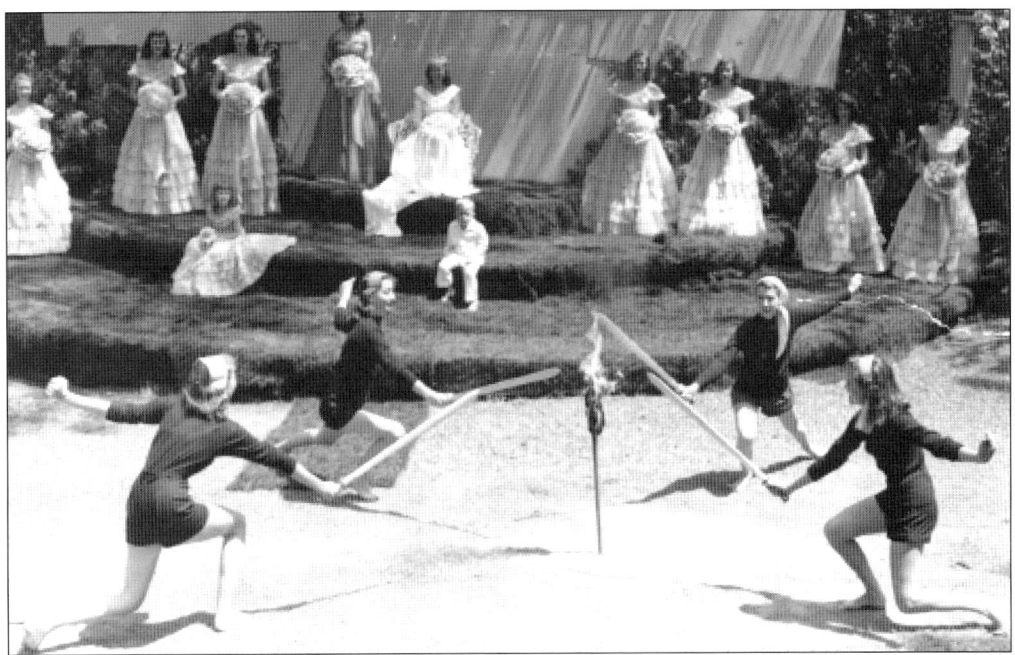
This image was captured during the swordfight scene in the May Day production of *Sinbad the Sailor* in 1949.

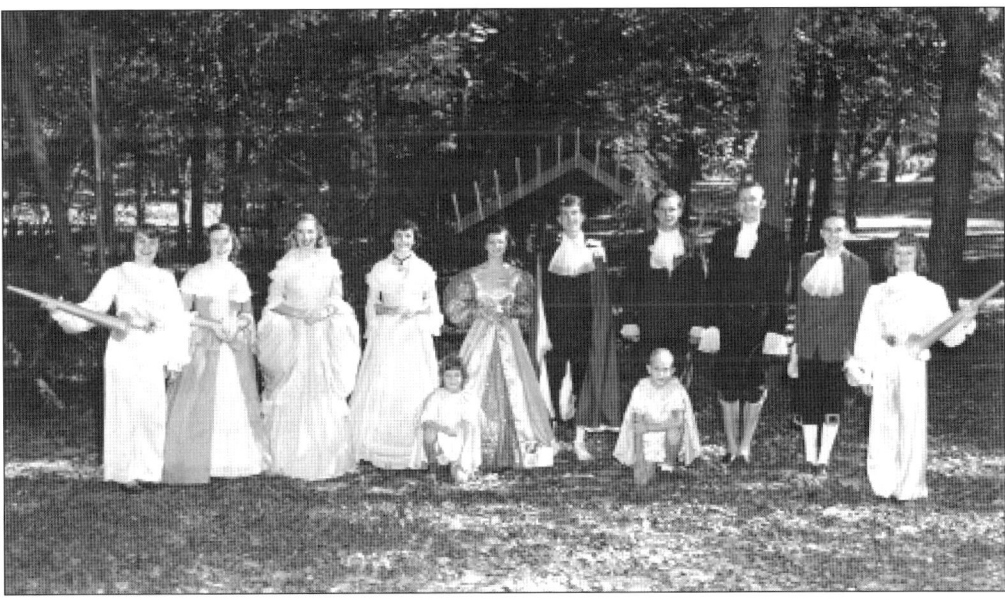
Pageantry and courtly processionals were not just reserved for May Day. A king and queen were crowned at the 1951 Harvest Festival and were honored with a program that included a parade and processional of the court, music by the Lander Lyrikers, tap dance by the Martin sisters, selections on the carillon bells played by music faculty member W.H. Ehrich, and a square dance. In this image, Joan Connor is queen and Lawrence McNair is king. Crown bearers are Jack and Jeanette Thompson. The court included princesses Opal Rush, Ray Belle Crowder, and Deebie Bessinger. Princes were Keith Fowler, Melvin Riley, and Billy Spivey; pages are June Hughes and Helen Howell.

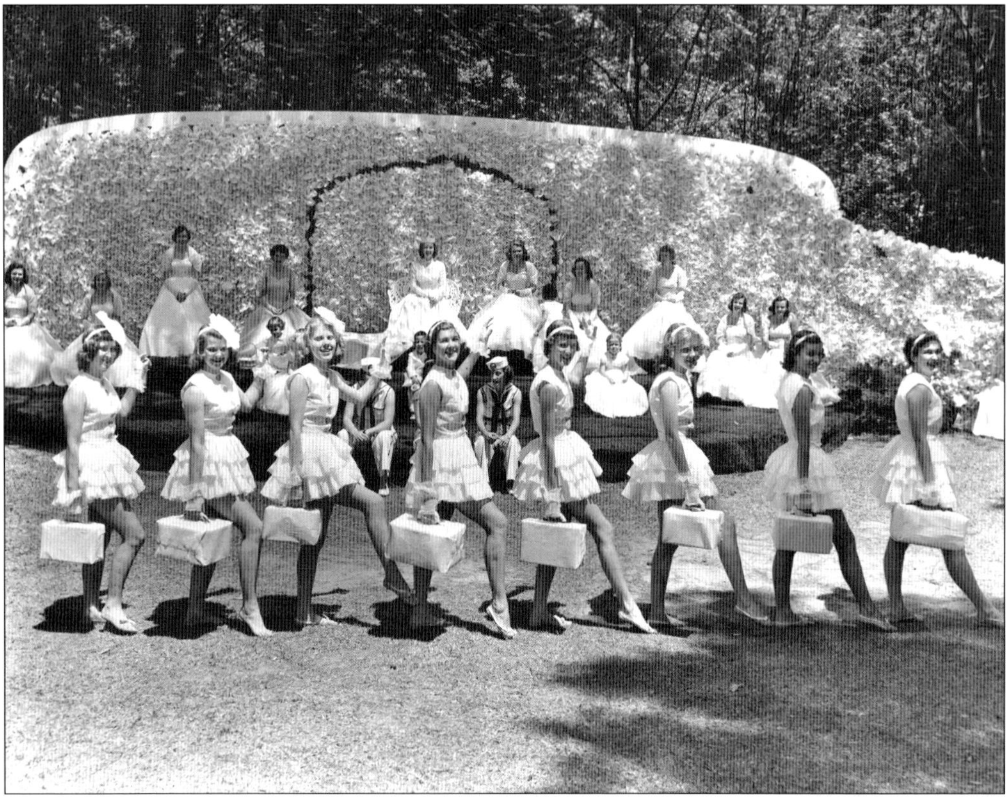

These are Lander students in a scene from the musical *Show Boat*, which was performed on May Day in 1952.

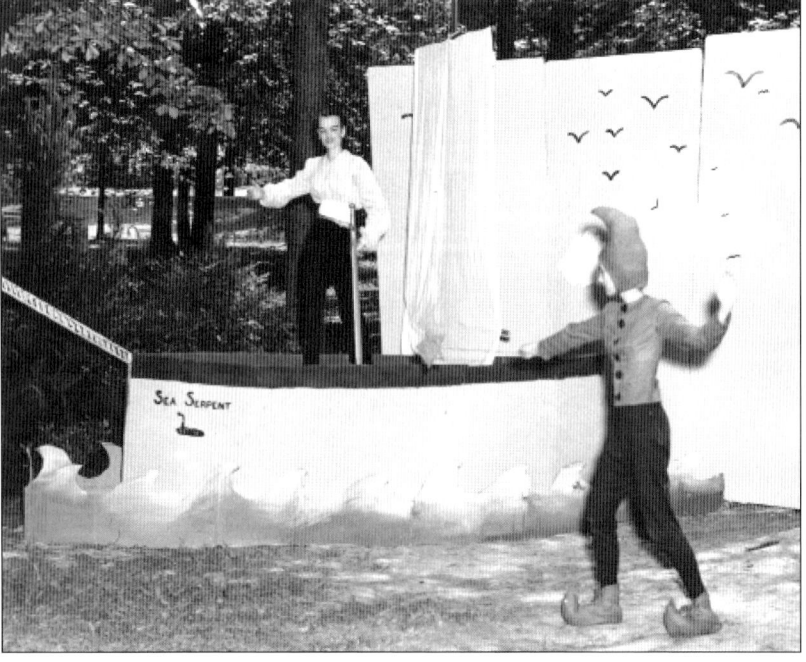

Students built and decorated a wooden ship outside in the campus Dingle as part of the set for the May Day production of *Sinbad the Sailor* in 1949.

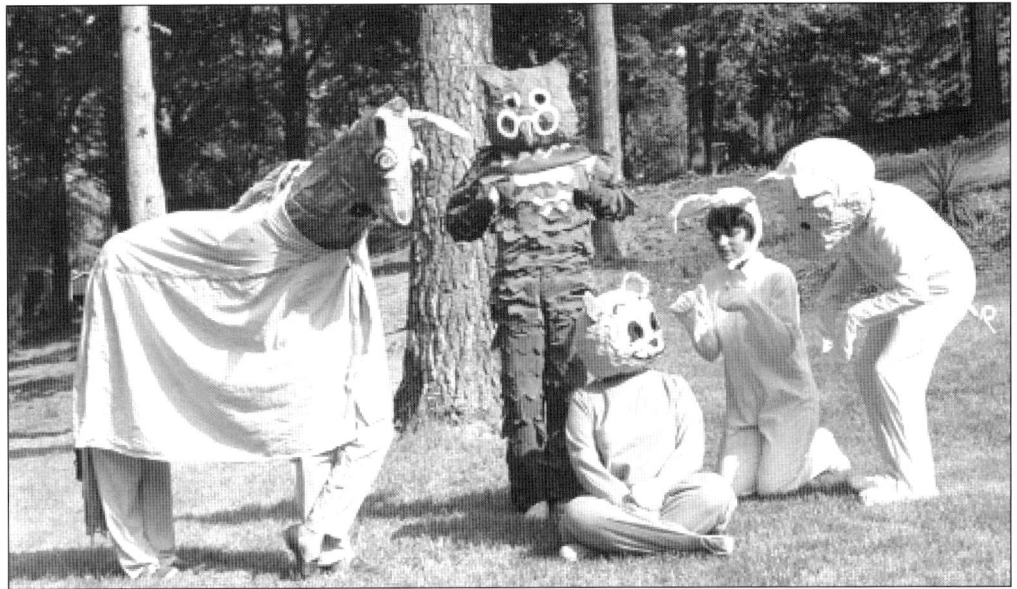

Large, quirky, papier-mâché animal costumes have appeared in photographs of various Lander plays, skits, and variety acts since the 1920s. This may have been the influence of art faculty member Marie Chisholm, who graduated from Lander in 1922 and went on to head the art department of the college before retiring in 1970. There are numerous photographs of Professor Chisholm instructing students in this art technique.

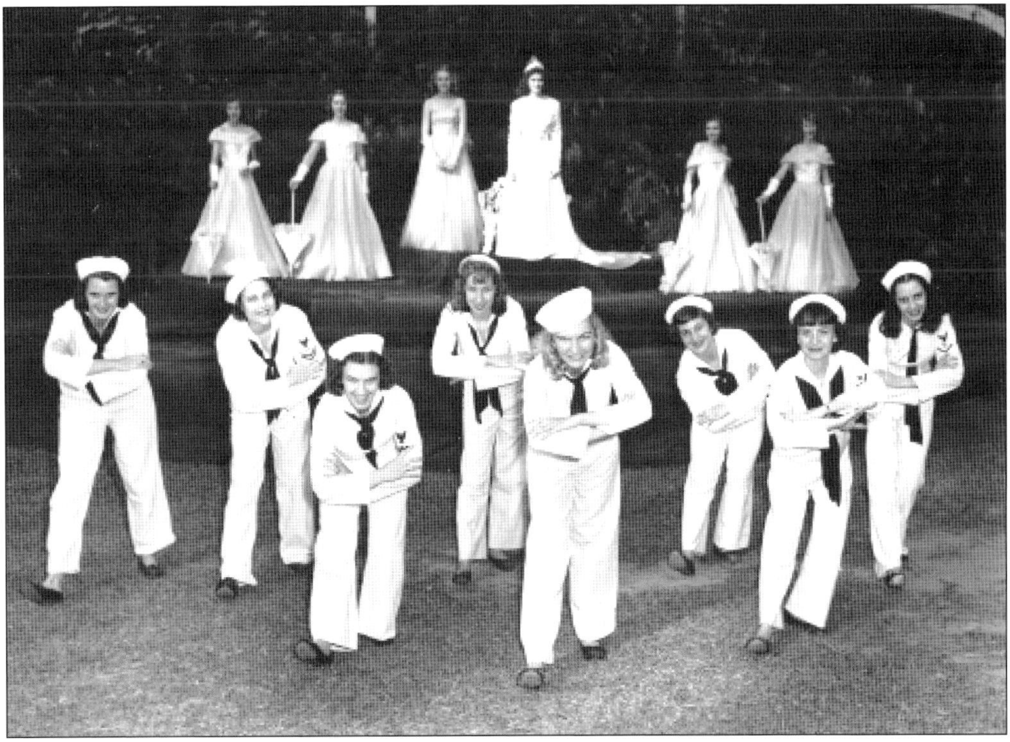

Sailors perform a high-flying dance to the reels of the Irish and the flings of the Scottish for the May queen and her court at the May Day pageant in 1951.

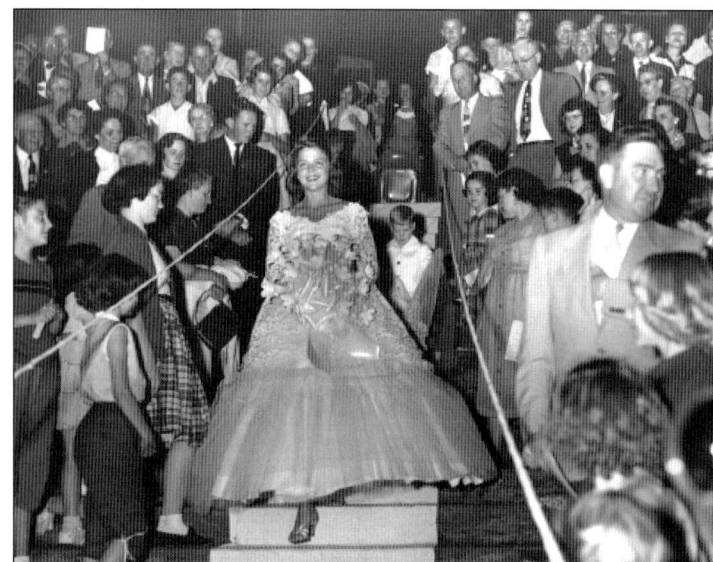

May queen Charles Andrews and train bearer E.B. Grier pass a large crowd of community members who joined Lander students, faculty, staff, and alumnae in viewing the 1954 May Day pageant. The theme that year was "The Enchanted Nutcracker."

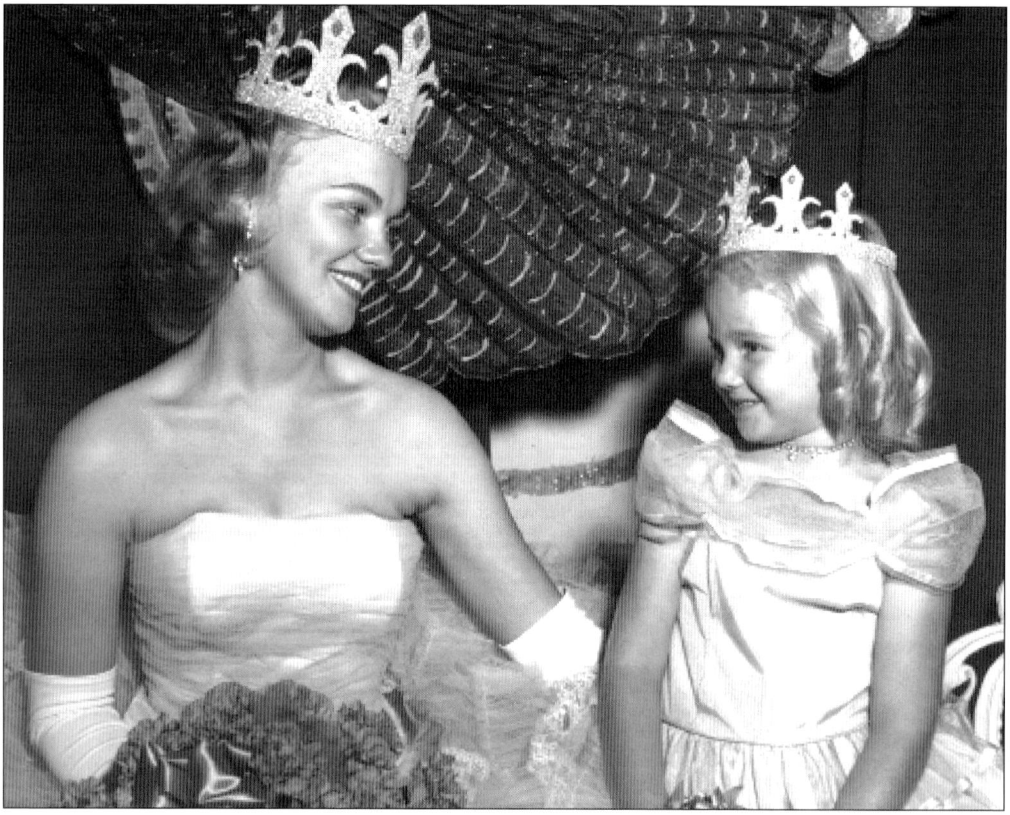

Miss Lander and Little Miss Lander are wearing matching crowns in this photograph taken at the Annual Beauty Review. Carol Ann Smith, an 18-year-old freshman from Easley was crowned Miss Lander of 1957. Smith was a home economics major and had been elected freshman bride earlier that year in the freshman-junior wedding. Six-year-old Sandy Buchanan was chosen Little Miss Lander. She represented Mathews Elementary School.

Biology major Betty Stone was crowned Halloween queen in 1955 at a dance held in the Sproles Recreation Center on campus. Stone was the president of the Student Government Association of the college and was sponsored by the Future Teachers of America Club at Lander.

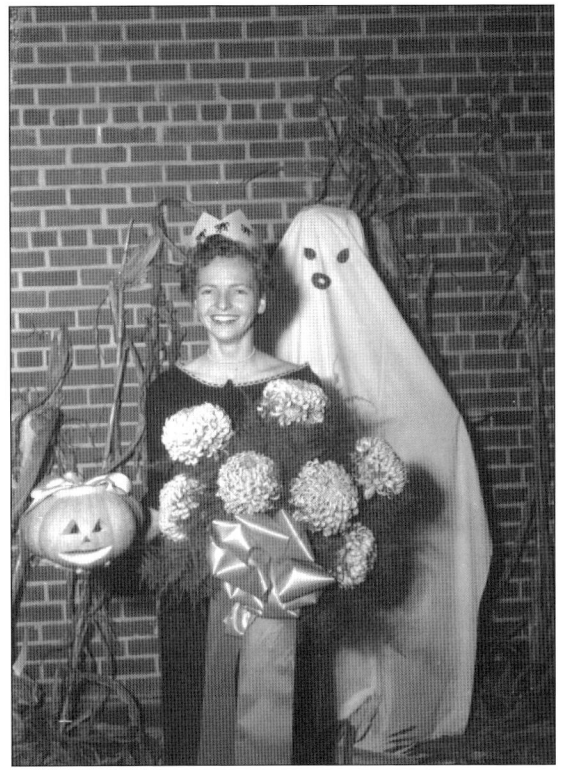

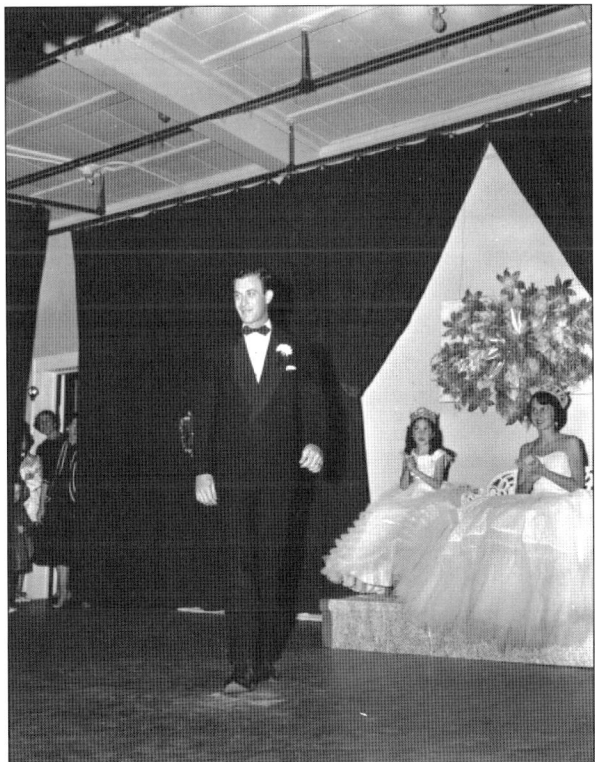

In this image from a beauty review in 1955, a group peers from behind a curtain just off stage at the man who was just selected to be Mr. Lander College, Carol Whatley. Whatley was a transfer from Wofford College and received his degree from Lander in business administration in 1956. Also pictured are previous year's Miss Lander, Barbara Bruce, and Little Miss Lander, Betsy Hoit.

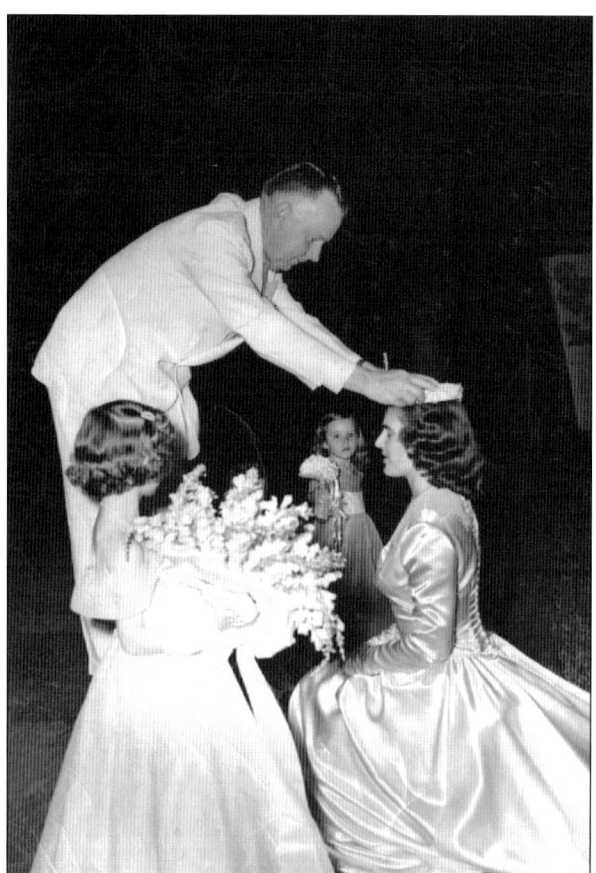

Dr. Boyce M. Grier, Lander's seventh president, crowns Cora Gunter as May queen in 1950. The child on the left is Anita Arnold; the child on the right is Lettie Baker.

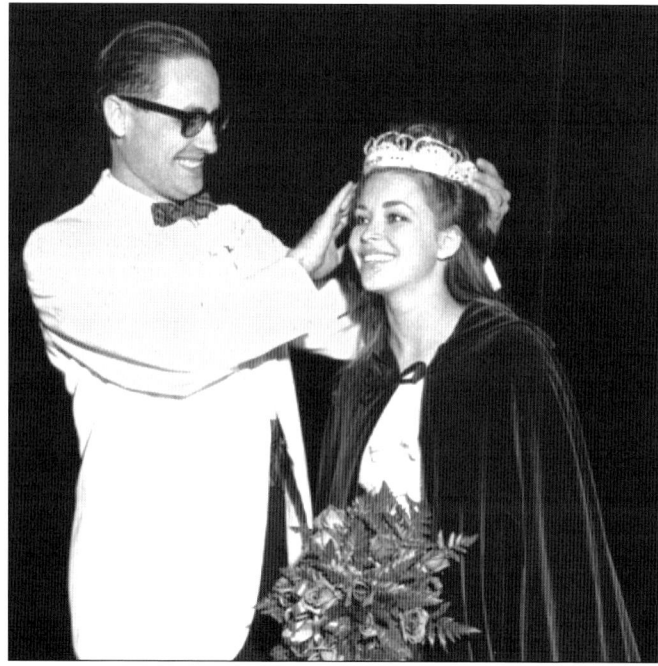

Dr. E. Don Herd Jr., Lander's eighth president, crowns Jayne Buchan McElrath as May queen in 1966. She had previously been crowned rat queen, Miss Lander, and Miss Valentine.

Brenda Freeman, Lander homecoming queen in 1973, is escorted by Anthony Dunlap III. Brenda was also a member of the student judicial council, the student centerboard, and the Pamoja Club. Pamoja is a Swahili word meaning "together," and the purpose of the club was to promote intercultural awareness and understanding. In 1972, Brenda was named Miss Pamoja.

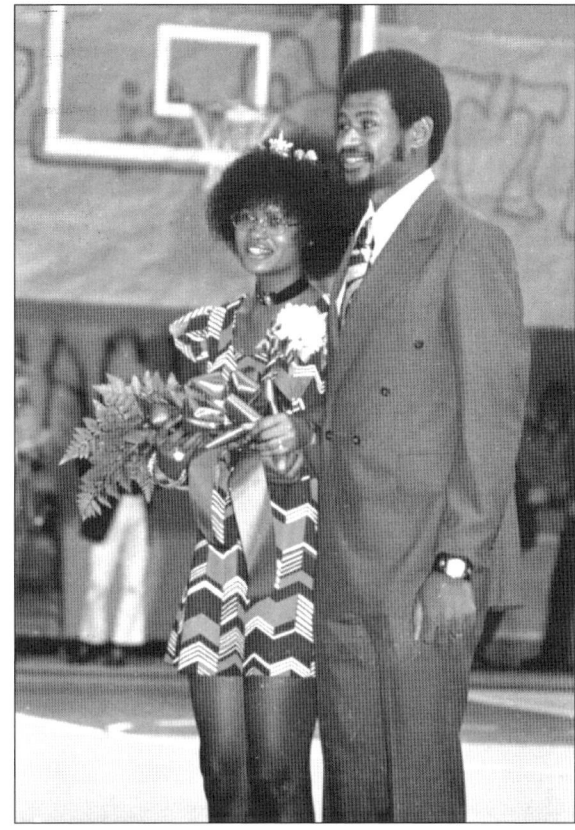

Past homecoming queen Brenda Freeman and Dr. Larry A. Jackson, Lander's ninth president, congratulate Rita Prater on her homecoming queen win in 1974.

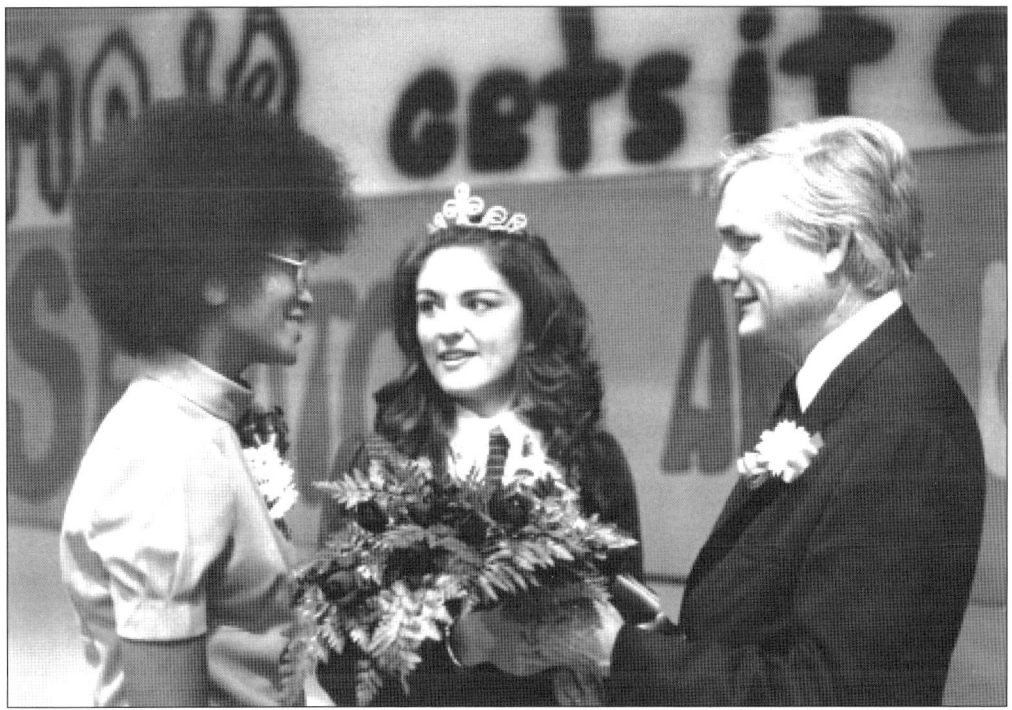

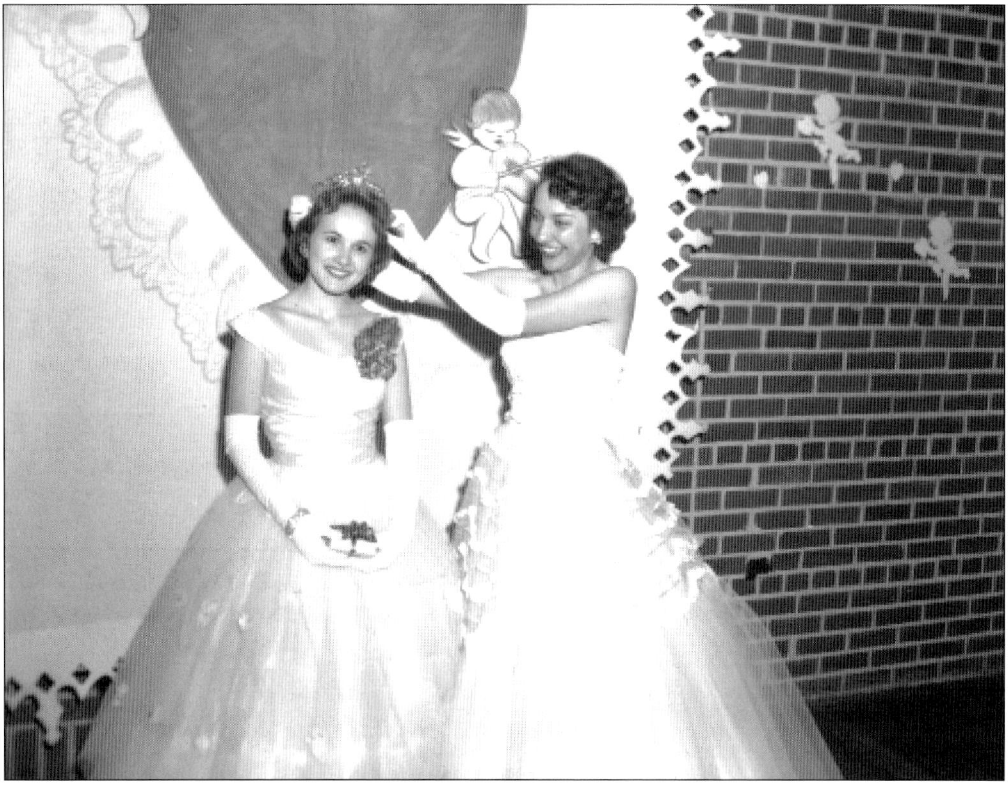

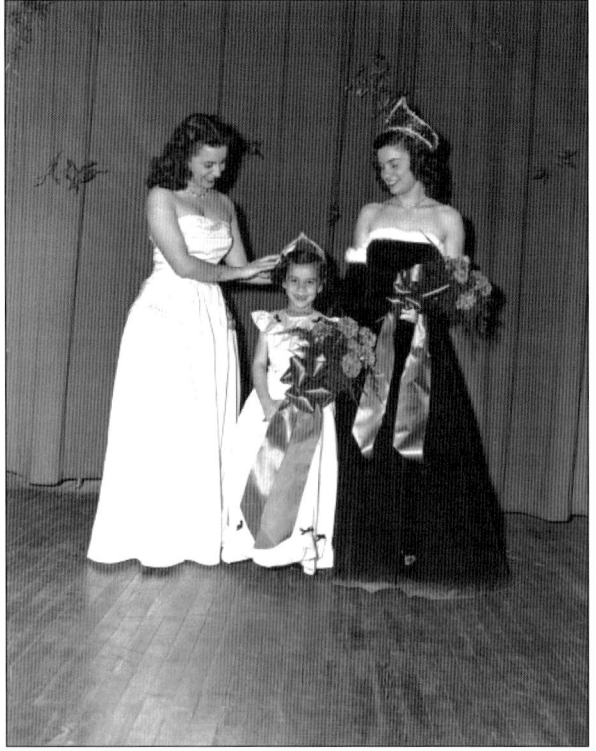

Senior Janet Butler crowns Jeanette Ward as Miss Valentine 1957. Eleven different Lander women competed in the contest, which was judged by the Alpha Tau Omega fraternity at the College of Charleston. The contest was sponsored by the Lander student newspaper, the *Rednal* (Lander spelled backward). The connection with the College of Charleston fraternity is not clear.

Raquel Canosa of Havana Cuba was selected to be Miss Lander in 1949. In this photograph from 1950, she crowns Jane Sparks as the new Little Miss Lander, while Peggy Martin, the incoming Miss Lander, looks on.

These contestants vied for the title of Miss Bullfrog in Lander's mock beauty review in 1963. The pageant was part of a variety show sponsored by the Lander Men's Club. According to the *Index-Journal*, the event was a night of fun featuring songs, music, skits, laughs, and a mock beauty show featuring the "Bullfrog Beauties." The first mock pageant at Lander occurred in 1948 and was sponsored by the N. Gist Gee Biology Club, whose symbol was, coincidentally, a green frog.

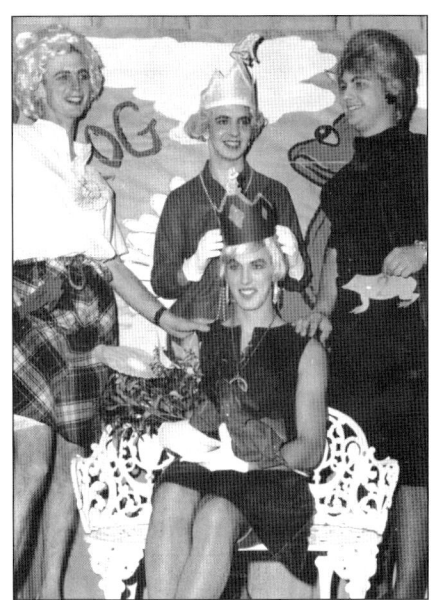

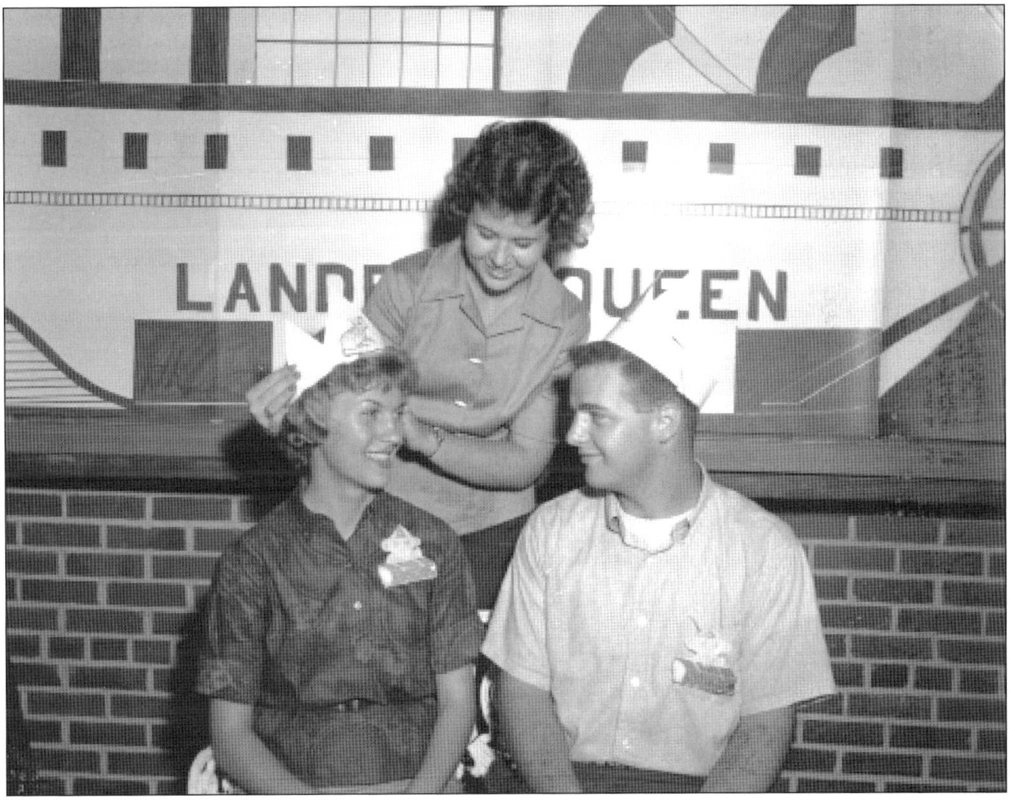

Student Government Association president Dottie Wise crowns Janice Jackson queen of the Freshman Rat Hop, or rat queen. Clifton Henry was selected as rat king. The two wear paper crowns decorated with illustrations of rats, and their name tags depict rats nibbling on books. In 1961, the dance was held at the end of orientation week in honor of all new students at the college.

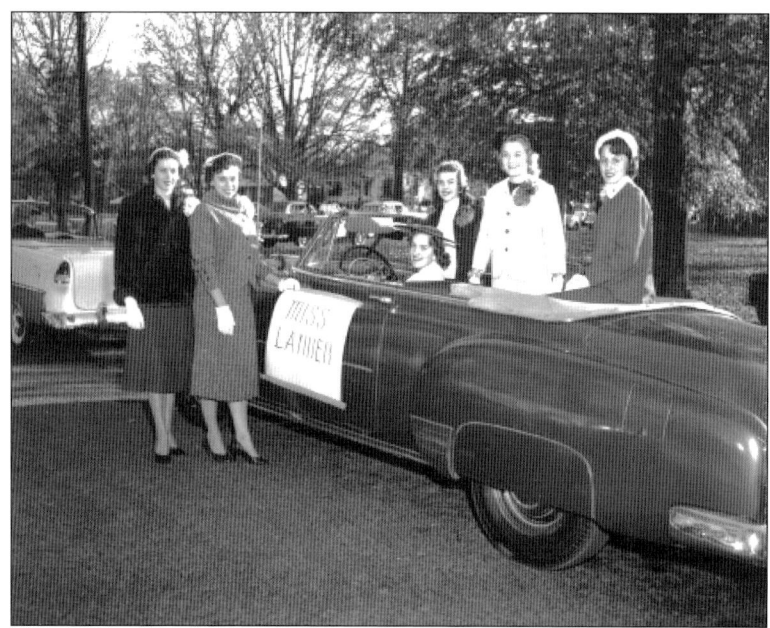

Miss Lander College, Barbara Bruce (seated far right), is about to head out to Greenwood's mile-long Christmas parade. That year, in 1955, area beauty queens each rode through the parade in convertibles.

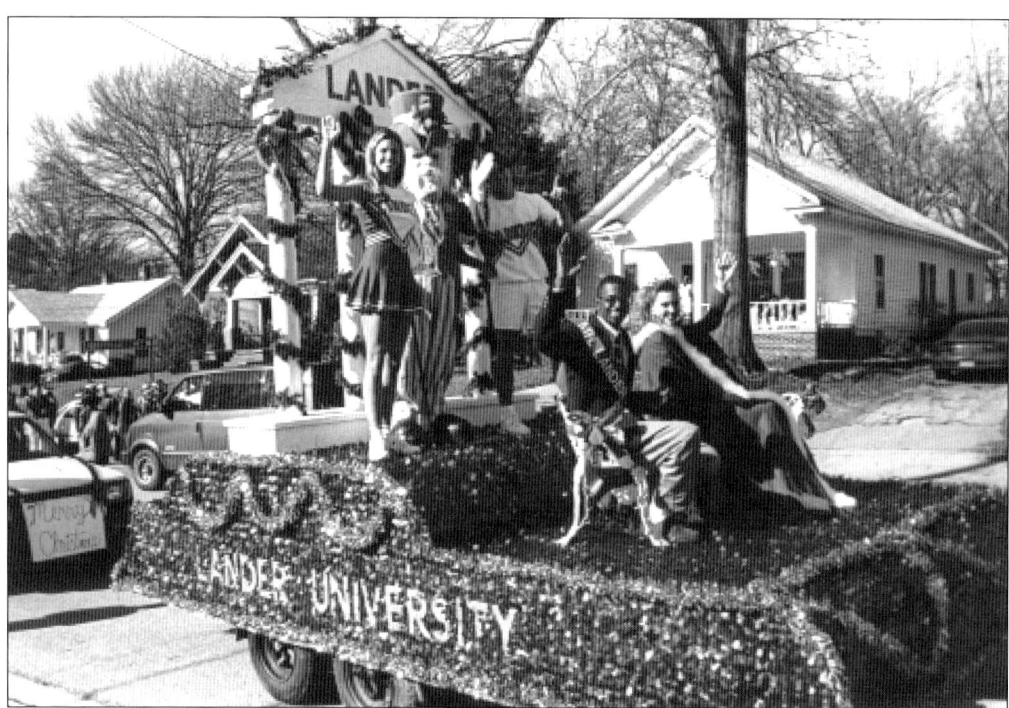

Mr. Lander University Terrence Harrell (left) and Miss Lander University Casi Begley (right) continue the tradition of participating in Greenwood's 1995 Christmas parade. Standing behind them flanking the senator are cheerleaders Courtney Goodman and Brad Kirby.

Six

Conclusion

In the first issue of the Williamston Female College newsletter (August 1884), called the *Naiad*, Rev. Samuel Lander wrote:

> In the olden time, the Greeks and Romans believed in a class of female divinities of a lower rank, to which they gave the name of nymphs. These nymphs were of different species, according to the department of nature over which they presided.
>
> The nymphs of the ocean were called Oceanides; those which inhabited the mountains were known as Oreades; while to those who had the care of fountains the name Naiades was given.
>
> The village of Williamston owes its origin to the discovery of the fine chalybeate spring, which still constitutes its principle native attraction. About 12 years ago, there sprang into existence near this fount of health, the fountain of learning which since then has sent forth copious streams of mental and moral culture, to adorn and gladden full many a happy heart.

He went on to say that the mission of Williamston Female College was to "impart health and vigor of body, mind, and spirit."

The Streams of Learning flowing from the spring at old Williamston continue to flow in Greenwood. They feed and are fed by one another, all tributaries flowing from the unique Lander wellspring.

Most of the photographs in this book were created for publicity and yearbook purposes. Some, including in this final chapter, were found in student and faculty memory books from a time when photographs in newspapers were rare and yearbooks did not exist. These memory books represent their own tributary, from the heart of Lander women a century past to "adorn and gladden" the Lander family today.

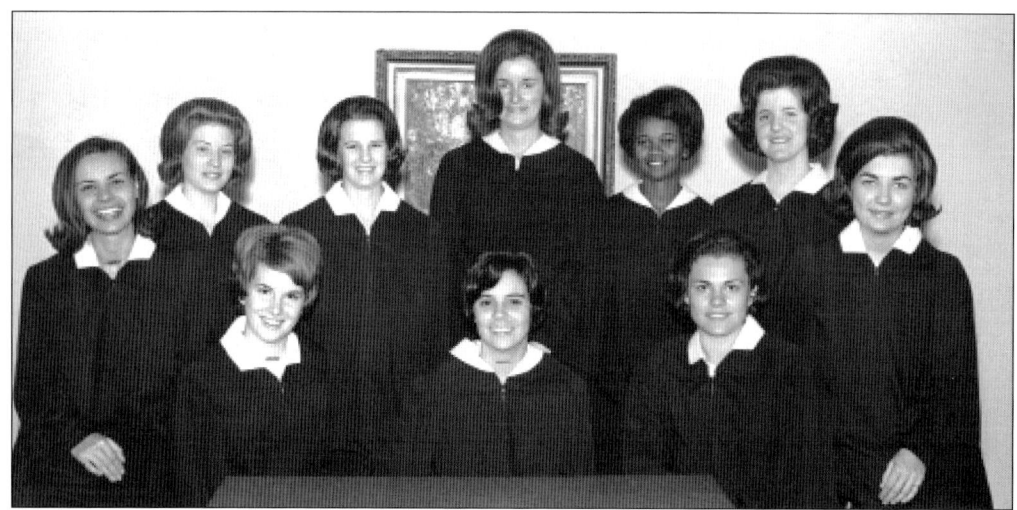

Members of the Alpha Chi national honor society are seen here in 1966. From left to right are (sitting) Connie Urquhart, Ellen Ayres, Ann Sparrow, Barbara Yonce, and Gay Timmerman.; (standing) Kay Mitchell, Laura Mims, Lynn Lewis, Mary Alice Brown, and Judy Lavender. Mary Alice Brown of Greenwood was the first known African American student admitted to Lander. She received the degree of BS in medical technology in 1968. This image is from the memory book of the Sr. Kenny Circle of Lander.

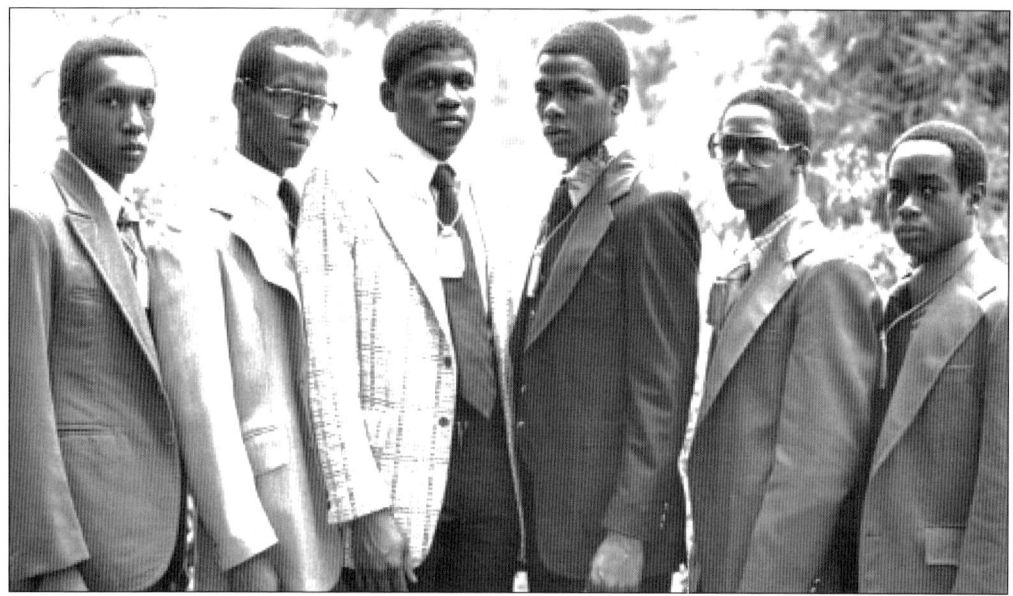

This photograph of pledges to the Omega Psi Phi Fraternity was taken in 1978. The fraternity was founded in 1911 at Howard University in Washington, DC. According to the 1980 *Naiad*, the principles upon which this fraternity is based are outlined in the four words: Manhood, Scholarship, Perseverance, and Uplift. The Upsilon Eta Chapter at Lander provided various social activities, such as discos and dances. In the community, they visited nursing homes and rendered their service in any way possible. The chapter also engaged in the four basic programs of the fraternity: Scholarship, Achievement Week, Talent Hunt, and Social Action. Pledges seen here are, from left to right, Bryant Sanders, Greg Childs, Alphonso Devlin, James Hawkins, Kenny Abrams, and Kenny Makins.

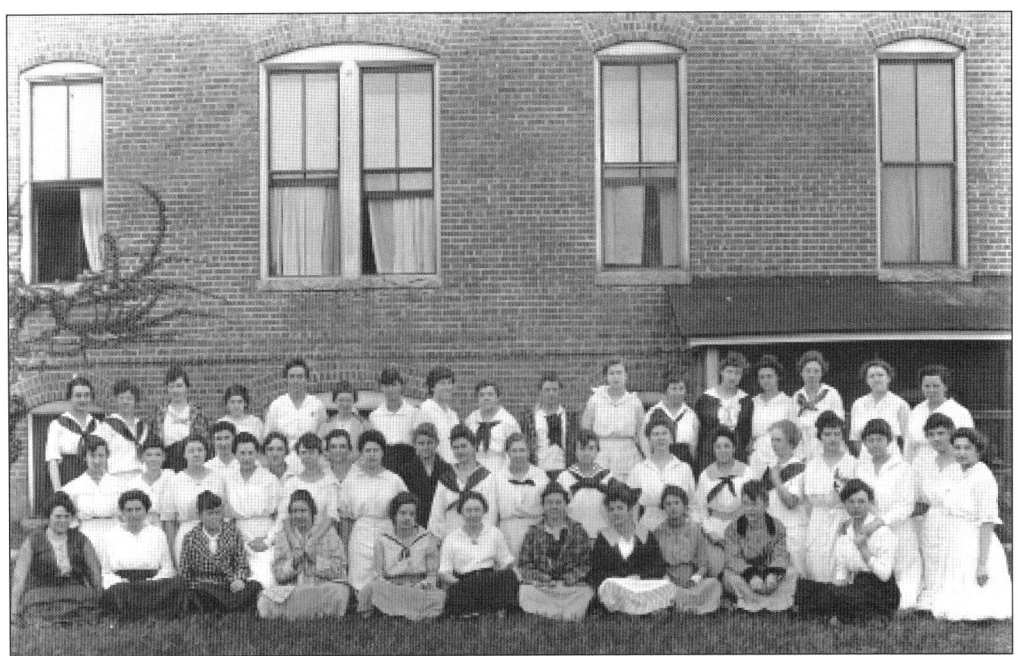

This is a group portrait of Opportunity School students in the 1920s. An article in the *Index-Journal* on July 21, 1922, announced a special summer program: "The faculty of the Opportunity School, a school to be conducted at Lander College for the benefit of women and girls who never had the opportunity of learning to read and write, was announced today. It will consist of a corps of specialists in adult school work from various parts of the state. Students from all sections of the state are expected to enroll." Arithmetic and spelling were also included in the curriculum. Scholarships for attendance were provided by the Greenwood City Council and local churches. The state superintendent of education for South Carolina mentioned the school in the 1922 annual report with the observation that "they came from all over the state and from all walks of life, the home, the mill, the farm, and the town. Thirteen counties were represented. The average number of years attended by the student body was three." A leaflet describing the Opportunity School was found in a scrapbook of clippings belonging to faculty member Annie Elizabeth Aunspaugh.

This photograph of Rev. B. Rhett Turnipseed (standing against pillar far right) was found in the memory book of student Cora Gilmore and was likely taken between 1917 and 1921, before his time as president. Prior to serving as Lander's third president, Reverend Turnipseed was the pastor of the college church, Main Street Methodist Church. He was also a member of Lander's building committee. The other man in the photograph is W.W. Weber, college secretary and professor of mathematics.

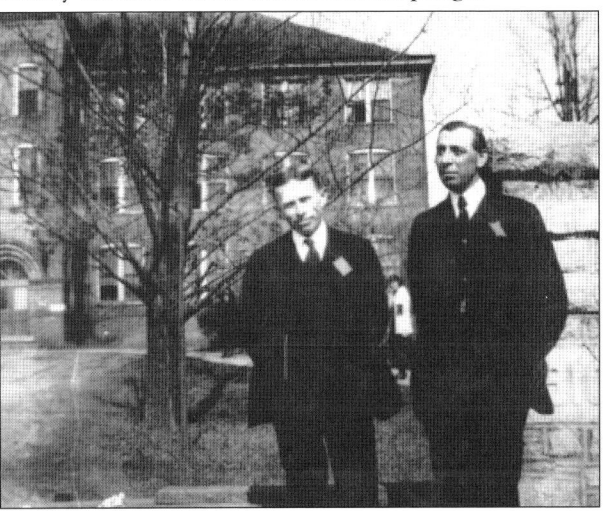

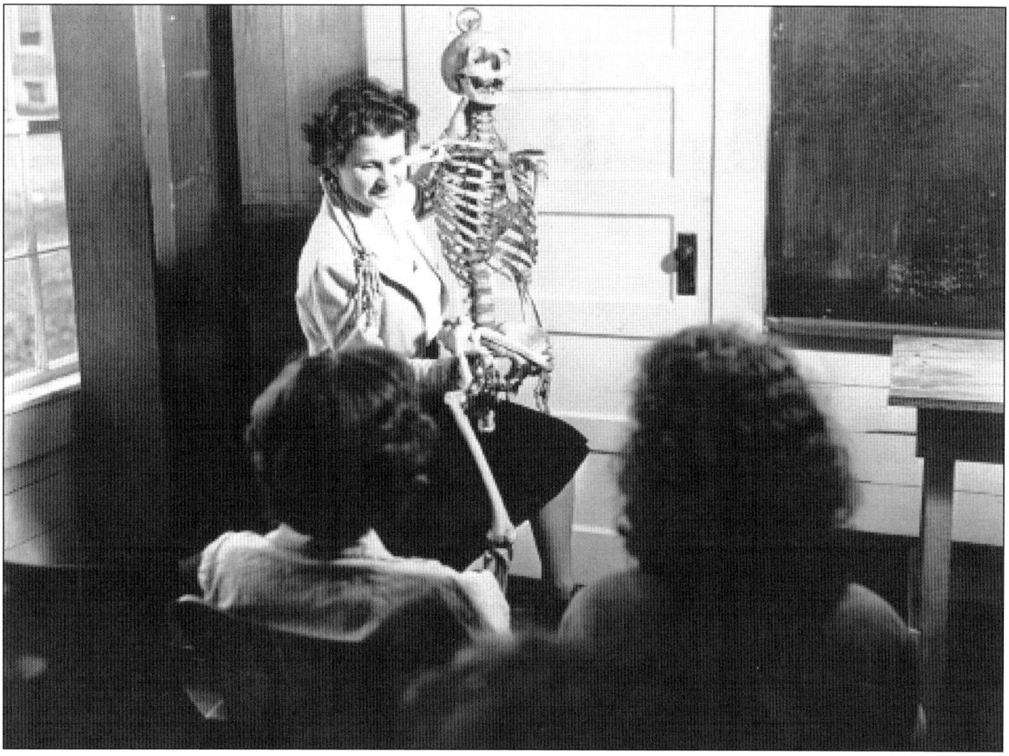

"Miss Susie" sits on the lap of faculty member Alice Spencer in anatomy class. The skeleton was not only a teaching tool but also played an important role in the Nathaniel Gist Gee Biology Club meetings, which were described in the 1941 annual: "Initiation of eleven new members was the program of the November meeting. Each initiate was introduced to 'Miss Susie'; each one shook her bony hand, kissed her fleshless lips, counted the bones of her back and toes; each one tasted of muscle to give her strength to feed dead spiders and snakes to Miss Susie. Cringing, protesting, each was forced through this ritual." This photograph is from the memory book of physical education faculty member Alice Spencer. (Courtesy of Allie and Glenn Williams.)

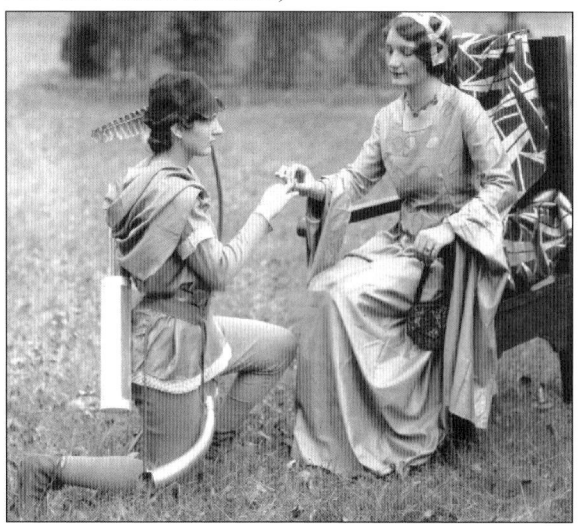

In this scene from a 1931 college production of *Robin Hood*, Gertrude Wiggington plays Robin Hood, and Audrey Shirley plays the queen. The photograph appeared in the *Naiad* annual, and the original photograph was found in the memory book of Mary Elspeth Stewart. Stewart was president of her graduating class in 1932 and received an AB in English. She was very active in campus life and served on the day student council, *Naiad* staff, and the Pan-Hellenic Council. Wiggington was also a class historian and a member of the Preachers' Daughters' Club.

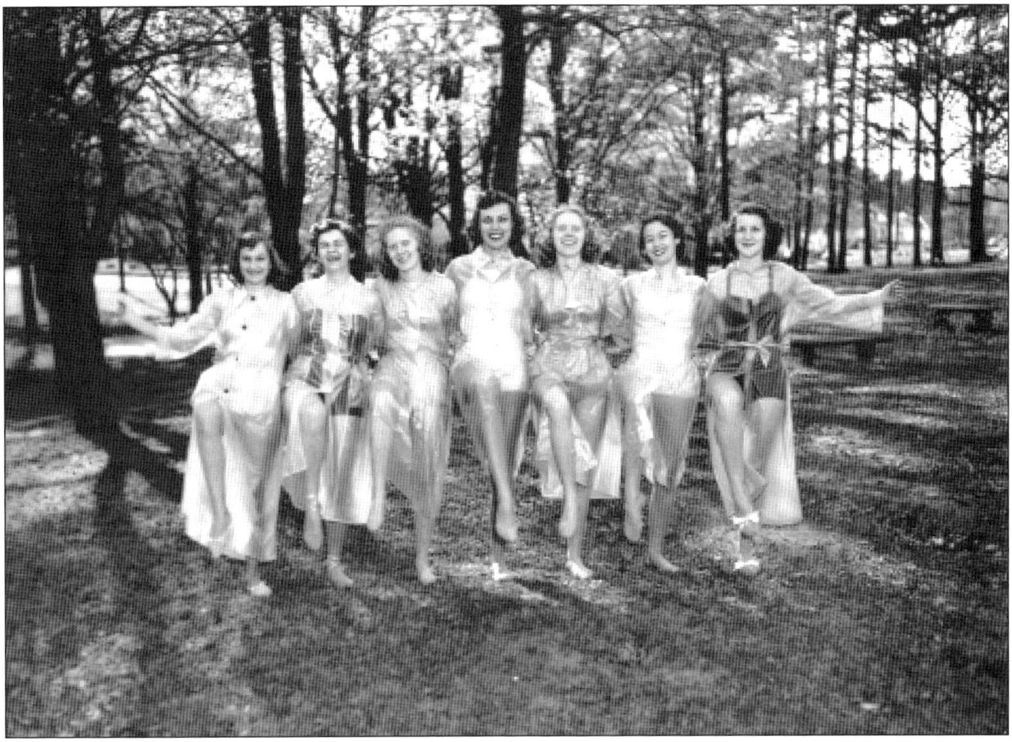

This image of students practicing their chorus-line kicks in the pines on campus was likely taken in the late 1940s in conjunction with a skit or variety show act, which was common on campus especially on May Day. In her essay "The Plants of the Lander Campus," Kathleen Lander Willson, wife of second president Rev. John O. Willson, describes the pine grove where this image was taken as part of a reforestation effort by her family: "Dr. W.T. Lander was laughed at when he transplanted to the west campus a group of little pines. These grew rapidly and it was not many years before a May queen and her court gave a party in 'the Pines,' where the drive now turns to Chipley Hall."

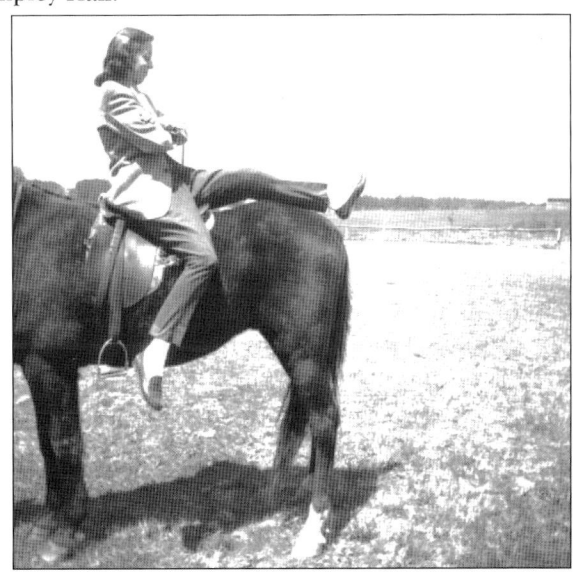

This photograph was taken from a set of instructive photographs demonstrating various mounts and dismounts. Lander students learned a variety of techniques to hone their equestrian skills in riding class. These skills would have come in useful in 1941, when students added a program to Field Day called "Gymkhana," which featured a race with riders carrying lances to spear potatoes with. The winner was the rider who collected the most potatoes.

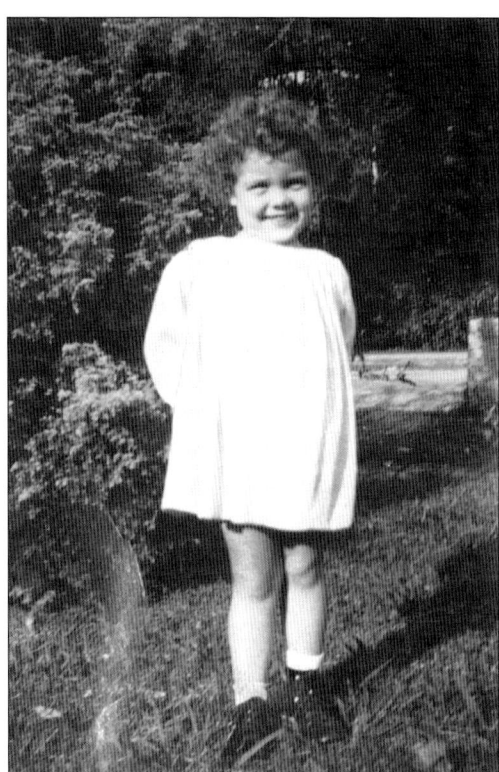

This portrait of 1930 senior class mascot Elizabeth Gray Scurry, daughter of local doctor C.J. Scurry, was found in the memory book of student Mary Major. The senior class mascots were treasured good luck charms, and Scurry may have been just the charm needed that year. According to reports in the *Index-Journal*, the class of 1930, with 55 graduates, was the largest in Lander's history.

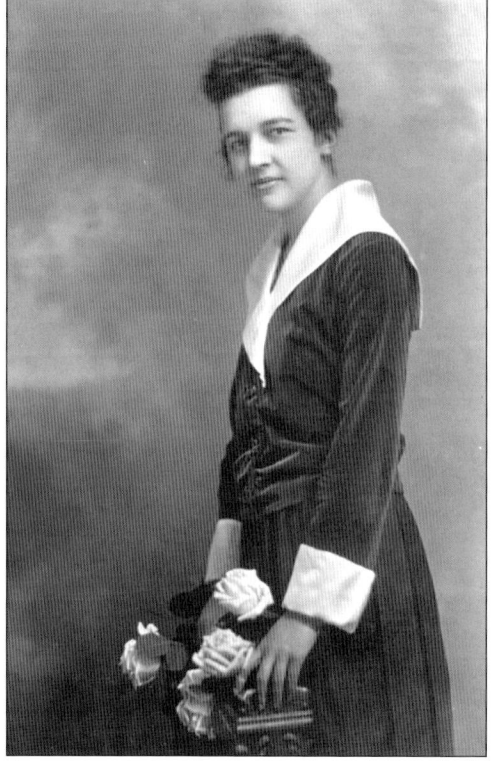

This is a portrait of student Kathleen Grier of North, South Carolina, who, upon graduating in 1914, summarized her time at the school by penning a version of a quote by poet Robert Browning in the memory book of classmate Ethel Anderson: "How sad and mad and bad it was. But, then how it is sweet!"